T0360707

Zhu Rongji and China's Economic Take-Off

Zhu Rongji and China's Economic Take-Off

John Wong

East Asian Institute, NUS, Singapore

Imperial College Press

ICP

Published by

Imperial College Press
57 Shelton Street
Covent Garden
London WC2H 9HE

Distributed by

World Scientific Publishing Co. Pte. Ltd.

5 Toh Tuck Link, Singapore 596224

USA office: 27 Warren Street, Suite 401-402, Hackensack, NJ 07601

UK office: 57 Shelton Street, Covent Garden, London WC2H 9HE

Library of Congress Cataloging-in-Publication Data
Names: Wong, John, 1939– author.
Title: Zhu Rongji and China's economic take-off / John Wong.
Description: New Jersey : World Scientific, [2015]
Identifiers: LCCN 2015035156 | ISBN 9781783268825 (alk. paper)
Subjects: LCSH: Zhu, Rongji, 1928– | Economic development--China. |
    China--Economic policy--1949– | China--Economic conditions--1949–
Classification: LCC HC427.92 .W65495 2015 | DDC 330.951--dc23
LC record available at http://lccn.loc.gov/2015035156

British Library Cataloguing-in-Publication Data
A catalogue record for this book is available from the British Library.

Copyright © 2016 by Imperial College Press

All rights reserved. This book, or parts thereof, may not be reproduced in any form or by any means, electronic or mechanical, including photocopying, recording or any information storage and retrieval system now known or to be invented, without written permission from the Publisher.

For photocopying of material in this volume, please pay a copying fee through the Copyright Clearance Center, Inc., 222 Rosewood Drive, Danvers, MA 01923, USA. In this case permission to photocopy is not required from the publisher.

Desk Editors: Chandrima Maitra/Lixi Dong

Typeset by Stallion Press
Email: enquiries@stallionpress.com

Printed in Singapore

To my dear wife Aline, a great intellectual companion

CONTENTS

ABOUT THE AUTHOR

John Wong is currently Professorial Fellow and Academic Advisor to the East Asian Institute (EAI) of the National University of Singapore. Prof. Wong was formerly Research Director of EAI, and Director of the Institute of East Asian Political Economy (IEAPE). Before these, he taught Economics first at the University of Hong Kong and subsequently at the National University of Singapore. He has written/edited 35 books, and published over 500 articles and papers on China, East Asia and ASEAN. He has also written numerous policy-related reports on development in China to the Singapore government. His first book is *Land Reform in the People's Republic of China: Institutional Transformation in Agriculture* (New York, Praeger Special Studies, 1973), pp. 354. His latest book is *The Political Economy of Deng's Nanxun: Breakthrough in China's Reform and Development* (New Jersey/London, World Scientific, 2014).

Part I

Part I

Introduction I

TAKING STOCK OF CHINA'S PAST ECONOMIC GROWTH AND ITS FUTURE PROSPECTS

China's Relentless Economic Rise

China's economy has chalked up a spectacular performance since its economic reform and the open-door policy in 1978, growing at an average annual rate of 9.8% for over three decades from 1979 to 2013, and about 10% for the two sub-periods of 1991–2013 and 2001–2013.[1] Its growth did not suffer much from the 1997 Asian financial crisis. It was also largely unaffected by the 2008 global financial crisis, which brought most economies to grief. In fact, China's economic growth in 2009, following the government's injection of a massive stimulus package of 4 trillion yuan, remained at 9.2% and quickly bounced back to 10.4% in 2010, leading the global economy to recovery. As the IMF Managing Director Christine Lagarde put it, "The global economic situation might have been even more calamitous had it not been for the impetus that China provided to growth and stability". In short, China's long streak of spectacular growth performance was simply historically unprecedented (Figure 1).

Economic growth has started to decelerate in recent years primarily due to structural problems and also because of the less conducive global economic environment, with 2014 registering only 7.3% growth, China's lowest in 24 years. For 2015, growth has been targeted at a still lower rate of 7%. China's economic slowdown is therefore very much in evidence, which has been widely reported and also sensationalized by foreign media, particularly for the first quarter of 2015 when its major growth drivers

---

[1]China National Bureau of Statistics, *2014 China Statistical Abstract* (Beijing).

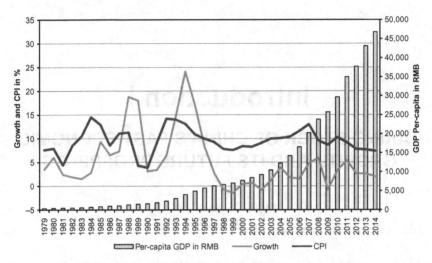

Figure 1.   China's GDP, CPI and economic growth, 1979–2014.
Source: National Bureau of Statistics.

like capital investment and exports plummeted sharply from their previous double-digit rates of growth to lower single-digit rates. By the mid-2015, however, growth held steady at 7% as a result of the government stimulus efforts, including four rounds of interest cut. By most forecasts, China looks to achieve 6.8–7.0% growth for 2015, as much desired by Premier Li Keqiang.

It is true that China's economy has lost its former high-growth momentum and is heading for a lower growth in a gradual manner. Put into proper perspective, China's present "lower" growth is "low" only on China's own terms, as its current level of growth at around 7% for such a huge economy is still remarkably high by any regional or global standard, and certainly well above the IMF's average global economic growth of 3.1% for 2015. This explains why the present economic deceleration had not much worried the Chinese leadership, which has officially taken it as the "New Normal". What is actually crucial for them is whether or not the next phase of more moderate growth would suffice to carry the country to fulfil its social target of becoming a *Xiaokang* (moderately affluent) society around 2020, and its economic target of reaching at the threshold of a developed economy before 2030.

In 2010, China replaced Japan as the world's second largest economy. In 2014, China's economy reached another landmark by becoming the world's largest economy (slightly exceeding the US level) based on the purchasing power parity (PPP) measure of gross domestic product (GDP), as so confirmed by the IMF. The PPP method of computing a developing country's GDP by using international prices inevitably exaggerates the real size of its total production. However, China's GDP, even in nominal terms, will inevitably catch up with the US level within a decade or so, given their glaring growth gaps. China's total nominal GDP in 2014 stood at 64 trillion yuan (US$10.4 trillion), which was nearly 60% of the US level. At its existing rate of growth, China in one year is generating twice as much GDP as the United States in one year.

For many years, China has already been the world's largest exporting country. In 2014, its total exports amounted to US$2.3 trillion, taking up 14% of the world market share. In the post-crisis world, China has further distinguished itself by holding the world's largest reserves of about US$4 trillion and as the only largest economy with large capital surplus and not being burdened by large external debts.

Beyond these GDP statistics (often imprecise due to changes in prices and valuation) one may look at the physical output levels of China's key industrial products and this can better convey a true sense of China's scale of economic production and the fact that it is really the world's foremost manufacturing powerhouse. Thus, China in 2014 topped the world in the production of coal (3.9 billion tons), steel (825 million tons), cement (250 million tons), automobile (24 million units), TV (140 million sets), refrigerator (103 million units), mobile phones (1.6 billion units), micro-computers (350 million units) and so on. For most of these commodity items, China's production statistics have been running into jumbo numbers as China's average global share of some key commodities run into 30–40%. Not surprisingly, three of the world's 10 largest companies in 2014 were Chinese: Sinopec, China National Petroleum and China State Grid. In fact, next to the United States, China had the largest number (95) of big corporations in the Fortune 500 global companies.

Regional and global impact

By its sheer scale that is further compounded by its high speed, China's levels of domestic production and consumption, and its imports and exports will continue to carry significant regional and global ramifications. On account of its massive industrialization as reflected in the mega output volumes shown earlier, China has become the world's top consumer of a wide variety of natural resources and primary commodities from steel and aluminium to oil and gas. China's rising demand for these products in recent years has driven up their world prices. China is responsible for the creation of the recent global commodity boom, with beneficial impact on a lot of primary producing countries from Southeast Asia and Australia to Latin America and Africa. In fact, over 80% of the primary commodity exports from Indonesia, Malaysia and Thailand are destined to China. At the same time, China's large-scale fabrication of many industrial products has also brought down their world prices, and the low-priced China-made merchandise has brought down inflation in the developed countries. For boom or for bust, the movement of China's economy has therefore created significant spillovers on the global economy.

Regionally, China's economy has become the most important engine of growth for its neighbouring economies, which are making use of China's huge domestic markets as a source of their own growth by exporting to China both manufactured products (machine and equipment, and parts and components) and primary commodities and natural resources. The process has also brought about closer regional economic integration. As shown in Figure 2, China has, in fact, become an important regional "integrator" through its many global and regional production networks. China's exports (about 50% being processing trade) embody raw materials, parts and components, technology and equipment, and financial and economic services from different Asian economies, converting "Made-in-Asia" into "Made-in-China" products for the world market. In this way, China's exports also generate large multiplier effects in these economies, sometimes even more than in China itself. In other words, China's economy operates not just as an engine of growth for the East Asia region, but also as a catalyst of regional economic integration. Globally, China's contribution to world economic growth in PPP–GDP terms increased from about 10% in the mid-1990s to peak at 30% in 2013.[2]

The pomp and ceremony that had accompanied China's hosting of the 22nd Asia-Pacific Economic Cooperation (APEC) Summit in Beijing on

---

[2]This comes from a study by the Bank of America-Merrill Lynch, "The Shadow of China over Asian Exports", September 5, 2014 (Jaewoo Lee).

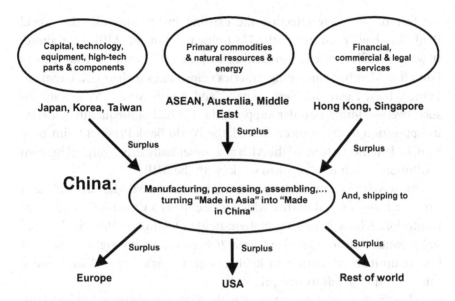

Figure 2. China-led regional growth and integration in East Asia.

November 10, 2014 was yet another unmistaken message to the world that China had already become emerging global economic superpower. Flush with China's capital surplus (resulting from persistent surplus in both its current and capital accounts), President Xi Jinping proposed to put up what Western media had characterized as China's "Marshall Plan" (this term was officially avoided by Beijing because of its Cold War connotation) by pledging US$40 billion to assist countries in its proposed Silk Road zone for infrastructure development under the operational term, the "One Belt One Road" scheme, which has been projected to comprise 60 countries and regions with a total population of 4.4 billion.[3] The first Silk Road Fund project has already started with China assisting Pakistan in developing its Karot hydropower project on the Jhelum River.[4]

    More concretely, China has proceeded to set up the Asian Infrastructure Investment Bank (AIIB) to assist in the funding of capital construction projects in the region by providing US$50 billion or half of the start-up capital. The United States initially opposed this China-sponsored project

---

[3]"China Sees More Exports, Investment Along Belt and Road", *Xinhua*, updated July 7, 2015.
[4]"Silk Road Fund Makes its First Investment", *China Daily*, April 22, 1015.

for fear of adversely affecting the existing institutions like the World Bank that have been under the US influence. But the AIIB went ahead. It was officially launched in Beijing in June 2015 with 57 countries as Founding Members, including America's close allies such as UK, Germany, France, Italy, Australia, New Zealand and South Korea. As a result of such overwhelming popular support, the US had subsequently softened its opposition to this project. Indeed, the World Bank President, Jim Yong Kim, had openly welcomed the AIIB as a "potentially strong ally" of his own institution, which was "ready to work" with the AIIB.[5]

Most Asian countries along with many from the Middle East and Latin America have joined the AIIB, which is essentially a China-led multilateral institution. China is its largest share-holder, taking up 30% of the total stake, which will in turn give China 26% of the voting rights. The AIIB has set up its headquarters in Beijing, with China's former Vice Finance Minister Jin Liqun as its first president.

Shortly after the birth of the AIIB, the New Development Bank (NDB), which is another new multilateral financial institution, initiated and backed by Brazil, Russia, India, China and South Africa (BRICS), was officially launched in Shanghai on July 21, 2015. This new institution will have its headquarters in Shanghai, with an Indian banker K.V. Kamath as its first president and China's banker Zhu Xian as its Vice President. Both the AIIB and the NDB critically depend on the injection of Chinese capital.

Addressing the opening of the Afro–Asia Summit in Jakarta on April 22, 2015, Indonesian President, Joko Widodo, gave a strong endorsement to this China-led AIIB by stating: "those who still insisted that the global economic problems could only be solved through the World Bank, International Monetary Fund and Asian Development Bank were clinging to obsolete ideas".[6]

China on its part had also assured that the operation of the AIIB would stick to the multilateral framework and basic market rules, and to operate in a transparent manner, much along the line of the World Bank's International Financial Corporation (IFC). China had also pledged that the

---

[5]"World Bank Chief Jim Yong Kim Says Lender 'Ready to Work' with AIIB", *South China Morning Post*, July 18, 2015.
[6]"Asian, African Nations Challenge "Obsolete" World Order", *Reuters* (Jakarta, April 22, 2015).

AIIB would work closely with other existing financial institutions. This new financial institution is expected to fill the crucial infrastructure funding gaps in the developing world. It suffices to say that China has scored a significant diplomatic coup by having attracted so many of America's allies to support its project.

In the meanwhile, China had also requested the IMF to include the Chinese *Renminbi* (RMB) in the basket of key international currencies that determine the Special Drawing Rights (SDRs). This would facilitate the further internationalization of the RMB. The main obstacle for China is that the RMB is still not fully convertible. The Central Bank governor, Zhou Xiaochuan, had originally announced that China would make the RMB convertible under the capital account by 2015.[7] However, with the unexpected turmoil of the stock market in July 2015 (as manifested in its turbulent boom-bust cycle within a few weeks) the healthy development of a much-needed capital market along with some aspects of the financial sector reform, particularly in regard to the scheduled liberalization of the RMB, might well be delayed.

In any case, the RMB has already gained a high international status in recent years. By 2014, about a quarter of China's trade was settled in RMB, which is now the seventh largest reserve currency in the world, ranking as the world's fifth payment currency after the US dollar, the Euro, the British Pound and the Japanese Yen. Given that China now is already the world's largest exporter and the world's second largest economy, it would just be a matter of time before the RMB would join these four key currencies in the IMF SDR basket.[8] It suffices to say that all the above, clearly signals China's growing economic muscle in the global financial arena.

In the geo-political arena, China has in recent years been pushing very hard its central foreign policy message of "peaceful rise". But this has not been wholeheartedly embraced by all its neighbours, partly due to China's lack of soft power. The situation has been further complicated by China's outstanding bilateral issues with some Asian countries over territorial disputes in the South China Sea. Chinese diplomatic postures are

---

[7]"China Close to its Goal of Full Yuan Convertibility on its Capital Account", *South China Morning Post*, June 22, 2015.
[8]"The Renminbi Deserves SDR Recognition", *China Daily*, June 18, 2015.

often seen as too assertive. Given so many obstacles, Chinese policy makers naturally see economic means as potentially a more effective instrument to advance its overall foreign policy interests. To use an economic parlance, China obviously possesses a stronger comparative advantage in economic diplomacy than its other options. In this way, China's stronger geo-economics arising from its sustained economic growth is expected to make up for its inherently weaker geo-politics.[9]

Thus, in 2000, Premier Zhu Rongji proposed the China–ASEAN Free Trade Area (CAFTA), the first and the largest "ASEAN Plus One" regional trade scheme. In 2010, the CAFTA came into effect, with the two-way trade reaching almost US$500 billion in 2014. In the meanwhile, China also put up the US$10 billion China–ASEAN investment Fund to deepen economic cooperation with individual ASEAN countries. More recently, China has been focussing on the larger, 16-member Regional Comprehensive Economic Partnership (RCEP), which is ASEAN-centric but mainly China-driven.

As China's economy grows and its external balances rapidly expand, China is becoming an increasingly important capital-exporting economy, particularly for 2014 when China's outbound overseas direct investment (ODI) exceeded its inbound foreign direct investment (FDI). With its total ODI amounting to US$140 billion, China had become the world's third largest source of FDI, with many Chinese corporations expanding their footprints to 156 countries.[10]

Apart from touting its strong financial and technological capability to develop infrastructure (e.g., its high-speed rail) for the emerging economies, China has indeed significantly expanded its Official Development Assistance (ODA) programme. During 2010–2012, China doled out a total of US$14 billion (largely grants and interest-free loans) to developing countries in Africa and the Asia Pacific. China's present ODA commitment is admittedly still small, compared to the traditional Organisation for Economic Co-operation and Development (OECD) donors. But China has the potential to catch up, particularly since many

---

[9] See John Wong, "China's Trump Card in Economic Diplomacy", *Straits Times* (Singapore, March 11, 2015).

[10] "China's ODI to Maintain Double-Digit Growth", *China Daily*, April 23, 2015.

OECD countries today have run into serious fiscal deficits. Thanks to its relentless economic rise, China is clearly in the thick of deploying all the major conventional economic diplomatic tools that Western powers and Japan have formerly used.

China's three decades of successful economic growth based on its own political system (one that is so different from the Western kind of liberal democracy) and fuelled by its own brand of capitalism (one with a special mix of state control and market operation), has already made a deep impression on many Third World countries. All the earlier-mentioned economic diplomatic activities, including the founding of the China-backed AIIB, could eventually contribute to the growth and spread of the so-called "Beijing Consensus" as a potential counter-weight to the existing "Washington Consensus". China's successful development experience can be seen as a unique development model from the South.

Towards the New Normal of Lower Growth

But the fact is that China is losing its former high growth momentum. Growth started to decelerate in 2012 with 7.8% growth, and then 7.7% for 2013, with no significant statistical difference. But the decline seemed more dramatic for 2014, which ended with 7.3%, the lowest in more than two decades and falling short of the official target of 7.5% originally set by Premier Li Keqiang. The 2014 slowdown in growth was in part due to some cyclical factors associated with the sluggish global economic outlook, i.e., sluggish growth in the EU and weak recovery in the US; but it was mainly due to the workings of many domestic structural factors arising from China's long periods of unbalanced growth patterns. Recent economic reform and other new policy initiatives like the anti-corruption campaign that were introduced by Xi Jinping had also dampened GDP growth as a kind of "policy-induced decline" in the short run.

No economy can keep growing at such high rates forever without running into various constraints. China has chalked up double-digit rates of hyper-growth for well over three decades, historically much longer than what the other high-performance East Asian economies of Japan, South Korea, Taiwan, Hong Kong and Singapore had experienced before — just a little over two decades of such high growth for Japan, Korea and Taiwan, and a bit shorter for Hong Kong and Singapore. As can be seen from Table 1, Japan experienced such high growth mainly in the 1950s and the 1960s, and then followed by Hong Kong, South Korea, Taiwan and Singapore after the mid-1960s, the whole of the 1970s and then much of the 1980s. Malaysia and Thailand also had high growth, but not nearly as high and lasting not as long while India's growth performance was even more lacklustre.

China has been the most remarkable for sustaining such high growth for so long. This is partly because China had enjoyed some latecomer's advantages in terms of reaping the technological backlog, but mainly because it had far greater internal dynamics in terms of having much bigger hinterlands along with a larger labour force, as compared to the other East Asian economies. Still, after its catch-up phase of phenomenal hyper growth, China's growth must come down due to the inevitable weakening of its various growth drivers or technically, the drying up of its sources of growth.

Weakening of the growth drivers

From a general economic development perspective, the major impetus of China's growth on the supply side was associated with the transfer of its surplus rural labour from low-productivity agriculture to higher-productivity manufacturing, *á la* Arthur Lewis.[11] But such growth potential has been rapidly exhausted in recent years. The population of age group 15–64 had started to peak in 2010 at 74.5%, with the labour supply coming near to the so-called "Lewis Turning Point". Though the situation is yet to be translated into immediate labour shortages, it does imply that China has already spent most of its "demographic dividend" and started to lose its comparative advantage in a wide range of labour-intensive manufacturing activities. *Pari passu* with its labour force decline has been the exhaustion of its easy productivity gains from early market reforms and institutional reorganization, and technological progress embodied in the imported machines and new equipment. Hence the hyper growth has to come to an end.

---

[11] This is the central argument of the two-sector model by the Nobel Laureate, W. Arthur Lewis. See his book, *The Theory of Economic Growth*, Allen & Unwin, 1955.

Table 1.   East Asia performance indicators.

Countries	Population (million) 2013	GDP Per Capital (USD) 2013	Total GDP (US$ Bn) 2012	Growth of GDP (%)							
				1960–1970	1970–1980	1980–1990	1990–2000	2000–2010	2011	2012	2013
China	1362	6747	8252	5.2	5.5	10.3	9.7	10.3	9.2	7.8	7.7
Japan	127	38,491	5984	10.9	4.3	4.1	1.3	1.1	-0.7	2.2	1.5
South Korea	50	24,382	1.151	8.6	10.1	8.9	5.7	4.2	2.4	2.7	2.8
Taiwan	23	20,980	455	9.2	9.7	7.9	5.7	3.9	1.1		2.2
Hong Kong	7.2	37,775	258	10	9.3	6.9	3.8	4.6	5.0	1.8	2.9
ASEAN-10											
Brunei	0.4	39,942	16.9	—	—	—	2.1	1.5	1.9	2.7	1.9
Cambodia	15.1	1075	14.3	—	—	—	6.4	7.9	6.9	6.5	7.0
Indonesia	243	3590	894	3.9	7.2	6.1	3.8	5.2	6.5	6	5.8
Laos	6.7	1476	9.3	—	—	—	6.1	7.1	8.0	8.3	8.3
Malaysia	30.2	10,547	307	6.5	7.9	5.3	6.5	5.5	5.1	4.4	4.7
Myanmar*	53.3	868	54	—	—	—	6.1	10.8	5.5	—	5.5
Philippines	99.5	2790	2407	5.1	6.0	1.0	3.3	4.9	3.7	4.8	6.8
Singapore	5.4	54,710	268	8.8	8.3	6.7	7.4	5.9	4.9	2.1	4.9
Thailand	64.1	5674	377	8.4	7.1	7.6	3.8	4.9	0.1	5.6	2.9
Vietnam	89.7	1901	138	—	—	—	7.3	7.4	5.6	5.1	5.3
India	1243	1615		4.4	3.1	5.2	6.5	7.5	6.9	5.4	4.7

Source: CIA Fact Book.
*Myanmar GDP data estimates based on 2006.

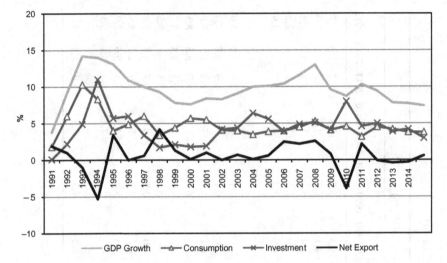

Figure 3.   Source of China's economic growth, 1990–2014.

Source: National Bureau of Statistics.

In terms of contribution to growth, China's economic growth since the early 1990s has been basically driven by total domestic demand, with domestic investment playing a relatively more important role than domestic consumption. This necessarily follows that the contribution of external demand (or net exports) to China's GDP growth has all along been quite negligible in gross terms, mostly around 5% in the 1990s and then up to around 10% in recent years. During the global financial crisis as China's exports plunged, the contribution of external demand to overall GDP growth even became negative. It had remained negative in the last few years, though turning slightly positive in the 2014. In fact, of the 7.4% growth in 2014, consumption accounted for 3.8% and investment 3.0% while net exports only 0.6% (Figure 3).

It thus appears that the export sector has not directly generated much GDP for China, particularly since China's exports carry high import contents with around 50% of China's exports being processing trade. This is because China is the base for numerous regional and global production networks and supply chains whose finished products usually contain a lot of imported materials and components, thereby netting only a small amount of domestic value-added for China. The classical example was the much publicized case of a China-assembled iPad from Apple that was sold in the US market for US$499, but yielding only US$8 to Chinese labour.[12]

However, the actual economic importance of Chinese exports to its economic growth has been seriously understated by this first-order simple analysis of gross export figures because it has missed out a lot important "indirect" economic activities and spillovers that are connected to China's export industries if we should go for more detailed inter-sectoral analysis. Most export-oriented industries have extensive economic linkages created by various local supporting service activities as well as investment in the upstream and downstream sectors. There are also the multiplier effects on the economy generated from the spending of millions of workers and employees in the export sector.

With rising operating costs and increasing wages, China's export competitiveness for labour-intensive exports is bound to suffer.[13] The sharp rise of China's unit labour cost in recent years has been widely reported, following its double-digit rates of wage hike. According to official data, the annual average wage of all employees had increased 5.5 times for the past 13 years from 9330 yuan in 2000 to 51,470 yuan in 2013. Minimum wages had also risen at double-digit rates for the past five years 2010–2015.[14] This, along with the gradual appreciation of the RMB (which has since appreciated over 30% against the US dollar since July 2005), had seriously eroded China's comparative advantage in its export markets. Consequently, China is now facing the same problem of "shifting comparative advantage" that had previously plagued Japan, South Korea and Taiwan. China would soon realize that its export sector is generating less and less growth potential for its economy. Accordingly, exports would no longer be a dependable engine of China's growth in the long run, not to mention that exports have often been the transmission mechanism of external risks and instability.

---

[12] For the assembling of an iPhone in China, which sold for US$179 but created a total value-added of only US$6.5 in China, see Xing Yuqing, "How the iPhone Widens US Trade Deficits with China: The Story of US$6.5 Value-Added to China for its Exports of US$179", *EAI Background Brief*, No. 629 (May 27, 2011).

[13] See HKTDC's report, "An Update on Production costs on the Mainland" (January 12, 2012).

[14] "China to Achieve Minimum Wage Growth Targets", *China Daily*, May 29, 2015.

This leaves domestic investment and domestic consumption as the principal drivers of China's future growth. It is well known that China's past GDP growth has been largely investment-led. Apart from infrastructure development, industrial upgrading and housing construction are the two other major components of fixed assets investment. To cope with the 2008 global financial crisis, Premier Wen Jiabao had hastily put up a huge stimulus package of 4 trillion yuan to pump-prime the economy, subsequently leading to serious over-investment as well as an overheated property market. Fixed investment had since come down substantially on account of industrial over-capacity (particularly serious for large industries like steel, cement and ferrous metals with over 20% excess capacities) and a downturn in the property market (real estate accounting for a quarter of total fixed investment). With domestic investment as the main engine of growth rapidly decelerating, GDP growth must also slow down.

Still more, the Chinese economy has been plagued by serious macroeconomic imbalance due to chronic over-investment and under-consumption, which has led to over-production and over-export, and eventually persistent trade surplus. In this way, China's macroeconomic imbalance has also contributed to global macroeconomic imbalances. The root cause of this unique problem is China's phenomenally high saving rate, which in recent years has been staying close to 50%.[15]

As shown in Figure 4, Chinese households and state enterprises have high savings, contributing to high national savings rates. The state had mobilized these massive domestic savings for capital investment, from building infrastructure and housing to the technological upgrading of key manufacturing industries. Heavy capital investment had therefore been the foundation of China's past pro-growth development strategy. However the same strategy had resulted in its unbalanced growth, with by far too much investment along with too little consumption. Hence the resulting phenomenon of over-investment and excess capacities were one of the key factors responsible for the lower growth in 2014.

---

[15]The basic macroeconomic identity $I = S$ can self-explain over-investment and over-consumption. Trade surplus can also be easily explained by another simple identity: $X - M = S - I$, i.e., "trade surplus" as the difference between exports (X) and imports (M) equals "saving surplus", as gross savings (S) minus gross investment (I).

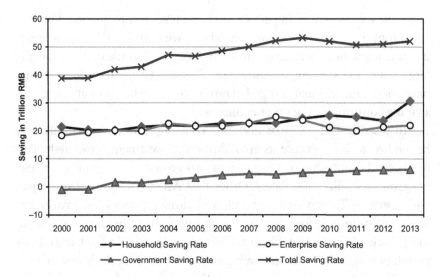

Figure 4.　China's saving rates, 2000–2013.
Source: National Bureau of Statistics.

But is the Chinese economy really under-consuming? At about 40% of its GDP, China's gross consumption level looks undoubtedly very low as compared to not just the US-level of 70%, but even India's level of around 56%. In an absolute sense, however, the Chinese people, particularly those in urban areas, have indeed been consuming quite a lot in recent years and emerging affluence is highly visible in China's big cities. Thus, in 2014, China topped the world's sale of more than 24 million units of automobile, 350 million units of micro-computers, and 1.6 billion mobile phones and so on. Also, Chinese tourists in 2014 made 3.1 billion domestic trips and 116 million overseas trips.[16] With growing urbanization, the next wave of consumption growth will come from new sources like social services, urban amenities and new lifestyle activities.

Closely related to the growing urban affluence is the rise of the middle class, which is estimated to be around 350 million. The size of the Chinese middle class will continue to rise rapidly along with China's future economic growth and further urbanization. It is destined

---

[16]China National Bureau of Statistics, "The 2014 National Economic and Social Development Statistical Communiqué" (February 2015).

to produce even greater impact on both the level and pattern of domestic consumption in the years to come, much like what America's baby-boomers had impacted the American economy and society. Because of its potentially large scale, the coming consumer revolution in China could in future have enormous regional and global ramifications in terms of affecting and shaping consumption in other countries.

In a sense, China's gross domestic consumption level currently may be too low mainly because its gross domestic investment is too high. This has been the outcome of China's past pro-growth development strategy of "grow first, distribute later". Other East Asian economies from Japan and Korea to Taiwan had also followed similar patterns of investment and consumption before. But such continuing investment-driven growth mode is clearly unsustainable in the long run. Specifically for China, as its population ages, its domestic saving rates are bound to decline over time as is already happening in Japan now. Viewed from a different angle, the fact that consumption is presently not the main driver of China's economic growth also means that it will be an untapped source of it future growth.

Also a kind of policy-induced slowdown

Beyond the foregoing "structural explanations", China's present economic slowdown can be further attributed to the workings of some short-term "policy factors", i.e., the slowdown could also be the outcome of some deliberate policy options on the part of the government. The case in point is Xi Jinping's relentless campaign against high-level corruption and rent-seeking activities in China, which, in helping him to consolidate his power, has also generated some dampening effects on economic growth in the short run.

Xi's war on corruption is supposed to be economically and socially beneficial in the long run. It is simply self-evident that getting rid of corruption anywhere would improve governance while promoting transparency and accountability. All these would in turn lower the transaction costs and raise economic efficiency, and eventually leading to higher economic growth. Paradoxically, however, China seems to be somewhat an exceptional case to the international debate on the relationship between corruption and growth. Though China has for years ranked quite high in the Corruption Perception Index by Transparent International, it has still chalked up double-digit rates of growth, outperforming all the other countries, including those that are manifestly less corrupt than China.[17]

Putting aside the controversial long-term relationship between corruption and economic development, the short-term effects of Xi's anti-corruption campaign are also mixed. Many of the government's anti-corruption and anti-extravagance measures (the "Eight-point Regulations") covering official travels, official dinners and other perks have evidently reduced domestic consumption, from dining and wining to purchases of luxurious goods and expensive gifts taking. The case of Macau's casino industry can be a good proxy for indirect evidence to substantiate this argument. Because of China's austerity drive, even the gambling revenue of Macau's casino industry had recently tumbled, the first since its gambling liberalization for mainland Chinese in 2002.

The more serious economic effect from Xi's corruption crackdown is the short-term disruption to the bureaucracy. The dismissal of many corrupt officials had already caused some delay in policy making and implementation. Corruption investigations at various levels of government by anti-corruption inspectors from Beijing have created widespread apprehension in the bureaucracy, leading to inaction of government officials and even some policy paralysis. Politically, Xi's severe crackdown on corruption has undoubtedly created a lot of uncertainty, which had unnerved many China scholars and prompted the veteran China-watcher David Shambaugh to hastily jump to an unwarranted conclusion that the Xi's regime was coming near the "end game" or about to "crack up"![18] It would actually be more realistic to argue that Xi's clampdown on corruption had exerted a toll on current economic growth by stalling the implementation of certain projects and even resulting in cutbacks on domestic investment, particularly at the local level.

Without doubt, Xi's overall reform package had also produced the same kind of "short-term pain for long-term gain" trade-off for economic growth, particularly in the area of financial sector reform. Sharp credit

---

[17] It is most ironical that just as Xi Jinping's anti-corruption campaign is reaping good results, China's ranking in the international corruption perception index for 2014 rose to 100 from 80 in 2013 (more corrupt in 2014 than in 2013!).

[18] David Shambaugh, "The Coming Chinese Crackup", *The Wall Street Journal*, March 6, 2015.

creation (officially called "total social financing"), the rapid growth of local government debt (arising from Wen Jiabao's anti-recession stimulus programme) and the rapid expansion of commercial banks' unregulated lending under the off-balance sheet (called "shadow banking") resulted in the sharp rise of China's total debt, which has reached a historical high, estimated to be around 250% of GDP in mid-2015, up from the 180% of 2008. Internationally, China's debt is at about the same level of Taiwan, Korea and Malaysia, but slightly lower than that of the US and much lower than that of Japan (almost 400% of its GDP).

It is actually not uncommon for a booming economy to incur high debt as easy credit is needed to charge economic expansion. For China, its debt problem has suddenly become more acute partly because of its current economic slowdown, which is further aggravated by the slump in its property market. Accordingly, its debt burden can operate as a serious drag on economic growth in next few years.

In the eyes of the former US Treasury Secretary Henry Paulson (who had dealt with the 2008 financial collapse in the Wall Street and is also familiar with China's financial structure) China's financial system "will face a reckoning and have to contend with a wave of credit losses and debt restructurings".[19] Nonetheless, Paulson believed that China's situation should be "manageable". Indeed, with its US$4 trillion in foreign reserves and high domestic savings, China would be able to defuse any large-scale financial crisis, especially since financial crisis, especially since most of the debt is basically domestic liabilities linked to the property sector and local governments.

China's debt is thus categorically different from that of other countries, because a lot of Chinese debt was primarily incurred for the purpose of economic and social development, not for financing social consumption as in Europe. They were mostly backed by substantial assets and underwritten by local governments. In this sense, China's debt problem is basically a reform problem. Currently, the government is making efforts to tackle the debt burden through restructuring and rescheduling them on the one hand; and it seeks to eventually digest the bulk of it through some securitization measures like converting debt into government or corporate loans.

---

[19]"A Veteran of '08 Crisis Warns China", *International New York Times*, April 22, 2015.

Still, China's current economic slowdown has inevitably increased the debt burden and thereby raised the level of short-term credit risk and possible default. A large debt overhang is just not conducive to economic growth. As the government is taking measures to manage the debt crisis through vigorous deleveraging, it is also creating at the same time the very macroeconomic environment that is squeezing economic growth. The case in point is the government's move to clean up local government debt by stopping runaway borrowing and loans, and the consequence of which is the weakening of one of the important economic growth drivers. In other words, Xi Jinping's policies of defusing the debt crisis and deepening the financial sector reform have also inevitably contributed to China's current economic slowdown.

Less obsessed with GDP-dominated growth

Another significant new policy option concerning economic growth under the New Normal has been the government's shift in its perception and mind-set related to what it considers the basic requirements of economic growth. Back in 1979, Deng Xiaoping launched economic reform to maximize economic growth for China, as manifested in the slogan: "To get rich is glorious". China's policy makers have since pursued such high growth strategy, almost at all costs. This had produced double-digit rates of growth for over three decades, with China's per-capita GDP in 2014 about 100 times more than that in 1979. However, such a blatant GDP pursuit (dubbed "GNPism") had also created a lot of social costs, ranging from high income inequality (with Gini ratio at 0.47 for 2014) to such undesirable by-products and negative externalities as serious air and water pollution.

In all fairness, the previous Hu–Wen leadership was actually aware of the problems of the fundamental GDP-dominated growth strategy. Wen Jiabao had at times called for a new development policy that would pay greater attention to the quality aspects of GDP growth, and not just high GDP numbers. However, Wen was fundamentally a pro-growth premier at heart. Much like his predecessor Zhu Rongji (who had openly vouched to "protect" economic growth at 8% or *bao-ba*), Wen himself was also highly obsessed with high GDP growth. Hence, as the global financial crisis struck China in 2008, Wen promptly put up a massive fiscal and monetary package to stimulate GDP growth, with many "over-kill" effects and many lingering problems such as the sharp rise of local government debt as discussed earlier.

This gave the new leadership under Xi Jinping an opportunity to make a decisive departure from China's time-honoured GDP-dominated pro-growth policy. Thus, China's National Bureau of Statistics (NBS), which compiles China's GDP accounts, recently declared that it had taken steps to end what it called "GDP Supremacy". It had radically revised its conventional GDP accounting to give higher weights to the "quality aspects" of GDP growth like innovation and R&D, and to factor in more welfare-aspects of economic growth like the social costs of pollution. The NBS also announced that it would provide a more comprehensive and multi-faceted assessment of China's growth performance beyond GDP. In future, along with the release of GDP data, the NBS would also provide some 40 or so core indicators that can better capture China's real economic and social changes, particularly in such crucial areas as industrial upgrading, technological development, environmental protection, rural–urban income gap, urbanization, people's livelihood and so on.[20] This clearly implies that China's future economic growth performance will not be epitomized by changes of just one GDP indicator alone.

Finance Minister Lou Jiwei, at the 2014 G20 Finance Ministers meeting in Cairns (September 2014), confirmed that China had indeed intended to downgrade pure GDP growth in formulating its economic policy and policy response. China's macroeconomic policy would in future focus more on comprehensive targets like stable growth, employment, inflation and so on. More significantly, the government would stick to the long-term goals of structural reforms and industrial upgrading, and would not, by and large, be distracted by short-term changes in certain GDP indicators.[21]

In broad principle, as economic growth fluctuates in future, the Chinese government is supposed to refrain from taking hasty stimulus measures just artificially boosting short-term GDP growth. In practice, however, the Chinese government has remained highly averse to any sharp volatility, be it in the stock market, economic growth or employment. Just for the

---

[20]"Chinese Statisticians to Broaden Focus from GDP", *China Daily*, September 12, 2014; "New Accounting Regime Ends "GDP Supremacy", *China Daily*, September 22, 2014.
[21]"China Will Not Alter Economic Policy", *China Daily*, September 22, 2014.

sake of maintaining social stability, the government would still be very much inclined to step in once a serious crisis is developing, as evidenced in the heavy government intervention to save the Shanghai stock market in July 2015.

Given its long central-planning mindset and legacies, the government is admittedly still adjusting to the hard reality of how to balance its intended reforms with the uncertain prospects of future growth. Thus, Premier Li Keqiang had quickly changed his initially more market-oriented macroeconomic policies to become highly interventionist in terms of openly boosting growth to 7% as the growth outlook in the early part of 2015 became very gloomy. Much as what Premier Zhu Rongji was doing to "protect economic growth at 8%" (*baoba*) in the late 1990s when China's economy was then threatened by the Asian financial crisis, Li Keqiang today has been taking a similar stand in "protecting his 7% growth" (*baoqi*) target for 2015.[22]

Overall, macroeconomic rebalancing and the related new policy initiatives are expected to bring about a gradual shift in the basic growth pattern, development priority and the basic economic structure over time. All these could slow down growth in the short run, but render future growth potentially more sustainable in the longer run.

Managing the new normal of lower growth

President Xi Jinping, in his keynote speech at the APEC CEO Summit in Beijing on November 9, 2014, confirmed that China had formally embraced the "New Normal" of lower but more stable growth. Referring to any risks of China's growth rate plummeting to the 7% level, Xi had simply dismissed it as something that "is actually not all that scary".[23] Economic growth is about increases in GDP at compound interest rates. As Xi had rightly pointed out, China's 7.7% growth in 2013 had added to China an increment of GDP in a single year that was equivalent to the entire GDP of 1994.

Xi himself is clearly not obsessed with simple high GDP growth, partly because he has realized that China's present rate of growth at 7% is not really low — an average annual growth of 7% would double GDP in 10 years —

---

[22]"Chinese Cabinet Expresses Confidence in Economy", *China Daily*, July 9, 2015.
[23]"Chinese President Says Risks to Economy 'Not that Scary,'" *China Daily*, November 9, 2014.

Table 2. Comparative economic performance of selected countries, 2014.

	GDP Growth %	Inflation (CPI) %	Unemployment %	Current A/C balance, % of GDP	Budget balance, % of GDP
China	7.4	2.0	4.1	2.4	−1.9
United States	2.3	1.6	5.6	−2.3	−2.8
Japan	−1.3	2.8	3.5	0.3	−8.2
Euro Zone	0.8	0.4	11.5	2.4	−2.5
Russia	0.6	7.7	5.2	2.6	0.4
India	6.0	7.3	8.8	−2.0	−4.3
Indonesia	5.0	6.3	6.4	−2.8	−2.3
Malaysia	6.0	3.1	2.7	5.7	−3.6
Singapore	3.1	1.1	2.0	20.7	0.5
South Korea	3.5	1.3	3.4	5.7	0.6
Brazil	0.1	6.3	4.8	−4.0	−5.5

Source: *The Economist*, January 17, 2015, pp. 80–81. Except for China's growth, inflation and budget balance, which comes from Chinese government, all other GDP, inflation and shares of A/C and budget balance in GDP, are estimates for 2014 by Economist Intelligence Unit. Unemployment data are official unemployment rates for October and November 2014. For India, the newest unemployment rate available is for 2013.

and partly because lower rates of growth in succeeding years could still create the same amount of GDP or economic activities. What is more crucial to him is whether or not the Chinese economy is on track to rebalancing its pattern of growth by rendering growth less dependent on investment and exports and more on domestic consumption, and continuing to upgrade its economic structure towards a more efficient growth based on higher productivity.

As can be seen from Table 2, China's so-called "lower growth" that has been widely reported by international media is actually not "low" at all by any regional or global standard. In fact, China today as a big economic mammoth of about US$11 trillion in GDP simply should not be growing at its former neck-breaking rates. Its mere 7% growth would add to it the amount of GDP in one year that is equivalent to about two-third of Indonesia's or one-third of India's current total GDP.

Having accepted the New Normal of slower growth, the Chinese government would hence be quite comfortable with a 7% growth or a slightly lower rate. A few years ago, it was often argued that China would need to sustain a high growth rate of 7.5–8% in order to generate sufficient employment opportunities. But such a high growth benchmark has since become outdated. With China's economic base today having grown so much bigger, it would need progressively lower rates of growth to generate the equivalent amount of GDP (economic activities) that are needed to create the equivalent number of new jobs. In the meantime, China's labour market has also stopped growing and an economic growth rate of around 6–7% would be quite sufficient to maintain employment stability for many years to come.

Thus, Xi's New Normal of lower but more stable growth is essentially a managed economic slowdown that will also facilitate the reform and rebalancing of the economy. He will use the stable growth environment to create more higher quality jobs as well as carry out reform and restructuring in various areas, ranging from land and labour to local public finance and state-owned enterprises (SOEs). In the short run, reform and rebalancing could, of course, put pressures on economic growth. In the long run, however, progress in reform and restructuring should yield sufficient "reform dividend" for the economy to make a successful transition towards the "developed economy" status.

In Transition to a Developed Economy

It is not enough for China just to rebalance its sources of growth to make growth more sustainable. In accepting the New Normal, it needs also to develop the *new* sources of growth. The kind of higher quality and more efficient economic growth in the future has to be based on opening up the new sources of growth associated with (a) innovation and technological progress; (b) deepening of market reform; and (c) accelerating industrial restructuring. Xi Jinping has repeatedly emphasized the importance of innovation and technological progress as well as more thorough-going market reform.

Cultivating new sources of future growth

For any economy, innovation and technological progress are the funda-mental sources of its productivity growth. China's past dynamic growth had indeed been fuelled by significant technological progress associated with imported technology and initial market reform. But China has now exhausted such easy source of technological progress, the so-called "picking the low-hanging fruits" way; and future productivity gains therefore will need to come from its own R&D efforts.

In recent years, China has rapidly expanded its R&D activities, which reached 2.1% of GDP in 2014, compared to the 2.8% for the United States and 3.4% for Japan. In total terms, however, China's global share of R&D spending is actually not low, being the world's second largest after that of the United States. In 2014 alone, some 2.4 million new patents were registered in China. The "Nature Index/Global" (which tracks the sources of publication of high-quality scientific papers) also ranks China, in 2014, for publishing the world's second largest number of scientific papers after the United States. With more than seven million new university graduates every year and an industrial base that is rapidly expanding and becoming increasingly more sophisticated, China is admittedly on track to develop a viable technological base that will eventually generate new sources of productivity increases to support future economic growth. Not surprisingly, the 2014 Bloomberg Global Innovation Index ranked China as the world's 25th most innovative country (the top 20 being mostly OECD countries) in total innovation score, being the first in manufacturing rank, the third in high-tech density rank, and the fourth in patent activity rank.

It may, however, be cautioned that a high R&D expenditure itself plus the training-up of a large number of high-levelled manpower, including many scientists and engineers, does not automatically translate into successful commercial innovations. Many patents and inventions do not end up in successful commercial applications, much depending on the conducive institutional environment like the protection of the intellectual property rights and the needed financial support like the availability of venture capital.

China will also face an even greater challenge of how to capture more productivity gains from "continuing institutional innovation" through more thorough-going market reform. Since China can no longer reap simple and easy productivity gains from its early phases of introducing the market system, its major task now is how to squeeze even greater efficiency and productivity through deepening market reform, including allowing the market to play a more central role in resource allocation in the critical areas of the economy. Whereas technological innovation is the "hardware", institutional innovation through further market reform and deregulation can be considered as the "software, or just the kind of needed "supply-side policies" to boost total factor productivity (TFP) growth for the next lap of growth. But all this, in turn, critically depends on the strong political will of Xi's leadership, first to initiate reforms and then implement the necessary changes.

At the Third Party Plenum in November 2013, Xi Jinping announced a bold and comprehensive reform package covering many critical areas that include financial sector reform, central–local fiscal relations, competition policy, SOE reform, rural land policy, foreign trade and foreign investment and so on. At the Fourth Party Plenum in October 2014, the main reform focus shifted to legal reform in order to strengthen China's "rule of law". Finally, China has come to recognize that an effective and functioning legal framework is simply indispensable for good governance, which in turn holds the key to the successful implementation of various reforms.

Xi had indeed laid out many reform plans on the table. They are all critical and they are also interdependent. So far, the financial sector reform and the reform of local public finance have made good progress while the rural land reform seems to get bogged down. For SOE reform, it is admittedly a difficult but a necessarily long-drawn-out process, as too many established interests are involved. Xi has followed a clever strategy of using his anti-corruption campaign to pry open some large SOEs for reform and re-organization. He has already restructured the SOEs related to oil and gas, the railway. He has since extended his target at the mass media, higher education and civil aviation.

Xi's reform endeavour will therefore be highly critical for the Chinese economy. As reform often gives rise to the inevitable trade-off of "the short-term pain for the long-term gain" in the short run, the Chinese economy will have to brace itself for many more headwinds from different fronts. For the next few years, therefore, it would be hard enough for China just to maintain growth at the 6–7% level. The government could still be able to play around with some pro-growth fiscal policy and some appropriate monetary easing measures such as the four rounds of interest rate cuts in the first half of 2015, should the external and domestic economic environment continue to deteriorate. But any large artificial stimulus to economic growth needs to be carefully applied lest it would undo the ongoing reform efforts.

Part of China's past growth was essentially derived from the sheer injection of a massive amount of capital (basically from its high domestic savings) along with abundant cheap labour. Now as China's fertility rates have sharply declined, it has also fast exhausted its "demographic dividend" for development. This follows that the next phase of growth will all the more have to shift from dumping in more inputs to fostering higher TFP growth based on not just technological innovation but also institutional innovation like deepening and broadening of the market reform. Once the reform has achieved a significant breakthrough, China's economy would then reap the "reform dividend" for its next lap of growth.

Last but not least is the need to step up industrial restructuring and upgrading. Successful East Asian economies like South Korea, Taiwan and Singapore had all started their industrialization based on labour-intensive manufacturing. In the course of time — normally after a decade or so of intensive industrialization, they experienced labour shortages as well as losing comparative advantage for their labour-intensive manufactured exports due to rising cost and increasing wages. Thus, they all had to undergo their second phase of industrialization, mainly in the late 1970s and the early 1980s, through industrial upgrading or restructuring their industries towards more capital-intensive and higher value-added activities.

As China has basically followed such "East Asian model" of economic development based on growing manufactured exports, China will also have to undergo similar process of economic restructuring — which was called the "Second Industrial Revolution" in Singapore, but it had not been a smooth-going process even for this small country. For China in recent years, its wage hike at double-digit rates is a clear manifestation of its increasingly tighter labour market while its sharply declining export growth from double- to single-digit rates is also the telltale sign of its losing comparative advantage for its labour-intensive manufactured exports. China's industrial upgrading is therefore long overdue.

It may be noted that the process of industrial upgrading had already started many years back; and it had in fact been emphasized as one of the central policy focusses in China's 11th Five-Year Plan (2006–2010). Over the years, the Guangdong government had vigorously pushed the industrial restructuring of its many small and medium labour-intensive industries in the Pearl River Delta region, while the Yangtze Delta region had also undergone significant industrial upgrading towards more capital-intensive and skill-intensive activities. In the Binhai region around Tianjin, however, the main focus had been on setting up large-scale, technology-intensive new industries related to space, aircraft manufacturing, new energy, new materials and so on, with heavy state support. Overall, China's manufacturing sector has no doubt made significant achievements in moving up the value chain, as evident in its increasing production of those high-technology items. However, China's manufactured exports have remained basically dominated by labour-intensive products or goods with low domestic value-added.

In a truly market economy, industrial restructuring is apt to be a gradual process of structural change to be properly guided by market signals. Xi Jinping and Li Keqiang are naturally impatient with such a market driven but slow-going process. Recently, the Chinese government unveiled the "Made in China 2025" plan, which is China's first action plan (reportedly to be quite similar to Germany's "Industry 4.0" plan or its Fourth Industrial Revolution) to promote "intensive manufacturing". Its main objective is to transform China's manufacturing sector from its present stage of being just a global manufacturing giant in terms of sheer volumes and output to a leading manufacturing power of the world in a quality sense. The key jargon is to upgrade China's manufacturing industries from "Made in China" to "Created in China". To this end, the focus for the next 10 years is to achieve significant breakthroughs in 10 crucial sectors comprising information technology, numerical control tools and robotics, aerospace equipment, ocean engineering and high-tech ships, railway equipment, energy saving and new energy, power equipment, new materials, medicine and medical devices and agricultural machinery.

It suffices to say that the implementation of this new manufacturing Master Plan will create a powerful new growth engine that should propel China's next phase of economic growth to reach the threshold of a developed economy by 2030, and also beyond.

Overcoming the middle income trap

The concept of "middle income trap" (MIT) has recently been widely discussed, but also widely misinterpreted. According to the World Bank, of the 101 or so middle income economies in the 1960s, only about 13 (mostly in East Asia) had graduated to become high income (or developed) economies by 2008. Such is the historical origin of the concept of MIT. But many commentators have since discussed this concept often in a misguided manner, with some linking the issue to a certain single factor like a sudden slowdown in economic growth or the emerging problem of ageing population.

Recently, China's Finance Minister Lou Jiwei had also sounded the warning that China might face a "greater than 50% chance" of falling into the MIT.[24] But Lou's sensational remark was clearly meant to be a political message that was calculated to warn the Chinese people against the many potential obstacles and challenges facing China's economy ahead. Just as successful economic growth of a country is underpinned by a comprehensive process of economic, social and institutional transformation, the failure to sustain continuing growth or falling into MIT cannot be attributed to just one or two factors.

In economic development literature, the term MIT was first applied to the development processes of many Latin American economies that were trapped in their prolonged periods of import substitution industrialization during the 1960–1970s, failing to achieve the successful transition to export orientation, as in Korea and Taiwan. The concept of MIT was subsequently also applied to some primary exporting Southeast Asian economies (e.g., the Philippines), which had been initially successful in their labour-intensive and resource-based industrialization. However, they subsequently failed to restructure and upgrade their manufactured sector to higher value-added activities.

In a sense, China as already an upper middle-income economy is on the verge of escaping the MIT, having sustained double-digit growth for over three decades, historically much longer than that of those economies that had successfully escaped from the MIT. Though China's recent growth has slowed to just about 7% (which is technically "very high growth"), it still has plenty of potential to sustain further growth, as already discussed earlier. China's nominal per-capita GDP in 2014 at around US$8,000 or US$13,000 in PPP terms is getting quite near to the threshold of a developed economy!

---

[24]"Nation Must be Alert to Middle-Income-Trap", *China Daily*, April 28, 2015.

More importantly, China's existing growth path and technological bases for growth do present a sharp contrast to those developing economies that had in the past fallen into the MIT. Apart from its high growth rates, China has already developed a huge and balanced industrial structure. Its manufacturing exports are still dynamic and competitive, while its superb physical infrastructure is of First-World standard. Furthermore, China's technological foundation has been growing stronger with rising R&D spending while its human capital is also developing rapidly on the back of having over seven million new university graduates a year along with an even greater number of graduates from technical institutions. In 2013, 35% of the relevant age-cohorts were enrolled in universities and colleges. All these have made China distinctively different from those developing countries that had fallen into the MIT.

It may be argued that if China's economy, so industrialized and with such stellar growth performance records behind it, should still fall into the MIT, it would simply imply that no other developing country would henceforth ever make it to a developed economy — quite an implausible supposition!

The negative impact of China's unfavourable demographics on its growth has also been exaggerated. Though China's labour force has started to slightly decline, it will not be facing serious labour shortages for many years to come. Indeed, the government in 2014 was still struggling hard to be able to create 13 million new jobs. The Lewis turning point is actually a gradual process.[25] Almost half of China's population is presently in the rural areas, and a lot of them are still waiting for the opportunity of migrating to urban areas for modern sector employment. The Lewis phenomenon of transferring surplus rural labour for industrial development in the urban areas should therefore continue for some time — and hence also the continuing source of productivity gains from this process.

The "demographic dividend" can actually be prolonged by stretching the quantity of the labour supply further through extending the retirement age, as in Japan and South Korea. In any case, China is unlikely to face acute labour shortages before 2025. In terms of quality, labour productivity

---

[25] See Mitali Das and P.N. Diaye, "Chronicle of A Decline Foretold: Has China Reached the Lewis Turing Point?" *IMF Working Paper* (WP/13/26).

can also be fostered through more intense human resource development as well as automation and robotization. As a matter of fact, China today has already widely used robotics in its major manufacturing industries. China today has overtaken Japan to become the world's largest market for robotics. In 2014 alone, it imported 57,000 such machines or one-quarter of the world's total production.[26]

Size really matters. China certainly still has a lot of potential for further development after its prolonged high growth. High-income economies of the West and Japan, and other smaller East Asian economies have all been facing the serious problem of demand-side constraint on growth, or lack of growth due to inadequate demand in both investment and consumption. For China, its vast interior and its northwestern regions are clearly still hungry for more growth and further development.

In 2014, China sold the largest number of cars in the world. However, China's car ownership ratio is just about 20 cars per 100 people, compared to 80 per 100 in the United States. Hence still a high demand potential, not just for cars, but also for all other consumable durables. In this sense, China's domestic-demand driven growth in future would be viable and sufficient for China to make a relatively easy transition to the developed economy before 2030.

At the threshold of a developed economy

The World Bank on February 27, 2012 released a study entitled, *China 2030: Building a Modern, Harmonious, and Creative High-Income Society*, which states that China has reached "a turning point in its development path". The report has also warned that "China's growth will decline gradually in the years leading to 2030 as China reaches the limits of growth brought about by current technologies and its current economic structure".

Together with China's government think tank Development Research Centre, the World Bank has done the growth trajectory made up of five discrete sets of average growth rates based on a series of China's Five-Year Plans: 9.9% growth for the 10th FYP (already achieved), 8.6% for the 11th, 7.0% for the 12th, 5.9% for the 13th and only 5.0% for the 14th (2025–2030), as shown in Table 3.

---

[26]"China Aims to be Leader in Robotics", *China Daily* (May 22, 2015).

Table 3. China: Projected growth pattern assuming steady reforms and no major shock.

Indicator	1995–2010	2011–2015	2016–2020	2021–2025	2026–2030
GDP growth	9.9	8.6	7.0	5.9	5.0
Labour growth	0.9	0.3	−0.2	−0.2	−0.4
Labour productivity growth	8.9	8.3	7.1	6.2	5.5
Structure of economy (end of period, %)					
Investment/GDP ratio	46.4	42	38	36	34
Consumption/GDP ratio	48.6	56	60	63	66
Industry/GDP ratio	46.9	43.8	41.0	38.0	34.6
Services/GDP ratio	43.0	47.6	51.6	56.1	61.1
Share of employment in agriculture	38.1	30.0	23.7	18.2	12.5
Share of employment in services	34.1	42.0	47.6	52.9	59.0

Source: World Bank, *China 2030: Building a Modern, Harmonious, and Creative High-Income Society* (2012).

Thus, projecting into the future, China's economy by 2030 is to surpass the US economy to become the world's largest, with a total GDP of US$24.4 trillion (compared to about $17 trillion for the US economy in 2014) at current US exchange rate. This projection now looks a little too conservative for the current state of the Chinese economy, as China is clearly set to fulfil this final target well before 2030!

Of greater importance is the fact that against the projected population of 1.47 billion, China's per capita GDP in 2030 will be about US$16,000–17,000 at current exchange rate, which is about the level of per capita GDP of South Korea in 2005, Singapore's in 1993 or Japan's in 1970. In any case, China will by then have definitely become a "developed economy", albeit still a low-income developed economy.

There are actually no universally accepted yardsticks to define a "developed economy". Beyond the per-capita GDP level, other common economic indicators like industrialization, infrastructure and human resource development have been used; but they are too complicated to compare across countries. Accordingly, the World Bank has simply classified countries into four categories of low, lower middle, upper middle and high

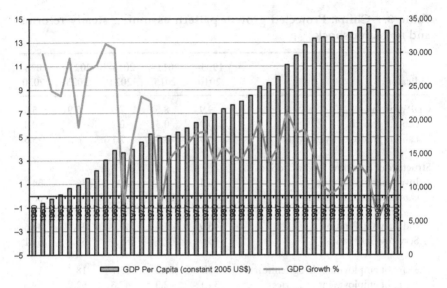

Figure 5.   Japan.

income economies on the basis of their (nominal) per-capita GDP level. For many years, the per-capita GDP of US$10,000 had been used as a convenient cut-off point to categorize a country to be a "high-income economy", or a proxy for a "developed economy".

Thus, Japan's per-capita GDP reached the US$10,000 level in 1965, just about 18 years from the start of its post-war high growth. Singapore reached this level in 1981, also 18 years after the beginning of its high growth in 1966. Taiwan reached this level in 1992, after about 26 years of its high growth. South Korea reached this level also in 1992, after about 25 years of its high growth (Figures 5–8). For China, its per-capita GDP by early 2015 still stood at US$8,000 (ranking only at the world's 78th position) after its 35 years of continuing high growth. On account of its huge population, China's per-capita GDP level is apt to remain low even after having sustained such a long period of high growth.

If the threshold of a developed economy were to be raised to the per-capita income level of US$15,000, as implied by the World Bank projection discussed earlier, it would take China from 2015 another 5 or 6 years to reach that level assuming a continuing 7% growth; or about 10 years for a continuing 6% growth. In this context, China would certainly become a "developed economy" well before 2030. However, it will still take China

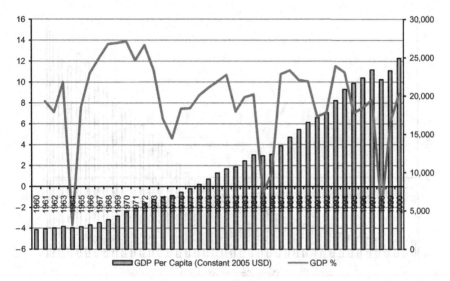

Figure 6. Singapore.

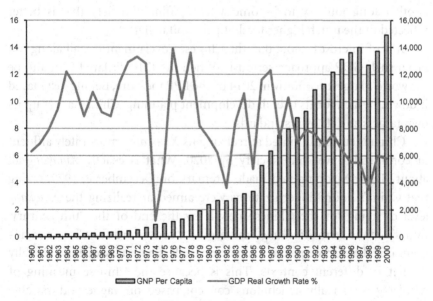

Figure 7. Taiwan.

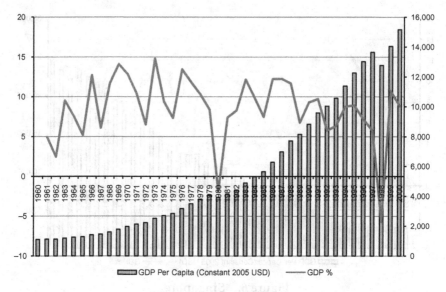

Figure 8.   South Korea.

another long journey to become a truly affluent society that is better reflected in the much higher level of per-capita GDP.

It is of interest to note that the Chinese government has all along not taken such GDP approach seriously. When the IMF declared China to be the world's largest economy in 2014 by the PPP measure, Beijing just played it down. In fact, for its overall development planning, China has set up its own targets and its own standards.

China is currently aimed at realizing its *Xiaokang* (moderately affluent or comfortably well-off) society by 2020. What is exactly *Xiaokang* all about? Deng Xiaoping first made a remark on December 6, 1979, saying that China's Four Modernizations were aimed at realizing the *Xiaokang* level of living for the Chinese people by the end of the 20th century. Ever since the term *Xiaokang* has become a code-word for China's socio-economic development, and China's top leaders had subsequently liberally used it in different contexts. This is because the Chinese meaning of *Xiaokang* is basically a nebulous concept based on vague and variable standards. To an ordinary Chinese, *Xiaokang* may convey the feeling of being "neither rich nor poor"; and in a concrete sense, this would imply having satisfied the material well-being of *wen-bao* or "enough to wear and eat".[27]

In economic development parlance, *Xiaokang* is simply about the satisfaction of the basic needs. But basic needs everywhere vary over time, and so it remains a moving target. China has since set the new target date of 2020 for becoming a *Xiaokang* society. In any case, the goal of the present Chinese leadership to realize *Xiaokang* by 2020 looks easily achievable. China being already an upper middle-income economy can easily develop the needed material base to satisfy such *Xiaokang* standard of basic needs like food and shelter for the common people.

The more challenging goal is admittedly the realization of the "Chinese Dream". For this, Xi Jinping has aimed higher and set his long-term vision of China developing into a fully-developed *Fuqiang* (rich and powerful) country by 2049, or exactly 100 years after the founding of the People's Republic (the Communist Revolution) in 1949.

Having escaped the "middle-income trap" to become a "developed economy" by 2030, China might still face another hurdle of how to grow rich or to achieve *Fu* after 2030 by overcoming yet another trap, the "low-income developed economy trap"! China's last challenge then is how to ensure that its living standard will finally converge with that of the developed countries of the West and Japan. China's success or failure in its future endeavour will matter most to millions of people in the South. They will watch closely how China will go about it if China's success will be potentially a good lesson of experience for them.

---

[27] For a more detailed discussion of the *Xiaokang* concept and its implications, see John Wong "Xiao-Kang: Deng Xiaoping's Socio-Economic Development Target for China", in Wang Gungwu and John Wong (eds.), *China's Political Economy* (Singapore University Press and World Scientific, 1998).

Introduction II

ZHU RONGJI AND CHINA'S ECONOMIC TRANSFORMATION

China's Growth and Development in Historical Perspective

Economic development is essentially a long-term process of economic growth with social change. For a better grasp of China's economic future, one may take a look at its immediate past. Going back with a bit of economic history would greatly help to unfold and understand better both its past and present development processes and their challenges.

Modern China scholars all agree that Deng Xiaoping's successful economic reform and open-door policy since 1979 has sparked off the present process of China's dynamic growth of the past three decades. But not many are aware that modern China in the 20th century also had periods of high growth before Deng's reform. Even more intriguing is the critical question: Why has the previous spurts of high growth fizzled out? This would then follow: Why has the present post-1979 high growth become self-sustained?

The take-off into self-sustained growth

The work of the eminent economic historian Walt W. Rostow, which had been criticized for its oversimplifications, is still useful for our purpose of analysis. He has generalized the sweep of modern economic history into a set of five stages of economic growth: the traditional society, establishing the precondition, the take-off, the drive to maturity, and the age of high mass consumption.[1]

---

[1] W.W. Rostow, *The Stages of Economic Growth: A Non-Communist Manifesto*, Cambridge University Press, 1961.

Using Rostow's conceptual framework, we can therefore characterize the period of Deng's post-1979 reform and development as China's "take-off", based on Rostow's key criteria: (a) the rise of productive investment from 5% of GDP to 10% or more; (b) the development of one or more manufacturing bases with high rates of growth; and (c) the existence or quick emergence of a political, social and institutional frameworks to exploit the dynamic expansion of the modern sector.

Indeed, the post-1979 China had embodied all these essential economic, social and institutional ingredients for the successful "take-off". In many senses, China had over-fulfilled Rostow's stated preconditions for "take-off". Economically, China's savings and investment ratios for the past three decades were well above the 10% benchmark, and had mostly been over 40%. Politically, Deng, emerging from his bitter experience of the chaos of the Cultural Revolution, had developed a strong penchant for social stability and a strong political will for economic reform. This in turn led to the introduction of the so-called "socialist market economy" with a pro-growth and pro-market social milieu.[2]

Never before in its modern history had China's post-1979 period developed a confluence of such strong institutional (particularly political and social stability and a pro-market government) and economic forces (strong domestic economic fundamentals and favourable international operating environment) conducive to economic growth. Hence China's successful "take-off into self-sustained growth" (i.e., combining Rostow's stages 3 and 4), for this post-1979 period, with most remarkable growth performance.

China's previous abortive take-offs

If the post-1979 period was unmistakably China's real economic take-off, based on Rostow's criteria of take-off, then we would also have to explain why China's several spurts of high growth prior to 1979 were only abortive attempts to take-off, i.e., a kind of false take-off that had never broken out into long-term self-sustained growth.

Another eminent economic historian, Angus Maddison, who had spent most of his academic career to meticulously assemble data to compute the

---

[2]See John Wong, *Understanding China's Socialist Market Economy*, Times Academic Press, 1993.

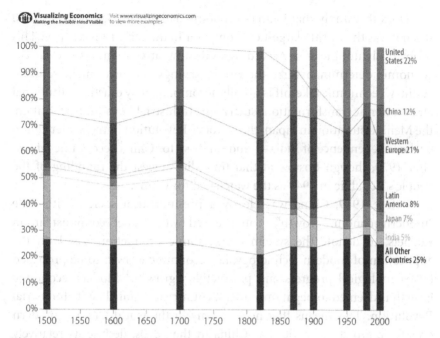

Figure 1. Percentage of World GDP (last 500 years) — China, Japan, Latin America, Western Europe and United States.
Source: Angus Maddison, University of Groningen.

world GDP for the last 600 years, had come up with the most intriguing findings in regard to the global GDP distribution of the large countries over the centuries. As can be seen from Figure 1, China and India were historically the two largest countries in terms of population and hence historically also the largest economies. In 1500, China and India accounted for 25% and 23%, respectively of global GDP in terms of purchasing power parity (PPP), simply because there was then little high value-added production before industrialization.

Specifically for China, it remained the world's largest economy well until the early 19th century, with its GDP in 1820 accounting for 31% of the world's GDP, even at the time of its rapid decline under the Qing dynasty. China's global GDP share had since started to shrink and much abruptly after 1900. By 1950, China's world share of GDP in PPP terms went down to just around 3%, or only 1.3% in nominal terms, compared to 1.2% for India.

Does this imply that China's economy had already taken off in 1500 when it was the world's largest economy? Or in the early 19th century? This is obviously not the case. According to Rostow, apart from some clear-cut economic determinants like the rise of savings and investment ratios, a country's economic take-off is usually accompanied by drastic institutional and economic transformations such as the Industrial Revolution in Britain, the Meiji Restoration in Japan, the October Revolution in the Soviet Union or the Independence of India — and surely so for China's economic reform after 1979, though Rostow at that time did suggest the founding of the People's Republic in 1949 as the watershed for China.

Before 1949, China was clearly a pre-industrial society with little "modern economic growth", a concept used by the Nobel economist Simon Kuznets, to denote the system of economic production based on the application of modern technology, i.e., economic growth to be propelled by technological progress and productivity growth.[3] Modern economic growth is deemed to begin only after a country has launched its Industrial Revolution. This means that no economy in the world had any modern economic growth in 1500. For China in the 1820s, despite its relatively large global GDP share, it was clearly still a pre-industrial economy with no "modern economic growth". Hence, clearly also, no real economic take-off for China.

It may be noted that prior to the its post-reform dynamic growth in 1979, China did have three short spurts of relatively high growth: the Republican period of 1914–1918, the Nanjing period of the Kuomintang government 1931–1936 under Chiang Kai-shek, and China's First Five-Year Plan period of 1952–1957 under Mao Zedong. All these three periods carried some significant institutional or economic landmarks that could potentially produce a real take-off, particularly the 1952–1957 period after the establishment of the People's Republic of China.

To begin with, the Republican China period of 1914–1918 started with the 1911 Revolution, which was an important political watershed conforming to one of Rostow's preconditions for take-off. But beyond this single event, no other strong institutional and economic prerequisites had

---

[3] Simon Kuznets, *Modern Economic Growth*, Yale University Press, 1966. Also, "Modern Economic Growth, Findings and Reflections", Nobel Lecture, December 11, 1971.

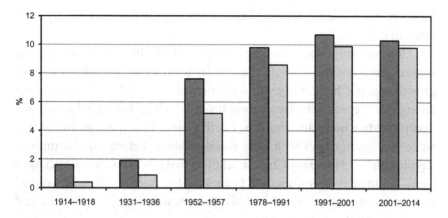

Figure 2.   China's GDP and per-capita GDP growth, 1914–2014.

Sources: World Bank Databank. Thomas Rawski, *Economic Growth of Pre-War China*, University of California Press, 1989; W. Galenson and L. Dachung, *Economic Trends in Communist China*, Aldine Publishing Company, 1968.

developed for a real economic take-off. This was essentially the warlord period in China with little or no political and social stability. Economically, it was only the nascent phase of modern economic growth for China with a few modern industries having been set up, even though 6,000 miles of railway tracks had been laid and modern banking had just come into being. Average GDP growth was also low, particularly in per-capita terms. Over all, there was hardly any economic development for the country as a whole, as GDP growth was less than 2% and GDP per-capita growth was less than 1% (Figure 2).

   For the Nanjing period of the Kuomintang government 1931–1936, China experienced for the first time in several decades a semblance of political and social stability under a "national" government. Politically, this would seem to fulfil one of Rostow's institutional preconditions for take-off. Economically, a wide range of modern industries, both national and foreign owned, also started to sprout, particularly in Manchuria, the Shanghai region, and several other modern enclaves in coastal provinces. Noted American scholars on China like Dwight Perkins have reassessed the importance of this period, pointing to its visible and significant economic growth and development, even though the extent of economic modernization was limited and fragmented — GDP growth for this period was still only 2%.[4]

However important the pre-war period of the 1930s was for the subsequent economic growth, this was far from a real take-off: its average growth was not high enough and the period of growth did not last long enough as the war with Japan soon broke out. The Japanese had already occupied Manchuria and much of North China. This was a period of war, strife and insurgencies with little social stability. Before the Communist Revolution in 1949, many Chinese scholars had labelled Chinese society as "semi-colonial and semi-feudal". Economically, there was lack of national economic integration, and economic growth was highly fragmented and largely in a haphazard manner.[5]

By comparison, the First Five-Year Plan of 1952–1957 seemed to display some solid institutional and economic characteristics that would meet Rostow's preconditions for a take-off. For the first time in more than a century, China was politically unified after the Communist Revolution in 1949. The economy had thoroughly recovered from its previous dislocation and hyperinflation. During the First Five-Year Plan period, China started to build several heavy industrial bases, including iron and steel, and automobile. Most significantly, the investment ratio had for the first time gone up to 20% level, well above Rostow's 10% benchmark. Accordingly, China achieved an average rate of 8% growth during 1953–1957. In many ways, this period could be a good candidate to be considered as China's real economic take-off.

In retrospect, this period was still a false take-off, as its high growth was soon dissipated. Hardly had the First Five-Year Plan been completed before Mao Zedong launched the collectivization of agriculture and then the Great Leap Forward movement. This led to the collapse of economic growth for the period of 1959–1962. Subsequently, Mao continued to intervene in the

---

[4] See Dwight H. Perkins (ed.), *China's Modern Economy in Historical Perspective*, Stanford University Press, 1975; and Thomas G. Rawski, *Economic Growth in Prewar China*, University of California Press, 1989.

[5] For further discussion on economic development of the pre-1949 period, see Cheng Yu-Kwei, *Foreign Trade and Industrial Development in China*, University of Washington Press, 1956; and also Wang Yuru, "Economic Development in China Between the Two World Wars (1920–1936)", in Tom Wright (ed.), *The Chinese Economy in the Early Twentieth Century*, St. Marin, 1992.

economy, with politics and ideology taking precedence over economics, culminating in the Cultural Revolution of 1966–1976. With such great political and social chaos, the foundation of orderly economic growth was therefore eroded, and economic growth itself was, in fact, not even the central social objective of Mao's own development strategies.

Indeed, American economists like Alexander Eckstein and Ta-Chung Liu, who were critical of the post-1949 Communist regime, had even argued that China's economic success in its First Five-Year Plan (1952–1957) owed a great deal to its pre-war economic heritages by providing a strong foundation for its industrial take-off.[6] Ta-Chung Liu and Kung-Chia Yeh even argued that by 1957 as Beijing was celebrating the successful conclusion of its First Five-Year Plan, China's per-capita GDP in 1957 (based on their computation) was only about 10% higher than in 1933 by the 1933 constant prices, or about 20% higher by the 1957 constant prices — implying that there had been hardly any substantial development progress for China's economy in the 1950s under Mao Zedong, as compared to the pre-war period.[7]

It suffices to say that by applying various institutional and economic determinants, we can cogently argue that these pre-1979 three spurts of high growth in China did not constitute a real take-off. High growth in each case was not self-sustainable. The real take-off should therefore go to the post-1979 period, whose high growth of 9.8% for three decades had really no historical precedence in China.

The post-1979 "real" take-off

The foregoing discussion of China's take-off pattern by applying a motley number of institutional and economic indicators is clearly unsatisfactory. We propose to use three more analytical and quantifiable economic determinants to explain why the post-1979 period has achieved the real economic take-off.

First, as discussed earlier, the single most important economic indicator of take-off used by Rostow is an increase in the ratio of savings and

---

[6] See Alexander Eckstein, Walter Galenson and Ta-Chung Liu, *Economic Trends in Communist China*, Aldine Publishing Company, 1968.

[7] Ta-Chung Liu and Kung-Chia Yeh, *The Economy of the Chinese Mainland, National Income and Economic Development*, Princeton University Press, 1965.

productive investment from 5% to 10% or more. This is primarily an empirical observation, rather than a theoretical yardstick to judge why 10% should be the key cutoff point for the take-off. It was commonly argued by development economists in the 1950s that capital shortage, or lack of adequate savings and investment, is the major cause of economic underdevelopment. The causation runs like this: lack of capital investment leads to low productivity, then low income, low savings, low investment and then back to low capital investment again. This ends up in the notion of "vicious circles" of poverty, which is a kind of cumulative causation.[8] A commonsense argument will then follow. A poor country must have enough investment in order for it to break out of the so-called "low-level equilibrium trap".[9] Thus, a high level of capital investment is essential for the take-off.

According to Perkins, there was hardly any significant investment in the Republican China period of 1914–1918 while the ratio of investment rose from 5% to 18.2% of GDP between 1931–1936 and 1952–1957, as expressed in 1933 prices, or from 7.5% to 24% of GDP in 1952 prices.[10] These small proportions are a far cry from the nearly 47% level of investment for the post-1979 period, so much so that China's post-1979 growth has been essentially investment driven until most recently when Xi Jinping was trying to rebalance China's economic growth towards more consumption-driven growth. Hence, the real economic take-off started in the post-1979 period, and not before that (Figure 3).

Secondly, any dynamic economy is also the one that is externally well integrated with the global economy, i.e., with a high proportion of GDP derived from foreign trade and foreign investment. This is actually the key feature of the successful development experience of the East Asian economies from Japan to the other newly industrialized economies of Korea, Taiwan, Hong Kong and Singapore, all of which followed export-propelled development strategies. Hence, all these economies had and still have high export-GDP ratios.

---

[8] See Gerald Meier, and Robert E. Baldwin, *Economic Development: Theory, History, Policy*, Wiley, 1957.

[9] The notion of low-level equilibrium trap was first developed by R. N. Nelson. See Benjamin Higgins, *Economic Development: Principles, Problems and Policies*, Constable and Company, 1968, 2nd edn.

[10] Dwight H. Perkins, *op cit.*, p. 126.

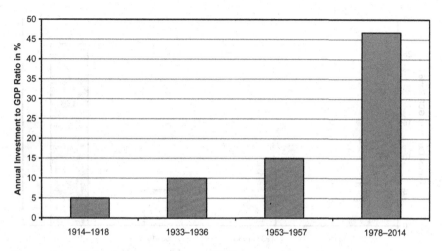

Figure 3. China's investment to GDP ratio, 1914–2014.

Sources: World Bank Databank. Thomas Rawski, *Economic Growth of Pre-War China*, University of California Press, 1989; W. Galenson and Ta-Chung Liu, *Economic Trends in Communist China*, Aldine Publishing Company, 1968.

It is sufficiently clear that in the two pre-Communist periods, China's manufacturing industries were primarily the kind of import substitution industrialization, producing mainly for the domestic markets and not competitive enough for exports. As for the third period of the First Five-Year Plan of 1952–1957, China as a centrally planned economy under Mao was virtually a closed economy. It was only after 1979 when Deng introduced both market reform and the open-door policy that China's economy started to become open and outward-looking, particularly after its accession to the World Trade Organization (WTO) in 2001. Hence the high average export-GDP ratio of over 26% for 1979–2014, as compared to only about 5% for the previous three periods (Figure 4).

Thirdly, modern economic development is effectively an industrialization process. A successful economic take-off is synonymous with a successful industrial take-off. Except for the city-economies of Hong Kong and Singapore, successful economic take-off in other East Asian economies was preceded by favourable agrarian preconditions, i.e., a successful agricultural revolution to precede their industrial revolution. The agricultural sector must be successfully transformed by becoming more productive so as to be able to produce a "surplus" that can be transferred to

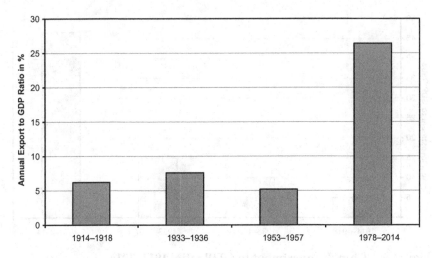

Figure 4.   China's export to GDP ratio, 1914–2014.

Sources: World Bank Databank. Thomas Rawski, *Economic Growth of Pre-War China*, University of California Press, 1989; W. Galenson and Ta-Chung Liu, *Economic Trends in Communist China*, Aldine Publishing Company, 1968.

the urban sector for industrial development. This line of argument was first put forward by the Nobel Laureate W. Arthur Lewis, and was later modified and extended by John Fei and Gustav Ranis.[11]

Comparing the different rates of agricultural productivity and the different levels of per-capita grain output of the previous three periods can clearly explain why they did not lead to a take-off. Before 1949, agricultural productivity in China was low and food supplies were often precarious. Even after the Communist revolution, Mao had never really solved the food shortage problem, and his obsession of the people's communes, in suppressing individual peasant incentives as a "capitalist tail", had only aggravated the agricultural production problem. Not surprisingly, China suffered a serious famine around during 1960–1962 following the collapse of the Great Leap movement.

In fact, most of the time China under Mao experienced some degrees of food scarcity. Eventually, it was Deng Xiaoping who had fundamentally resolved China's centuries-old food problem with reform. Today, with its

---

[11]See, W.A. Lewis, "Economic Development with Unlimited Supplies of Labour", *The Manchester School*, 22(2), 115–227, 1954. J.C.H. Fei and G. Ranis, "A Theory of Economic Development", *American Economic Review*, 51(3), 1961.

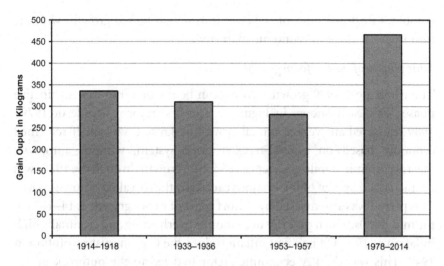

Figure 5.   China's grain output per capita, 1914–2014.

Source: National Bureau of Statistics; Dwight Perkins, *Agriculture Development in China*, 1368–1968, Aldine Publishing Company, 1968.

population more than double than in the 1960s and with its cultivated acreage sharply lower, China can still feed itself. As shown in Figure 5, the average per-capita grain output in China for these three periods of abortive take-off was only about 300 kilograms, compared to over 450 kilograms for the post-1979 period.

Indeed, Deng's first shot in his economic reform was the introduction of pragmatic agricultural policies emphasizing both individual incentives (i.e., the household responsibility system) and technological progress that had finally brought about the critical agricultural transformation needed to support long-term industrial expansion. In this sense, agricultural success not only spearheaded Deng's market reform but also laid the foundation for China's economic take-off.

Zhu Rongji's Role in the Take-Off

It has thus become abundantly clear that the post-1979 period of economic growth truly signifies, on all accounts, China's "real" economic take-off. This was in fact the beginning of China's long streak of hyper-growth process at double-digit rates, which was accompanied by significant economic and social changes as well as technological progress. In a sense, it actually combines Rostow's stage of "take-off into self-sustained growth" with the next stage of "drive to economic maturity".

Four phases of post-reform growth

The whole post-1979 growth process can be divided into four distinctive phases, as clearly shown in Figure 6. The first reform decade of 1979–1989 registered an average annual growth of 8.6%. It was a half-reformed economy based on a dual-tracked price system, without automatic macroeconomic stabilizers. Hence economic growth through the 1980s was characterized by a lot of fluctuations caused by the so-called "reform cycles". This period was also marked by a short spurt of hyper growth at 14–15% in the mid-1980s, which gave rise to economic overheating and eventually high inflation at 19%, China's first inflation since the Communist revolution in 1949. This was the key economic factor that led to the outbreak of the Tiananmen event on June 4, 1989.

The second period of 1989–1991 saw growth plummeting to 6.5%. This was clearly a "politically induced cycle" caused first by the outbreak of the Tiananmen incident and then the post-Tiananmen economic retrenchment and adjustment. The top leadership was mired in intense political debate

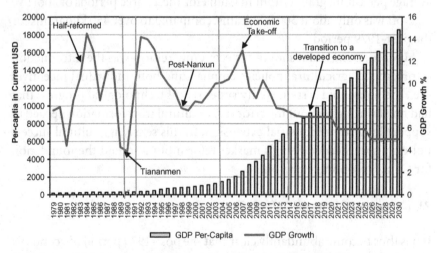

Figure 6.   China's growth and per-capita GDP, 1979–2030.

Source: World Bank for per-capita GDP from 1979 to 2014. For per-capita GDP from 2015 to 2030, it is calculated on growth forecast from 2015 to 2030; United Nations forecast for China's population from 2015 to 2030.

and then split over the issue of whether or not to slow down the economic reform.

The third period of 1992–2002 was marked by the return of high economic growth averaging at 9.9%, which was initially sparked off by Deng Xiaoping's *Nanxun* in early 1992. Deng not only reignited the market reform after the post-Tiananmen lull, but called for the deepening and broadening of the market reform so as to convert China into a "socialist market economy". The extensive marketization that followed had greatly enhanced economic efficiency and productivity of China's economy, giving rise to another high spurt of double-digit growth (at record 14% during 1992–1994) until the outbreak of the 1997 Asian financial crisis. This phase of high growth was clearly the outcome of what may be called the "*Nanxun* effect".

The fourth period of 2003–2013 was featured by another upsurge of high growth averaging at 9.9%, with a short spurt of super-growth of 12% occurring in the first few years until the outbreak of the global financial crisis in 2008. Much of the high growth of this phase can be attributed to the "WTO effect", which marks the rapid integration of China into the global economy. It was also the climax of Deng's open-door policy that started in the early 1980s. China's accession to the WTO has made it possible for China to capture the mechanism of international capitalism — mainly through trade, foreign direct investment (FDI) and technology transfer — to raise its economic growth to an even higher level.

Deng Xiaoping vs. Zhu Rongji

It goes without saying that the underlying driving force behind these three phases of high growth was Deng Xiaoping's economic reform and opening or *Gaige Kaifang*. His economic reform was epitomized in the creation of China's socialist market economy while his open-door policy culminated in China's accession to the world trade body of WTO. Both policies, reinforcing each other, had sparked off the processes of high growth. This explains why Deng was officially called the "architect of China's economic reform and development" and given the full credit for China's subsequent economic growth and prosperity.

Deng's key role is not just in his role as the "architect" of the market reform in the sense of shaping the basic policy or laying down the grand strategy. He had indeed taken great pains to prepare the necessary political and ideological groundwork for the reform to start. He launched the reform programme shortly after his return to power (the third time) but barely before he had completely consolidated his position. In the immediate post-Mao aftermath, he had faced enormous challenges in convincing the many Maoist ideologues and conservatives to give market reform a trial. Some of his senior colleagues like Chen Yun (who opposed Mao's leftist policies but was himself still a central planner at heart) were not totally in agreement with Deng's radical approach to market reform. Hence, Deng had to proceed cautiously at the start of the reform.

This, in turn, had given rise to Deng's unique reform strategy based on a gradualist and experimental approach, as opposed to the "Big Bang" of the former Soviet Union. Having realized that there was no textbook to teach him how to proceed to "unplan" a socialist planned economy, Deng had to grope his way around by falling back on to the traditional Chinese way of doing things as aptly expressed in his famous dictum of "crossing the river by feeling the stones". It was essentially a gradual and piecemeal process, by "trial and error" and "learning by doing". Such a gradualist reform strategy not only reduced initial political opposition to his reform plan, but had actually proved to be highly effective for China's reform in the long run.

It suffices to say that Deng Xiaoping fully deserves all the credits for launching the reform and laying down important tactical guidelines on how to proceed. He was truly the chief architect of China's reform and development from every perspective.

As Deng was the architect, who then would be the builder, i.e., someone as an able technocrat and administrator, who would follow up on all the detailed implementation of various reform plans? Viewed from a different angle, as Deng had successfully introduced economic reform and open-door policy in 1979 that had transformed China's economy leading to a successful economic take-off, who then was the person to manage such a dazzling take-off? That Zhu Rongji was such a person seems much like a self-evident truth.

Zhu in managing the marketization

To begin with, Zhu Rongji's involvement in managing the Chinese economy spanned his whole career in the central government, 1991–2003, first as Vice-Premier and then Premier. In 1991, Deng Xiaoping specifically plucked him from his job as Shanghai mayor for his new position in Beijing as Vice-Premier in the State Council (which is essentially China's economic cabinet). Deng considered Zhu as the only person in high position who "understands economics", though he was originally an engineer by training from Tsinghua University. Zhu was thus immediately put in charge of economic affairs under Premier Li Peng, who was then not very popular because of his role in the Tiananmen crackdown in 1989.

Looking back, Zhu's tenure in office with the central government was one of the most turbulent periods for China's post-reform economy, with a lot of ups and downs. But this period was also the most critical in modern Chinese economic history, as it not only marks the breakthrough in China's economic reform, but also lays the precondition for China's economic take-off.[12]

To break the post-Tiananmen political stalemate on reform, Deng Xiaoping in February 1992 launched an inspection tour of South China or *Nanxun*, calling for a bold move towards market reform. This sparked off an immediate economic boom as FDI from Hong Kong poured into Guangdong virtually within weeks following Deng's *Nanxun* speech (which was quickly leaked out to the press in Hong Kong). The upsurge of foreign trade and foreign investment had in turn given rise to three years of double-digit rates of hyper economic growth, leading to serious economic overheating.

Thus, Zhu's first challenge as the "Economic Czar", as he was so dubbed by the foreign press, was to stabilize the economy and reduce economic overheating by bringing down the runaway inflation, which shot up to 22% in 1994, even higher than the previous peak of 19% in 1988 that contributed to the Tiananmen crisis. Zhu was then learning the job, and it was a difficult job in any case because China was then still a half-reformed economy with no built-in automatic macroeconomic stabilizers. Zhu could not employ macroeconomic fine-tuning techniques of the market economy to cool the economic overheating. In the end, he had succeeded in stabilizing the overheated economy by applying a combination of tough administrative

---

[12] See John Wong, *The Political Economy of Deng's Nanxun: Breakthrough in China's Reform and Development*, World Scientific, 2014.

measures and some aspects of conventional monetary and fiscal policies meant for the market economy.

Zhu's early career with the State Planning Commission had made him a good "regulator". Thus, in dealing with economic overheating, he was naturally very much at home in applying direct state intervention measures by controlling lending and prohibiting "chaotic and illegal raising of capital" as well as regulating the real estate market. At the same time, he had also used some monetary policy tools like controlling money supply (M2) and leveraging on interest rates. He had indeed learnt fast on how to operate monetary policy after he became (simultaneously) the Governor of the People's Bank of China during 1993–1995.

In this way, Zhu had developed his unique brand of macroeconomic management that was henceforth officially called *Hongguan Tiaokong* or "macroeconomic control", which was highly effective for China's transitional economy at that time. It was essentially a delicate combination of direct administrative control measures characteristic of a centrally planned economy with some indirect levers associated with the conventional monetary and fiscal policies of the market economy. He had subsequently perfected this specific policy tool that may be called "macroeconomic control with Zhu Rongji's characteristics". One of Zhu's Western admirers, Laurence Brahm, had thus stated: "Zhu has created a practical approach to transitional economics that is deserving of recognition as a new brand of economic theory, tried and proven through his actual application to China's circumstances".[13]

Zhu had barely succeeded in stabilizing the economy before the Asian financial crisis suddenly struck in the middle of 1997. The double-digit rates of inflation were brought down to 8.3% in 1996 and further down to 2.8% in 1997. But as the Asian financial crisis had quickly spread to other Asian economies in Southeast Asia and also made Hong Kong jittery, he had to turn his attention to preventing the contagion effect of the financial crisis from reaching China and Hong Kong, which had just returned to China's sovereignty. Technically speaking, China was most unlikely to fall as the next financial domino, mainly because China's Renminbi was not

---

[13] Lawrence J. Brahm, *Zhu Rongji and the Transformation of Modern China*, Wiley, 2002, p. 3.

convertible on the capital account. Furthermore, China's foreign exchange reserves had increased from US$22 billion in 1991 to a sizeable amount of US$140 billion in 1997. Zhu's success in stabilizing the economy prior to the 1997 outbreak had also greatly strengthened China's resilience against potential external shock.

Still, Zhu was under considerable pressure from this financial crisis, not least because international speculators had then repeatedly made use of the foreign media to spread rumours of the imminent devaluation of the Renminbi. This was subsequently known as a ploy used by speculators to prepare positions for them to attack the Hong Kong dollar, which was under the currency board system but directly pegged to the US dollar — and hence most vulnerable to a speculative attack. In response, Zhu had repeatedly reaffirmed China's position of maintaining the exchange rate stability of the Renminbi. The devaluation rumours had nonetheless caused some illegal capital flights from China, even though technically international speculators just could not possibly deliver any speculative attack on the Renminbi because of capital control. For his decision to stand fast on maintaining the exchange rate stability of the Renminbi, Zhu was subsequently lauded by several ASEAN governments for preventing the crisis from getting worse, while this had also contributed to the financial stability of both China and Hong Kong.

Having staved off the direct onslaught of the Asian financial crisis, Zhu had to cope with the post-1997 downturn of China's economy, which was slipping into a mild deflation during 1998–1999, partly as a result of his over-zealous implementation of the earlier retrenchment policies to fight overheating and partly due to unfavourable external economic environment in the wake of the Asian financial crisis. In March 1998, Zhu was confirmed as a full Premier at the ninth National People's Congress. But economic growth in 1998 plunged to 7.3% with a negative inflation. Some of his reform policies related to the state-owned enterprises (SOEs) and the banking sector at that time also had the tendency to dampen growth further. Thus, he declared his famous pro-growth slogan *Baoba* or striving to maintain growth at 8%.

In fact, he spent the last few years of his tenure as Premier partly to continue revamping the economic structure and partly to restore and then build up the high economic growth momentum. By 2003, as he handed over the premiership to his successor Wen Jiabao, he had left behind for Wen many of his legacies, including a booming economy growing at the double-digit rate of 10.5%, which was partly fuelled by China's accession to the WTO. So much for how Zhu had managed the economy under his watch.

Zhu in implementing crucial economic reform

But what Zhu had done in the area of economic reform is by far more significant. This is where his long-term legacies lie. Experts and commentators on China, both in and outside China, have generally pointed to the three waves of reform initiatives that Zhu was involved in and had achieved breakthroughs with last effects. The first was the package of reform that was approved at the Third Party Plenum in November 1993, but was left to Zhu to carry it out throughout 1994. This included the tax reform in terms of unifying the tax code and simplifying the taxation system, the foreign exchange reform by abolishing the dual-exchange system, and banking reform by making the People's Bank of China the country's real central bank and converting the four specialized state banks into commercial banks. Without fundamental reform in these critical areas, Deng's "socialist market economy" just could not function. All these reforms had produced immediate effects. Whereas the banking reform had proved to be a continuing process, the taxation reform had shaped the central–local political and economic relationships that have lasted to this day.

The second wave of reform initiatives was targeted at the SOEs and other related reforms involving the banking sector and the social security area. The SOE reform had proved to be a long-drawn process. Zhu actually started this reform in 1994, initially by modernizing the management structure of SOEs (then over 100,000) and their enterprise governance through corporatization and by converting large SOEs into shareholding companies. But the SOE problem persisted.

Later, at the Fifteenth Party Congress in September 1997, Zhu was given a new mandate to "deepen the reform of SOEs". He then tried out the strategy of *Zhuada Fangxiao* (holding on to the large strategic SOEs while letting go the smaller ones), which involved restructuring and consolidating large SOEs before putting them under the central government control while passing on smaller ones to local governments at their disposal.

Finally, he started to apply the more drastic measures of retrenchment, which was carried out under a very imaginative term *Xiagang* (or "off post"), whereby redundant workers were not nominally laid off outright, but were gradually removed from their duty or gradually pensioned off. China's strong economic growth through these years had much cushioned the political and social impact of such retrenchment by creating new employment opportunities for many laid-off workers from SOEs.

When Zhu was to step down as Premier in 2003, the state sector had been greatly trimmed down, with the remaining 120 or so large centrally-owned SOEs (the *Yangqi*) becoming much more market-oriented and also going international (*Zou-chu-qu*). The SOE issue had ceased to be a serious problem until most recently when Xi Jinping decided to apply a new round of more rigorous reform and restructuring.

Zhu and China's WTO membership

It may be stressed that from the very start, Deng Xiaoping had, quite rightly, linked his market reform to his open-door policy. Progress in domestic market reform inevitably stokes economic growth, which in turn stimulates foreign trade and foreign investment. This is especially the case for China which adopted the export-oriented development strategies. For over three decades, China's exports had been growing at double-digit rates. Thus, China naturally wanted to seek institutionalized international protection against trade protectionism and also to benefit from such schemes as reciprocity and non-discrimination with its trade partners. For all these, China had to be a member of the General Agreement on Tariffs and Trade (GATT) and later the WTO so as to be a participant of the multilateral trade negotiation (MTN) process.

China was originally a founding member of the GATT. When the Nationalist government retreated to Taiwan in 1949, it took with it the China membership but was later forced to give it up. So China had to apply to re-join, which it formally did in 1986. But this had proved to be a complicated and protracted process, especially since the United States was trying to delay China's entry on the ground that China's domestic market reform had not gone far enough to meet the "GATT compatibility". In the wake of the Tiananmen, the US government had further imposed direct obstacles to the China–US trade by requiring the annual renewal of the most favoured nation (MFN) clause for China. If China were already a GATT member, it would be technically difficult for the United States to continue with this annual MFN pressures on China, because such a move would be against the multilateral trade negotiation principle of reciprocity and non-discrimination. Thus, Zhu from the outset recognized the crucial role of all those international bodies, from the GATT to the IMF and the World Bank, in facilitating China's reform and development.

In January 1995, the GATT was superseded by WTO. China, not being a GATT member, had also failed to become a founding member of WTO. To Zhu, the WTO membership was now even more important as China's economic growth had increasingly become export-driven. He instructed his foreign trade minister Madam Wu Yi to intensify diplomatic efforts to gather more international support for China on the one hand; and on the other, he took serious efforts to liberalize China's foreign trade sector such as lowering the average tariff rates and opening more areas to foreign investment. Zhu reckoned that such liberalization reforms were good for China's own development in any case.

In the meanwhile, as China's economy continued with its dynamic growth with strong potential to be a rising trading power, the developed country members led by the United States also wanted to pry open the vast China market as much as possible by raising the "admission price" of the China's WTO membership with even more stringent technical require-ments as a precondition, including treating China not as a developing economy.

In November 2001, China finally signed the protocol for its accession to the WTO. By then, China was already the world's fifth largest trading nation — becoming the largest one about 10 years later. For the WTO membership, Zhu had no doubt carried out extensive reform in the related areas. In the process, Zhu was criticized by many in China for paying too exorbitant a price for this membership. Sure enough, some of China's inefficient SOEs along with many of its small and medium enterprises, and producers of a large number of agricultural products such as soya beans, wheat, corn and cotton — which were above international prices — had indeed suffered a great deal in the first few years of China's becoming a WTO member, due to fierce competition from more efficient international producers. It had been argued that if China were then a Western-style democracy, there would have been many lobby groups in China to delay its WTO membership!

Zhu stood his ground. He was not unaware of those problems, which he saw as the short-term adjustment costs. He (and his like-minded technocrats under him) took the view that the long-term benefits of the WTO membership would eventually outweigh those short-term costs. Since the Chinese economy was set to carry on with even more economic reforms and more liberalization ahead, such short-term adjustment costs associated with the WTO membership would in any case be the foregone costs of China's final transition towards a functioning market economy. Furthermore, the "dynamic benefits" of China's WTO membership were quickly borne out. In the wake of its WTO membership (December 2001) China experienced double-digit rates of economic growth for six full years until the global financial crisis struck in 2008.

Such is the "WTO effect" for this phase of hyper growth, as mentioned earlier. Zhu was fully vindicated for his vision in the WTO. He certainly deserved credit for his many deeds, not just for the WTO membership, but also his successful management of the post-*Nanxun* process of marketization along with the introduction of many crucial reforms. In this way, he had truly contributed to China's economic take-off. This is essentially what this book is about.

Zhu was well known for his no-nonsense, straight-talking leadership style, intolerant of incompetence and inefficiency. He was then regarded as China's most popular Premier after Zhou Enlai. He was well-liked by the general public, though much feared and also respected by many bureaucrats. The common people or *Laobaixing* had been greatly impressed by his determination to fight corruption and rent-seeking activities. His clean and incorruptible image was best epitomized in his open statement: "Prepare for me 100 coffins, 99 of them for corrupt officials and the last one for myself". Accordingly, he must be shocked by the widespread high-level corruption existing in China's leadership today that was recently revealed by Xi Jinping's war on corruption. Ironically, this anti-corruption drive was carried out by Wang Qishan, one of the many able technocrats whom Zhu had groomed.

In retirement, Zhu has maintained a low profile, making very few public appearances. In 2011, his speeches, articles and directives from the time when he was Vice Premier (May 1991) to when he was Premier (February 2003), were collected and edited to be published into four volumes as *Zhu Rongji Jianghua Shilu* (A Compendium of Zhu Rongji's Speeches). These speeches were subsequently edited and translated into English, and published as *Zhu Rongji on the Record* by the Brookings Institutions in Washington, D.C., 2013, with a foreword by Henry Kissinger and Helmut Schmidt each.

It should come as little surprise that Zhu's two books immediately became best sellers in China, yielding him handsome royalties of 24 million yuan (US$4 million). That is another measure of his huge popularity in China. Eventually, he donated the royalties to an education foundation, and that had made him even more popular as he was put on the list of the 2014 Hurun Philanthropists in China, with Jack Ma of Alibaba topping this list.

Most Chinese people would probably not see Zhu as their "people's Premier". He is more like a modern technocrat or perhaps a legendary Mandarin. He is also like Deng Xiaoping for being practical, pragmatic and blunt. That is perhaps why Deng had picked Zhu to work with him in the first place, and the two had since been well complementary with each other in ability and aspirations for reform. But Deng was also a national leader and a politician. If Deng was the political leader to prepare the political and institutional precondition for China's economic take-off by launching the market reform, Zhu was the person to carry it through and manage the take-off with great success.

About this Book

The 14 chapters selected for this volume were written by the author during 1997–2003, originally as *EAI Background Briefs*, which were circulated to the Singapore government (ministers and senior civil servants) for information or as policy briefings. Most had not been formally published. They cover a variety of topics, including a brief survey of the state of the economy at the beginning and at the end of Zhu's term as Premier; how he had tried out his "macroeconomic management with Zhu's characteristics", how he had fended off the contagion effect of the 1997 Asian financial crisis, as well as how he started to reform the SOEs, banking and financial liberalization.

The collection also includes special studies of such topics as China's service sector, its export structure, and the sources of its high growth.

The collection ends with a social chapter on China's rapid population transition of falling fertility and a political chapter on how Zhu had finally embraced capitalism. Taken together, these chapters should provide a comprehensive review of various aspects of China's economic and social development along with its reform and marketization processes during China's critical period of economic growth when Zhu was in charge. This should amply reflect Zhu's legacies in managing China's economic take-off.

The original papers as policy reports were necessarily succinct and concise. Hence each chapter is preceded by a lengthy introduction, which not only highlights the main issues and arguments, but also provides a broad background to interpret those issues and arguments from today's perspectives based on updated information and fresh research. In a way, this book has a certain dualistic feature. While the individual chapters are historical essays that reflect events taking place at that point in time, the long introductions to each chapter are essentially self-contained essays that discuss the related issues and perspectives in a broad sweep. Some readers may find the introductions more relevant to what is happening in China today.

China's economy for over three decades has been basically a continuing process of reforming, growing and changing. A lot of its salient economic problems and burning reform issues that China is facing today, such as the SOEs reform or financial liberalization, are rooted in the past. A good understanding of how Zhu Rongji had tried to tackle those issues then would certainly throw light on the kind of challenges that are currently confronting Xi Jinping in his efforts to deal with many similar problems. Xi needs to come to grips with these problems effectively in his national rejuvenation before his "Chinese Dream" for a *Fuqiang* (rich and powerful) China can be realized.

Part II

Part II

1

GOOD POLITICAL ARITHMETICK
FOR THE 1997 FIFTEENTH
PARTY CONGRESS

Introduction

This chapter carries considerable historical significance from several angles. It is based originally on the EAI Background Brief No. 1, which was the first research briefing that the newly constituted East Asian Institute (EAI) sent out to the Singapore government (ministers and senior civil servants) on September 2, 1997. In April 1997, the Institute of East Asian Political Economy (IEAPE) was dissolved and renamed East Asian Institute to become an autonomous research organization within the National University of Singapore.

IEAPE (whose predecessor was the Institute of East Asian Philosophies or IEAP) was originally set up by Singapore's first Deputy Prime Minister Dr Goh Keng Swee as a "think tank" for the Singapore government. As IEAPE used to circulate regularly its research reports to the government, EAI decided to continue this "think tank" practice of sending out informative and readable policy-related briefings to the government while it also publishes books, monographs and journal articles to cater to the academic community at large.

This chapter is about the Fifteenth Party Congress (held in September 12, 1997), which was historically of great personal importance to Jiang Zemin and Zhu Rongji as this was the first post-Deng Party Congress, with both Jiang and Zhu fully in charge. The Fourteenth Party Congress held in 1992 was the post-Tiananmen meeting, which was dominated by Deng Xiaoping, though Jiang as the General Secretary of the Party delivered the report. The main theme of Jiang's report at the Fourteenth Party Congress was how to carry out "Socialism with Chinese characteristics", which clearly reflected the ideological victory for Deng. Jiang also made the key report at the Fifteenth Party Congress, whose main theme was to "hold high the great banner of Deng Xiaoping's theory for building socialism with Chinese characteristics." In other words, the Fifteenth Party Congress still carried Deng's ideological hallmark.

Deng's ideological shadow apart, Jiang had to face many real policy challenges (what he called "cross-century problems"), as he was to lead China into the 21st century. Deng's Nanxun in 1992, by embracing more daring market reforms and the further opening up of the Chinese economy, had sparked off an unprecedented economic upsurge with double-digit rates of growth. But the post-Nanxun period was also marked by economic chaos, overheating and runaway inflation, partly because the operation of the market forces was not at harmony with the existing socialist institutional structure. In other words, there were lots of practical problems when the market was put to work within the still socialistic institutional framework.

No one was then more familiar with the inherent "contradictions" of the "socialist market economy" than Zhu Rongji, who was originally hand-picked by Deng to become China's Executive Vice Premier in charge of economic affairs. Zhu had learnt the hard way of how to cope with the frequent post-Nanxun macroeconomic instabilities in China's half-reformed economy due to the absence of the built-in stabilizers that are the normal part of a functioning market economy. In the event, Zhu had successfully brought down inflation from the high of 28% in late 1994 to just over 2% in the early part of 1997; and Zhu had done this mainly by relying heavily on administrative intervention.

Thus, China's economy on the eve of the Fifteenth National Party Congress had again confounded observers with its highly creditable performance. Instead of the expected slowdown after its successful soft landing in 1996, it still turned in another robust growth of 9.5% for the first half of 1997, with inflation falling further to 1.6%, a truly enviable situation of high growth with low inflation.

What was most heartening to the Chinese leadership was, in fact, the realization of its much-cherished price stability, a key precondition in China for its overall social stability. With the retail price index (RPI) for July 1997 falling to 0.6%, China had clearly broken the backbone of its four-year long inflation with apparently no significant trade-offs for lower growth. Indeed, the Chinese economy seemed to be heading for an era of sustainable strong growth. *(At that point of time, the Asian financial crisis had broken out just two months ago and its contagion effects had not reached China yet.)*

Such a buoyant economic outlook on the eve of the crucial post-Deng Party meeting naturally raised the political capital of the Party's General Secretary, Jiang Zemin, and won him support for his policy lines. A good "report card" on the economy thus served to legitimize the pending reform programmes and emboldened Jiang and Zhu to take stronger reform initiatives.

The title of the original report carried the term, "Good Political Arithmetick", which was highly relevant then as it is still now. Economics cannot be separated from numbers. Modern economics today is getting increasingly technical and all the more concerned with numbers and measurements. Thus, an eminent 17th-century English philosopher Sir William Petty in his famous essay "Political Arithmetick" referred to such an aspect of economics as "the art of reasoning by figures upon things related to government".

How fitting it was when put into the Chinese context! This is not just about the inherently close relationship between politics and economics in China, but also how "good economics" can lead to "good politics", and vice versa. "Bad politics" or political and social instability is clearly harmful to economic growth while "good economics" with its strong economic growth, in creating employment for the people and generating revenue for the government, will ensure political and social stability.

This kind of thinking was appropriate for Jiang and Zhu in 1997 as it is today for Xi Jinping and Li Keqiang. Good economic performance, i.e., strong GDP growth, is always good "political arithmetick" that would smooth the way for more reforms. A caveat though for Xi and Li today: As China's economy has chalked up more than three decades of hyper growth, they have become much less obsessed with pure GDP increases in quantity terms and emphasize instead the quality aspects of GDP growth. This clearly marks a fundamental shift in the concept of economic growth from Jiang–Zhu's time two decades ago when a good "political arithmetic" would mean the single-minded pursuit of maximum economic growth in terms of the highest GDP increases.

Back to 1997, all the pre-Congress clues at that time suggested that the reform of state-owned enterprises (SOEs) would occupy the Congress's main economic agenda. This was later proved right. At the Fifteenth Party Congress on September 12, 1997, Jiang delivered a rather tedious report which, after *paying a lengthy tribute to the ideological significance of "Deng Xiaoping Theory", set focus on the two important but interrelated aspects of reform: readjusting and improving the ownership structure, and accelerating the SOE reform. For SOE reform, attention at that time was focussed on the Chinese way of transforming the ownership structure by converting SOEs into shareholding cooperatives, thus explicitly avoiding any open implications of "privatization", which was still ideologically a taboo.*

Not surprisingly, from the outset, the SOE reform was destined to be a long-drawn process, and this topic kept cropping up throughout Jiang–Zhu's tenure in office. Indeed, in the following years, Zhu Rongji had spent much strenuous efforts in order to crack the SOE problem. In retrospect, though Zhu had achieved significant breakthrough in the SOE reform, the SOE problem continues to linger on to this day as China's unfinished business of reform.

Indeed, some 16 years later, Xi Jinping at the Third Plenum of the Eighteenth Party Congress in November 2013 still put SOE reform on top of his reform agenda. While Jiang Zemin at the Fifteenth Party Congress called for SOE reform against the background of the dominance of state sector and prevailing public ownership, Xi Jinping today has downplayed the role of public ownership and instead allowed the market to play a more decisive role in resource allocation. In this way, Xi stands a good chance of settling once and for all the remaining outstanding issues of the SOE reform.

This chapter, in dealing with the politics of economic growth and reform as well as the central issue of sustaining high economic growth along with price stability, actually epitomizes the major tasks that Zhu Rongji had to cope as the country's "Economic Czar". When the economy had built up a strong growth momentum, he had to watch for signs of overheating, and as economic growth was losing too much steam, he had to put up appropriate policy response to ensure a "soft landing" for the economy. In the meanwhile, he still had to mind the various reform programmes that were being implemented.

It suffices to say that this chapter, in discussing the many key problems and issues that had cropped up from time to time to become recurrent throughout Zhu's tenure as Premier, also serves as an appropriate opening chapter. It offers a foretaste of all the major problems and challenges that Zhu had to manage during this critical period of China's economic take-off.

Good Economics to Boost Jiang's Politics

Economics as a science is mainly about measurement, involving numbers and figures. Among the early precursors of modern technical economics was an essay by a 17th century English philosopher Sir William Petty, entitled "Political Arithmetick", which was meant to be "the art of reasoning by figures upon things related to government . . .".

In mid-September 1997, as the Chinese Communist Party held its Fifteenth National Party Congress, its General Secretary, Jiang Zemin, was in need some good "political arithmetick", not for governing China, but for him to manoeuvre his own agenda through this critical Party gathering. Jiang wanted the Party to embrace his main policy lines for the post-Deng Xiaoping era and endorse the selection of his younger protégés in key positions so as to lead China into the new millennium of the 21st century.

The First National Party Congress (NPC), held in Shanghai in July 1921 to mark the formation of the Chinese Communist Party, was attended by 12 delegates including Mao Zedong and represented only about 50 Party members. The Sixth NPC was held in Moscow in June 1928, representing about 57,000 Party members. The Seventh NPC was held in Yenan in April 1945, representing some 210,000 Party members. After the establishment of the People's Republic in 1949, the first meeting was the Eighth NPC, held in Beijing, representing about 10 million Party members. Since then, every NPC meeting has been eventful. The Ninth NPC was held in 1969 amidst the Cultural Revolution; the Tenth NPC in 1973 marked the downfall of Lin Biao; the Eleventh NPC in 1977 was the first post-Mao meeting. But the Third Plenum of the Eleventh NPC, held in December 1978, was historically the most crucial as it officially sanctioned Deng Xiaoping's economic reform and the open-door policy. . . . the Fourteenth NPC in 1992 was "post-Tiananmen" meeting, and the Fifteenth NPC (September 1997) is therefore "post-Deng".

Since the Eleventh NPC, after the death of Mao, the NPC meeting has been held regularly once in five years. The Eleventh NPC represented a total Party membership of 58 million.

The Chinese economy, after its successful soft landing in 1996 with a 9.7% (subsequently adjusted to 10.2%) real growth and a much reduced inflation of 6.1% (subsequently adjusted to 8.3%), had once again confounded foreign observers with this continuing high growth performance.[1] Instead of the expected slowdown for the first half of 1997, it still turned in another robust growth of 9.5% with inflation further falling to 1.8%. Strong economic fundamentals had led Chinese leaders to confidently predict that China's economy could possibly achieve 10% growth for the whole of 1997 with reasonable price stability.[2]

The external sector performance was even more impressive. Despite the general deterioration of the international economic environment, China's exports in the first seven months of 1997 registered 26% growth to US$96 billion while its imports grew by only 1.9% to US$76 billion, thereby yielding a substantial trade surplus of US$20 billion. This, along with a 15.6% increase in foreign direct investment (FDI) to a total of US$26 billion in the same period, had contributed to the further swelling of China's growing foreign reserves (hitting US$126 billion) and the stability of the *Renminbi*. Indeed, China's strong external financial balance presented a sharp contrast to the financial turmoil that swept across Southeast Asia. (The Asian financial crisis started first in Thailand on July 1, 1997.) The Chinese leadership understandably took considerable comfort for China's apparent immunity to such financial instability, but they also took the lesson of Thailand to heart.[3]

At that time what was most heartening to the Chinese leadership on the economic front was not, however, China's success in sustaining high economic growth (a regular occurrence since the economic reform), but the realization of its much-cherished price stability, which was the key to overall social stability. It might be remembered that China's past high economic growth had also spawned double-digit rates of inflation. Vice Premier Zhu

---

[1] See "Chinese 'Miracle' Confounds Predictions", *International Herald Tribune*, July 23, 1997.

[2] The prediction was made by China's Central Bank Governor Dai Xianglong. See "Nation Sustains Strong Growth, Low Inflation", *China Daily*, August 15, 1997.

[3] See "Will the Thai Baht Crisis Affect China?", *Renmin Ribao* (*People's Daily*, Beijing, August 20, 1997). At that point of time, it was too early to judge if the Asian currency crisis rendered Chinese policy makers over-cautious in their planned financial liberalization process, which include the full convertibility of the *Renminbi* by 2000.

Rongji had to apply tough macroeconomic stabilization measures to cool the overheating economy.

After the RPI for July 1997 fell to 0.6%, it was evident that Zhu had undoubtedly broken the backbone of the inflation. Even more significantly, Zhu had achieved this with apparently little adverse trade-off for lower economic growth (and hence the "soft landing"). Zhu's remarkable achievements in macroeconomic management had thus strengthened Jiang's core leadership, so much so that Zhu was slated to succeed Li Peng as China's next Premier.[4]

With major economic troubles behind him, Jiang had turned his full attention to managing the politics of the Fifteenth Party Congress. An NPC was usually an occasion for intense behind-the-scene politicking among different factions in order to exert their influence on high-level appointments (*Renshi-anpai*, literally, "personnel arrangements") and on the Party's major policy lines. This was particularly the case during the Fifteenth Party Congress, which was the first post-Deng meeting without the domination of a single strong personality. Accordingly, Jiang had spared no efforts in mobilizing all his personal and institutional resources, firstly, to extol the economic and social achievements of Deng Xiaoping's theory of building socialism with Chinese characteristics, secondly, to feature himself as the legitimate heir to Deng's main policy legacies, and thirdly, to use the label of "primary stage of socialism" to preempt leftist critique.[5]

In the run-up to the Party Congress, some Party ideologues had brought back the old debate on the relative virtues of socialism and capitalism (the so-called "Mr. Socialist vs. Mr. Capitalist"). A motley group of leftists, conservatives and remnant Maoists had also exploited the dissatisfaction of the losers of the reform by mounting attacks on the central authorities

---

[4] For Zhu's achievement in inflation fighting, an American journalist had nicknamed him "China's Inflation-Taming 'Greenspan'". See *International Herald Tribune*, August 22, 1997.

[5] The "People's Daily", the Party's main propaganda organ, had carried many articles and commentaries extolling Deng's economic reform and open-door policies, and China's past economic and social achievements since the reform, as well as Jiang's speech at the Central Party School on May 29, expounding the theme that China was only at the transitional "primary stage of socialism". These documents were issued for Party cadres to study as their ideological preparation for the upcoming Party Congress.

for being responsible for those undesirable "social contradictions" such as rising unemployment, including the widespread *xiagang* (off-post) phenomenon created by the SOE reform.[6]

True, economic reform and the open-door policy had given rise to many negative social fallouts, many of which were transitional in nature and could best be disposed of with continuing rapid economic growth in the longer run. Such was the basic rationale underpinning the government's pro-growth strategies, which were unfortunately not shared by leftist detractors on ideological grounds. But in the short run, especially on the eve of this crucial Party Congress, China's continuing robust economic growth, as was manifested in all the impressive economic numbers and statistics, certainly strengthened Jiang's hands in countering his critics and doubters of economic reform. Few, of course, had expected such ideological attack on the central leadership, be it from the left or the right, to undermine Jiang's leadership.

More importantly, a good "report card" on the state of the Chinese economy, prior to the Party Congress, legitimized the ongoing reform programmes. This in turn had emboldened Jiang to take stronger initiatives or even hard decisions for the next round of economic reform. Jiang was widely expected to put the reform of the SOEs at the centre of his economic agenda.

The problems of SOEs were in fact well known to the Chinese leadership, which had also realized that without accomplishing the reform of the state sector, the Chinese economy would continue to operate with all the well-known inefficiency of a partially reformed economy. But just how best or how effectively the new reform measures could be carried out remained to be seen. Jiang prepared the political ground to push for the Chinese way of privatization by transforming many

---

[6]See, for example, "Jiang Accuses Leftist of Exploiting Anxieties", *South China Morning Post* (Hong Kong, July 31, 1997); and "The Counter Attack of Beijing's Conservative Group", *Ming Pao* (Hong Kong, August 15, 1997). "Xia Gang" is retrenchment of redundant workers by SOE, and it became a serious problem. According to the State Statistical Bureau, some 15 million workers had been made redundant by SOEs, representing 12.5% of the total urban labour force. Then there were rural surplus labour and the new entrants to the labour market ("Promising Reemployment Project", *Beijing Review*, August 18–24, 1997).

SOEs into "shareholding companies".[7] He had Zhu Rongji in charge of implementing this.

Growth vs. Stability

The Chinese economy had been growing at about 10% since its economic reform in 1978 (Figure 1). Growth was particularly spectacular during 1991–1996, averaging at 12.1%. But such high growth gave rise to serious economic overheating, with inflation soaring to the record high of 27% in October 1994 (Figure 2). Since then, the restoration of price stability

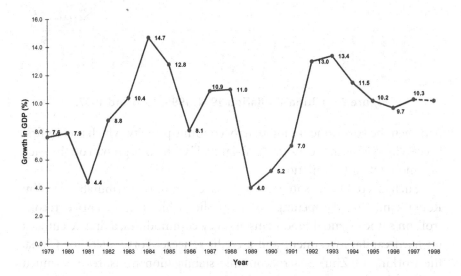

Figure 1.   China's economic growth and fluctuations (1979–1998).

---

[7] The Party's Propaganda Department had requested cadres to seriously study Jiang's speech given at the Central Party School, in which Jiang called for the "third liberalization of thought, based on seeking truth from facts". The "first liberalization" was advocated by Deng Xiaoping in 1978 for a more open interpretation of Mao's thought in order to prepare China for the economic reform and open-door policy. The "second liberalization" was again advocated by Deng in January 1992 during his tour of South China, and Deng had asked people to put an end to the futile debate over "Socialism vs. Capitalism" so that China could move forward to the "socialist market economy". At that time, for the "third liberalization", Jiang had asked people to skip the debate over "public vs. private ownership" so that he could push ahead for a fundamental reform of SOEs. See "Jiang Promotes the Third Thought Liberation of the Communist Party", *Xinbao* (*Hong Kong Economic Journal*, August 15, 1997).

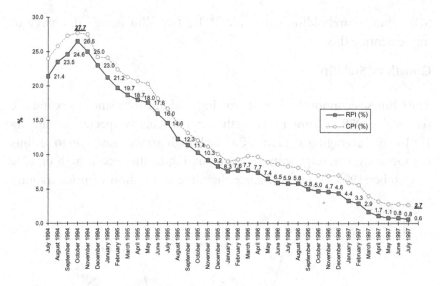

Figure 2.   China's inflation 1994, 1995, 1996 and 1997.

had been the government's top macroeconomic priority, which met its first success in 1996 as the economy "soft-landed" with 9.7% growth on the back of a moderate 6.1% inflation.

Such a creditable soft landing was commonly attributable to Zhu Rongji's inflation-dampening austerity policy, which included price "recontrol" on some essential food items and key commodities, a drastic cutback on fixed capital investment and a credit squeeze. Fortunately for China, the working of Zhu's macroeconomic stabilization measures was much facilitated by bumper agricultural harvests two years in a row and by the continuing influx of FDI. Hence, Zhu was able to squeeze out inflation without squeezing output.

The Chinese economy entered 1997 on a distinctively deflationary note, especially for the first quarter. As inflation, measured by both RPI and CPI, continued to drift downward month by month, industrial growth had also slowed down while both unemployment and stockpiling of unsold goods soared. Above all, the most significant growth-dampening factor had been the marked decline in the growth of fixed capital investment, which went down to 12% for the first six months of 1997 from the 1992 peak of 59%.[8]

---

[8] See "Macro Controls Anchor Growth Rate", *China Daily*, August 21, 1997.

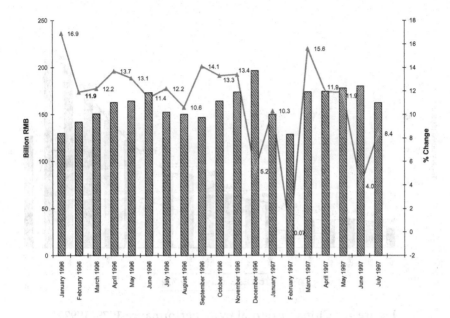

Figure 3. China's monthly industrial value-added 1996–1997.

The Chinese economy at the beginning of 1997 was widely expected to slow its growth to some "healthy" level of 8% in order to be compatible with the low inflation.

However, much to the surprise of many foreign observers, China still posted a 9.5% growth for the first half of 1997 together with a very low inflation of 1.6% on RPI. As can be seen from Figure 3, the upturn occurred during the months of June and July, probably as a result of the loosening up of the tight monetary policy through two rounds of interest rate cuts along with corresponding increases in money supply (M2) and loans, at 19% and 18%, respectively. Apart from increases in domestic demand, exports also recovered, growing at 26% for the first seven months of 1997 (Figure 4).

What were the good "structural reasons" to explain such an unexpected strong growth performance? Before Zhu Rongji, the Chinese government relied on blunt administrative means to fight inflation, often resulting in boom-bust cycles. Since 1993, Zhu had learned to apply a mixture of market-based instruments with some subtle but firm administrative devices for appropriate macroeconomic controls.

For instance, the People's Bank of China had put in place a more effective system for monitoring credit and loans at its local branches, thanks

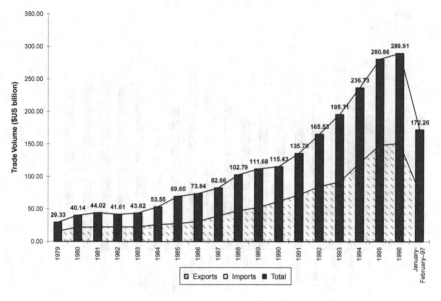

Figure 4.   China's external trade performance 1979–1997.

to its computerization efforts and the related administrative reforms. In other words, China had been learning how to use macroeconomic fine-tuning techniques in previous decades. Accordingly, Zhu's increasing skill in macroeconomic management was paid off in the form of more favourable output-inflation trade-off — technically speaking, causing a shift of the traditional type of Phillips Curve towards the left. If this were true, the Chinese economy were headed for an era of sustainable high growth with low inflation.

There were no signs that the low inflation trends were to reverse in the second half of 1997. But it was far from certain that the high growth momentum would continue throughout 1997 as to end up in a 10% growth. The Chinese leadership had already revealed its preference for stability to growth, and the underlying political condition for such a preference was not likely to change so drastically as to justify a large measure of reflation after the Fifteenth Party Congress. This was because further economic reforms would still call for a stable macroeconomic environment.

However, China found it increasingly difficult to sustain its existing strong export growth (mainly driven by a sharp rise in the export of textile and garments) for the rest of 1997 because the depreciation of several Southeast Asian currencies had turned regional export comparative advantage against China, thus reversing the very force which used to favour China in the past few years over its competing Southeast Asian economies. All in all, there was still much uncertainty over China's economic growth in the second half of 1997, but it was not serious enough to cause a shift in Jiang–Zhu's basic policy stand over the economy.

New Approach to the Old SOE Problem?

The immediate economic challenge Jiang had faced was actually how to put forth his own programmes of economic reform for the endorsement by the Party Congress. Judged by his pre-Congress speeches to top Party leaders, the reform of SOEs occupied the Party Congress's main economic agenda. Indeed, the SOE reform was one crucial area which had till then not achieved any significant breakthrough.[9] This was because SOE reform was technically more complicated, and politically and socially more difficult to implement than any previous reform items. But China had to thoroughly reform and restructure its SOE sector before it could complete its transition to a full "socialist market economy".[10] A simple bottom-line approach

---

[9] In 1978, SOEs accounted for 78% of China's total industrial output; but the figure declined sharply to only 31% by 1995. The relative decline of the SOE sector over the years may just reflect the dynamic expansion of the non-state sector, which included township and village enterprises (TVEs) and various forms of individual and foreign-owned enterprises. Despite its relative shrinkage, the SOE sector remained large in terms of employment, fixed assets and exports. In 1995, there were about 118,000 *industrial* SOEs, of which approximately 16,000 were considered "large and medium", and they together provided 55% of total urban employment. Most SOEs were engaged in raw material and energy production as well as in heavy industry, including a wide range of capital-intensive industries that had to operate on the economies of scale. In fact, the bulk of China's basic industrial raw materials and intermediate products are produced by SOEs.

[10] As Premier Li Peng said during his visit to Singapore, "Not all SOEs are bad; and their problems have been exaggerated by foreign media", he is quite right in a way. China has compiled its own equivalent to the "Fortune's 500", and most of them, including the annual top performers, are SOEs. So were those listed on the Hong Kong Stock Exchange as H shares, and "Red Chips".

However, the overall performance of the SOE sector had remained consistently weak, fundamentally because they still operated under some kind of "soft budget constraints". According to a report from the State Planning Commission, in the first part of 1997, some 46.8% of all SOEs reported losses, upto 2.7% over the same period of 1996.

was to allow the many ailing SOEs to go bankrupt or to wait until a workable national social safety net was in place (so as to take care of any massive retrenchment of redundant workers). Obviously, neither was a viable option then. Thus, all eyes were on the kind of new SOE reform strategies Jiang was to unravel at the Congress — how much of them just for the rhetoric, and how much for implementation.

To crack the SOE problem, the Chinese government, to its credit, had actually been quite open-minded in experimenting with various reforming strategies. Prior to 1993, the reform focus was placed on improving enterprise governance such as greater managerial autonomy and greater accountability of enterprises. Later, progress in price reform had also provided a much improved external economic environment for SOEs to operate. At that time, especially after the enactment of the new Company Law, the main emphasis had shifted to "corporatization" by encouraging SOEs to restructure themselves into modern enterprise groups, or to convert themselves into "shareholding companies".

It suffices to say that the government continued to attack the SOE problem on many fronts. In terms of the actual implementation strategy, the slogan then was about the *Zhua-da fang-Xiao* strategy, (concentrating on large SOEs and letting go smaller ones). In this regard, over 2,500 large and medium SOEs were earmarked for trying out various ways of reform, half of which had been converted into "shareholding companies", with some having been formed into huge 57 modern enterprise groups (subsequently increased to 120) to become under direct central control.[11]

The pre-Congress debate on the SOE reform policy clearly pointed to a growing interest in the shareholding system, indicating that Zhu's new

---

Regardless of the real extent of the SOE losses and their real causes, China's SOE sector posed at least two serious problems to the Chinese economy: (1) an ailing SOE sector, controlling a disproportionately large share of physical and human resources, badly distorted the whole economy — clearly a classic case of misallocation of resources on a gigantic scale, and (2) the existence of an inefficient state sector had become an obstacle for the reform efforts of other sectors, particularly the financial sector reform. When large SOEs were making losses, the state banks bailed them out, leading to the accumulation of too many bad loans for the state banks — the official figure for non-performing loans in the state banks were 18%. And the problem of bad debt, in turn, hindered banking reform.

[11]"A Review of SOE Reform Since the 14th Party Congress", *Renmin Ribao*, Beijing, August 28, 1997.

SOE reform strategy focussed on the conversion of the majority of the SOEs into some kind of shareholding companies, particularly the so-called shareholding co-operatives. It is well known that a lot of SOE problems could be traced to their weak internal incentive mechanism associated with state ownership and control. Without owning a stake in the enterprise, workers and management would not have the inherent incentive to perform well.

Thus, China started its first experimentation of a shareholding system as early as in 1983, but it was only after 1992 that more SOEs were converted into shareholding companies. By 1997, China had 9,000 registered shareholding companies, mostly small to medium in size. For the 1,000 or so large SOEs, the government had been reluctant to diversify its ownership by converting them into shareholding companies. But why such a renewed interest in the shareholding system at that time?

From all the pre-Congress clues, Jiang's leadership had apparently taken the view that for the numerous small and medium SOEs, especially those controlled by local governments, privatization was the most effective approach to tackle such thorny problems as incentive mechanism, property rights and depoliticization of economic management.[12] But privatization had to be tactfully promoted without openly running afoul of the open ideological taboo involving the controversy of *gong* vs. *si* (or public vs. private ownership). Hence, the limelight on the "shareholding cooperative", which was considered quite similar to the "collectively owned" TVEs in terms of combining capitalist mode of production with socialist (or collective) elements of ownership. Ideologically, the shareholding cooperative would thus suit quite well the current label of "primary stage of socialism" for China, which was used by Jiang to rationalize his new reform initiatives with hidden privatization.

The shareholding cooperative, if successful, were destined to be the Chinese way of privatization. Not enough operational details were known as to how exactly a typical shareholding cooperative was to be organized and how the scheme would be promoted.[13] Admittedly, the government

---

[12] See, for example, the Reuters dispatch "China's Leaders Look Set to Promote Private Enterprise", *Business Times*, Singapore, August 18, 1997.

[13] An important question was how a shareholding company would have valued its assets and how it would have divided up the shares for allotment among the state or local government,

had to sort out a number of conceptual and empirical difficulties before it could be effectively used as one of the main instruments to attack such a "cross-century problem" as of the reform of SOEs.

Deng's eminent success in the first phase of economic reform owed a great deal to his flexibility and pragmatism, based on his celebrated "Two-Cat Theory" — "It does not matter if the cat is white or black, so long as it can catch mice". If Jiang and Zhu had similar pragmatism and strong political will for the SOE reform, they too would have similarly declared, "It does not matter whether an enterprise belongs to the public or private sector, so long as it makes profits!"

---

the enterprise's own employees, and the legal entities like banks, pension funds, etc. In 1997, a lot of debate was on whether or not each worker was allowed to vote as one shareholder regardless of the number of shares he has, and whether or not his shares can be bought and sold on the secondary market.

Some legal scholars had also argued that a shareholding cooperative is "neither a horse nor a mule", as it displays a contradictory mixture of the capitalist element of shareholding with the socialist element of a cooperative. See, e.g., "Shareholding Cooperatives are in Urgent Need of Proper Legal Rulings", *Xinbao* (*Hong Kong Economic Journal*, August 30, 1997).

2

INTERPRETING ZHU RONGJI'S ECONOMIC STRATEGIES FOR THE 1990s

Introduction

This chapter was written in March 1998 against two backdrops. First, the Fifteenth Party Congress, held in September 1997, confirmed Jiang Zemin as China's supreme leader, who in turn appointed Zhu Rongji as one of the seventh Politburo Standing Committee members. Zhu's substantive position was China's Premier of the State Council. The Party's list of nominees for top posts (called "personnel arrangement"), as always, had to be officially rubber-stamped by the National People's Congress (NPC), or China's Parliament. The Ninth NPC in mid-March 1998 had just endorsed Zhu as China's new Premier.

Second, much of Southeast Asia was then in the throes of the Asian financial crisis, which, started in the latter part of 1997, had spread to parts of East Asia, particularly South Korea and Hong Kong (which was just newly returned to China on July 1, 1997). Unlike Hong Kong, China's financial sector was then basically closed to the outside world, with the Renminbi being inconvertible on the capital account and under strict capital control. Still, China's economy was feeling increasing external economic pressures as other Asian countries had sharply devalued their currencies and the region's foreign trade and foreign investment were seriously disrupted. In fact, in the following few months, the Hong Kong dollar was under severe speculative attack, adding further pressures to China.

Apart from a myriad of domestic economic and social challenges associated with the development of the "socialist market economy" that the Fifteenth Party Congress had adopted, China also had to contain the spread of the Asian financial crisis. Thus, all eyes were on China's new Premier Zhu Rongji. At his maiden press conference shortly after he was confirmed Premier, the no-nonsense Zhu dwelt freely and confidently on his immediate missions and future tasks. He made no bones about the various challenges ahead that he equated to a "mind field or an abyss", and he was bracing himself to cross it.

Frank, straight-talking and full of convictions, Zhu had thus greatly impressed both domestic and foreign media, which labelled him as China's "Economic Czar". Never before had the media come across such an open Chinese Premier, bearing in mind that his predecessor Li Peng was by nature very shy and also highly unpopular both at home and abroad because of his alleged role behind the Tiananmen Square crackdown in June 1989.

Zhu put what he set out to do in a motto of 12 Chinese characters: Yege quebao; sange daowei; wuxiang gaige — literally meaning, "Ensuring one", "putting three in place" and "Reform in five areas". Some of his views were already well known as he had been dealing with China's economic reform and development for many years as Vice Premier. The key questions then were: What do all these mean for the Chinese economy, now that he is Premier? Can he deliver?

In policy terms, Zhu's immediate objective was to maintain China's economic growth in 1998 at 8% with inflation below 3%. Because of the deteriorating international economic environment, Zhu could only reflate China's economy by boosting domestic demand. This would have to be done by mainly increasing fixed assets investment, from 10% in 1997 to 15% in 1998, with more money pouring into infrastructure like a "New Deal". Ever since, the Chinese economy had got "addicted" to increasing fixed investment for high economic growth. In fact, for the following decade and a half, China's economic growth had become basically investment driven.

Zhu had apparently changed from a kind of "Monetarist" for macroeconomic stabilization a few years ago (when he was fighting high inflation) to now more a "Keynesian" for expansion! But it was far from certain that he could achieve his 8% growth target for that year, partly because the economy was then facing so many headwinds both domestically and externally, and partly, his growth-stimulus package was just too moderate.

In fact, 1998 ended the year with only 7.8%, falling short of Zhu's magic rate of 8% growth, while inflation plummeted to below zero. With hindsight, Zhu would later come to know that 1998 and 1999 were two years of serious deflation for China, with consumer price index (CPI) dropping to −0.8% and −0.14%, respectively. This was China's first deflation since the start of economic reform in 1978, which clearly implied that Zhu's former macroeconomic control policies had been working too well. In other words, Zhu's policies had overshot its original targets such that their lingering effects were carried over to this period.

In retrospect, because of the two bouts of serious inflation — one in the late 1980s and the other in the mid-1990s, China's economic planners and policy makers had since developed a kind of inflation phobia, and such inflation-targeting bias had also built into Zhu's economic strategies. In all fairness, the gloomy regional and international economic environment at that time had also contributed to China's domestic deflation in this period. It has since also come to light that China's exports in 1998 actually fell by 1.5%, a far-cry from its dynamic growth in the early 1990s. Thus, for the first time in many years, many Chinese factories experienced over-production and over-capacities, with domestic markets glutted with surplus merchandise.

Accordingly, one of Zhu's central economic policy objectives for 1998 was bao chengchang or maintaining growth. At the same time, Zhu looked beyond this short-term growth objective by placing even greater emphasis on his longer-term reform programme, particularly his commitment to "fix" China's state-owned enterprise (SOE) problems in three years. Actually, he had staked his reputation on the SOE reform. To facilitate this task, he was also pushing other supportive reforms like administrative reorganization, and banking and housing reforms at the same time.

The biggest obstacle to his SOE endeavour came from China's rapidly growing urban unemployment, which had reached 7%, higher than what was considered "acceptable to China based on its social and economic conditions". If Zhu were really a good politician, he would have to take heed of the Party's constant fear of disorder or pa-luan and would have to tailor the progress of the SOE reform with the need for maintaining social stability.

Zhu appeared to be increasingly aware of the high social costs associated with reforming SOEs at the time of China's economic slowdown. There were indications that he would even go slow on the SOE reform to allow him to concentrate first on other related supportive reforms such as downsizing the bureaucracy to improve governance and putting in place a better social safety net. This would then enable him to build up a more viable institutional framework for the decisive attack on the SOE problem later when the socio-economic conditions had improved. With this smart tactic of balancing reform with stability, Zhu was hopeful that he might still be able to accomplish a lot of what he had promised to do in next three years.

> *No Matter what lies ahead of me, be it a minefield or an abyss, I will brace myself for it. I have no hesitation and no misgivings, and I will do my best and devote myself to the people and my country until the last day of my life.*
> *— Premier Zhu Rongji at his maiden press conference,*
> *March 19, 1998, Beijing*

The Right Man at the Right Time

On March 17, 1998 Mr. Zhu Rongji was confirmed by the Ninth NPC as China's new Premier with an overwhelming majority — 98% of the 2950 deputies voted for him. This had been a much anticipated event, to which both foreign and local media had devoted extensive coverage. Zhu was commonly portrayed as a tough and resolute ("A Blunt Pragmatist" by *International Herald Tribune*; and "The Man with the Iron Face" by *Asiaweek*) but talented and dedicated administrator. His track record as Vice Premier in charge of China's economy (nicknamed China's "Economic Czar") had won wide acclaim, particularly for bringing the Chinese economy to a successful "soft landing".

At his maiden press conference on March 19, 1998, the much confident and straight-talking Zhu "projected a relaxed, personal style, bantering with foreign and domestic journalists and fielding questions on everything",[1] which was rather unusual for China's political leaders. Zhu outlined his immediate mission and his broad strategies for the Chinese economy. Was he able to deliver? This chapter attempts to separate Zhu's rhetoric from China's reality, and interprets his broad development strategies in the perspective of China's existing problems and constraints at that time.

It was almost decades ago in December 1978 when the historic Third Plenum of the Party's Eleventh Central Committee approved Deng Xiaoping's economic reform and open-door policy. Based on a cautious,

---

[1] "New China Leader Vows to Blaze Trail", *International Herald Tribune*, March 20, 1998.

gradualist (*Mozhe shitou guohe* or "Crossing the river by touching the stones") strategy, Deng's reform efforts achieved eminent success in the first part of the 1980s, especially in agricultural reforms. However, the reform met resistance as it was extended to other sectors and broadened to non-economic areas. This culminated in the June 1989 Tiananmen incident. In retrospect, both the Tiananmen event and the subsequent collapse of the Soviet Union had convinced Deng that the only future for China was (1) to accelerate economic reform rather than holding it back, and (2) to continue to let economic reform precede political reform, i.e., the exact opposite of the Soviet strategy of putting *glasnost* before *perestroika*.

Accordingly, Deng embarked on his celebrated tour of South China in the spring of 1992 to preach more thorough-going economic reform in order to transform China into a "socialist market economy". This marks the beginning of the second phase of China's economic reform, which in the short span of five years had changed China almost beyond recognition, both economically and socially. As a result of the dynamic growth at the average rate of 11% during 1992–1997, the Chinese economy had indeed been extensively transformed in terms of structure and orientation. By 1997, China's economy had already been substantially integrated into the global economy, as China in 1997 became the world's 10th largest trading economy with US$183 billion of total exports, and the world's second most favoured destination for foreign investment with an inflow of US$45 billion. Viewed from a different angle, China's economy had since also become more vulnerable to the ebbs and flows of international capitalism.

As for economic reform, following the endorsement by the Fourteenth Party Congress in 1993 for a comprehensive reform programme, China made important reform progress in the areas of finance, taxation, foreign exchange, pricing and investment.[2] By 1997, the Chinese economy had also become by and large market driven, with the prices of most consumer goods and intermediate products including some key raw material items like petroleum and steel products, basically set by supply and demand. However, in the crucial areas of SOEs and banking (which are closely interrelated in operations), their reforms had failed to achieve significant breakthroughs.

---

[2]"Premier Li Peng's Report on Work of Government", *China Daily*, March 23, 1998.

The Chinese leadership at that time had already recognized that without cracking the SOE problem, China could not modernize its banking and financial sector. As long as these two critical reform areas remained in limbo, China would not be able to complete its transition to a full market economy and would instead continue to suffer from the inefficiency of a partially reformed economy.

That explains why the SOE reform was catapulted to the top agenda of the Fifteenth Party Congress in September 1997.[3] However, reforming SOEs, for China as for the other transitional economies, was politically and technically very difficult to manage because of serious political and social ramifications. What was critically needed for success was a strong political will. And Zhu Rongji knew that.

Thus, Zhu had immediately set out to clear the decks for this daunting task. First, he streamlined China's unwieldy government structure by eliminating 11 out of 40 government ministries. A number of outmoded ministries (which were originally created for central planning purposes) were merged into one powerful "mini-economic cabinet" called "State Economic and Trade Commission" for more effective policy implementation (see Table 1).

Second, he pushed forward an even more vigorous plan to downsize the entrenched and overstaffed government departments, which were themselves often obstacles of reform. Over the next two years, about half of the estimated eight million government and Party officials were set to be transferred or simply laid off under the euphemism of *fen-liu* or "streamed out".

Third, he had hand-picked a team of younger, professionally qualified technocrats, including a number of well-tested state entrepreneurs (e.g., Sheng Huaren and Wu Jichuan), to help him push through his reform plans. The average age of his 38-strong cabinet was 59.7 years, four years younger than that of the previous cabinet headed by Li Peng.[4]

---

[3] For a more detailed discussion of the SOE reform problem, see John Wong, "Reforming China's State-owned Enterprises: Problems and Prospects", *EAI Background Brief No. 3*, October 10, 1997.

[4] "Technocrats Selected for Zhu's Cabinet", *South China Morning Post*, March 19, 1998. This issue was widely reported in the foreign media. See also, "China Approves Cabinet of Younger Technocrats", *Asian Wall Street Journal*, March 19, 1998.

Table 1.   Zhu's new state council.

Old: 40	New: 29
State Planning Commission	State Development and Planning Commission
State Science and Technology Commission	Ministry of Science and Technology
State Education Commission	Ministry of Education
Ministry of Foreign Affairs	Ministry of Foreign Affairs
Ministry of Defence	Ministry of Defence
State Economic and Trade Commission	State Economic and Trade Commission
Ministry of Power	
Ministry of Coal Industry	
Ministry of Metallurgical Industry	
Ministry of Machine-Building	
Ministry of Chemical Industry	
Ministry of Internal trade	
• Textile Industry Council	
• Light Industry Council	
• General Company of Petroleum and Gas	
• General Company of Chemical Industry	
Ministry of Electrical Industry	
Ministry of Post and Communication	Ministry of Information Industry
Ministry of Radio, Film and Television	
State Nationalities Affairs Commission	State Nationalities Affairs Commission
Ministry of Public Security	Ministry of Public Security
Ministry of State Security	Ministry of State Security
Ministry of Supervision	Ministry of Supervision
Ministry of Civil Affairs	Ministry of Civil Affairs
Ministry of Justice	Ministry of Justice
Ministry of Personnel	Ministry of Personnel
Ministry of Finance	Ministry of Finance
Ministry of Construction	Ministry of Construction
Ministry of Railway	Ministry of Railway
Ministry of Posts and Telecommunications	Ministry of Posts and Telecommunications
Ministry of Water Resources	Ministry of Water Resources
Ministry of Agriculture	Ministry of Agriculture
Ministry of Foreign Trade and Economic Cooperation	Ministry of Foreign Trade and Economic Cooperation
Ministry of Culture	Ministry of Culture

(*Continued*)

Table 1.   (*Continued*)

Old: 40	New: 29
Ministry of Public health	Ministry of Public Health
State Family Planning Commission	State Family Planning Commission
People's Bank	People's Bank
Auditing Administration	Auditing Administration
Commission of Science, Technology, and Industry for National Defence	State Science, Technology, and Industry Commission for National Defence
• Department of National Defence of the State Planning Council • Governmental functions of Military Industry Companies	
Ministry of Labour	Ministry of Labour and Social Security
• Social Security Department of Ministry of Personnel • Social Security Department of Ministry of Civil Affairs • Insurance Department of Ministry of Public Heath	
Ministry of Geology and Mineral Resources	Ministry of Land and Resources
• State Land Administration • State Maritime Bureau • State Survey Bureau	
Ministry of Forest — Forest Bureau under SC	
State Physical Cultural and Sports Commission	
State Commission for Economic Systems Restructuring	

Note: • refers to organs previously managed directly by the State Council.
Source: *China Daily*, March 11, 1998.

Bao Chengchang or Maintaining Robust Growth

Zhu Rongji revealed his strategic plans and policy initiatives in his famous 12-character motto: *Yi-ge que-bao, san-ge dao-wei, wu-xiang gai-ge* (literally, "One ensuring, Three putting in place, and Five reforms"). To spell out, his first objective was to confront the challenge of the Asian financial crisis by ensuring China's economy in 1998 maintained a reasonably strong growth of 8% with inflation below 3%. Secondly, he wanted to realize his policy aims of (a) relieving China's large and medium SOEs of their "most difficult problems" by restructuring them into modern enterprises; (b) overhauling China's banking system, and (c) completing the reorganization of China's government structures at various levels, all in three years. Thirdly, he wanted to achieve reforms and changes in five areas pertaining to grain distribution, investment and financing, housing market, healthcare and taxation and revenue.[5]

To fulfil his first objective of maintaining China's past high growth momentum, Zhu had broached his ideas of boosting domestic demand by (a) increasing investment for infrastructural development in highways, railways, agricultural reclamation, water conservancy, municipal facilities and environmental protection, (b) speeding up the development of high-tech industries and their technical upgrading, and (c) promoting residential housing construction as a "new growth point".

As the Chinese economy had emerged by then from the three-year long macroeconomic control programme, Zhu reckoned that he could channel more financial resources to expand domestic demand without stoking inflation. These measures to boost economic growth through expanding domestic investment would look like Roosevelt's New Deal, which Zhu was reported to have been studying very closely over the past few months.[6] Zhu had evidently changed from a kind of "Monetarist" for stabilization (that was needed to reduce overheating) to now more like a "Keynesian" for expansion!

To begin with, Zhu's decision to reorient China's economic growth strategy from excessive dependence on external demand towards greater emphasis on domestic demand appeared quite rational. For years, the growth of China's economy, much like that of the other export-oriented East Asian economies, had been fuelled mainly by strong external demand. For example, China's exports grew at 23% in 1995, 11% in 1996 and

---

[5]"Zhu Charts Development Course", *China Daily*, March 20, 1998; "The First Press Conference of the 9th NPC", *Renmin Ribao* (*People's Daily*, March 20, 1998).

[6]"Zhu Charts 'New Deal' Policy", *South China Morning Post*, February 20, 1998; "Zhu Vows to Boost Economy", *ibid.*, March 20, 1998.

21% in 1997.[7] Since 1993, China had consistently been the world's second largest recipient of foreign direct investment (FDI), and by 1997, China had captured a total FDI inflow of US$222 billion.[8] The financial crisis must have made the Chinese leadership also realize the potential vulnerability to the Chinese economy by further relying on external economic factors as a major source of growth.

The 1997 Asian economic crisis had certainly produced significant impact on China's external economic growth engine, as over 70% of China's FDI originated from sources which had been affected, in varying degrees, by this crisis.[9] A study from Ministry of Foreign Trade and Economic Cooperation (MOFTEC) put China's FDI in 1998 at US$35 billion, down by 25% from 1997.[10] There had even been cases of reversed FDI flow as some ethnic Chinese from the troubled Southeast Asia liquidated some of their assets in China in order to ease their debt problems at home.[11] In any

---

[7] See "Statistical Communique of the State Statistical Bureau of the People's Republic of China on the 1997 National Economic and Social Development", *China Daily*, March 14, 1998.

[8] In 1995, foreign-funded enterprises, including those owned by Hong Kong and Taiwan, accounted for 14.7% of China's total value-added in manufacturing and provided a total employment of 8.9 million workers, or about 6% of China's total manufacturing employment. Above all, foreign enterprises in 1996 were responsible for US$62 billion worth of exports, or 40% of China's total exports. See "Foreign Capital Aids Growth", *China Daily*, March 10, 1998.

[9] It may be pointed out that some ill-informed commentators have exaggerated the direct effect of Southeast Asian economic crisis on China because only about 7% of China's total exports are destined for the Association of Southeast Asian Nations (ASEAN) economies including Singapore. It would also take months for the beleaguered ASEAN economies to reorganize their manufactured exports to compete directly with China in the third country markets, especially since China's major manufactured exports like textiles and garment, shoes and toys have remained very competitive for the time being even without the devaluation of the *Renminbi*. However, China's exports will face great challenges from its East Asian neighbouring economies of South Korea, Taiwan, Japan and Hong Kong, with which the Chinese economy has established closer linkages.

[10] "A MOFTEC Researcher Pointed that FDI this Year Would Decline", *Xinbao* (Hong Kong, March 4, 1998). Apart from the Asian financial crisis, over-capacity and depressed retail markets in China have also caused a slowdown in the FDI inflow to China.

[11] The case in point is the Charoen Pokphand or CP group, which is one of the largest and most successful investors in China from Southeast Asia. The CP group was at that time reported to be withdrawing some assets from China. See "Asian Crisis Tests Thai Firm's China Investment", *International Herald Tribune*, March 28–29, 1998.

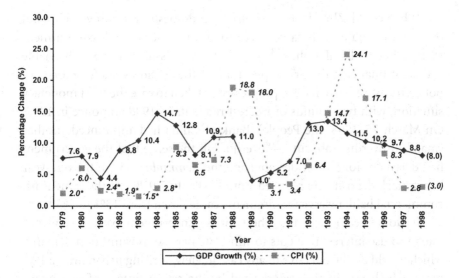

Figure 1.   China's economic growth and inflation (1979–1998).

case, China's external sector performance in 1997 was so strong that it was hard for 1998 to repeat that even under normal circumstances. To sustain continuing high growth, therefore, Zhu simply had to reflate the economy through boosting domestic demand. But was this effective?

It was certainly not easy to reflate an economy that had just achieved a "soft landing". As can be seen from Figure 1, China's growth rates, following Zhu's vigorous macroeconomic stabilization measures, had since 1993 been on a steady decline. This means that any domestic demand stimulus package had to be equally vigorous in order to force the economy to reverse gears towards a new "take-off" again.

From the official statistics, however, industrial growth in value-added terms for the first two months of 1998 recorded only 8% increase over the same period last year, a 2.4% point lower than that of 1997, while inflation had become negative (−1.9% by retail price index (RPI) and −0.1% by CPI).[12] Clearly, the Chinese economy was still suffering from the after-effect of Zhu's macroeconomic "squeeze", and was possibly even heading for a deflation.

---

[12]"Industrial Production Growth Decline and Contraction Continues", *Xinbao*, March 19, 1998.

What could Zhu do to revitalize the domestic economy? His fiscal options were quite constrained because of the government's commitment to a stringent fiscal policy.[13] This left bond issues as the only viable source of financing the prime pumping of the economy. As for monetary policy, measures were indeed progressively taken to ease the tight monetary situation, with two rounds of interest rate cuts in 1996 and once in 1997. On March 25, 1998, the People's Bank of China had announced another small but overdue rate cut — "overdue" in the sense that the government had delayed it for fear of destabilizing the *Renminbi* — with the one-year benchmark deposit rate reduced from 8.64% to 7.92%. At the same time, commercial bank reserve requirements came down from 13% to 8%.[14]

It would seem clear that the Chinese government basically did not intend to use interest rate cuts to stimulate private consumption demand, which would not be effective in any case in view of rising urban unemployment, which was in turn aggravated by the retrenchment of redundant workers due to SOE reform. Nor would many private businesses rush to seek bank loans for expansion because of the existing market glut in all kinds of consumer goods, from food stuffs and traditional daily commodities to modern durables like colour TVs, VCD, refrigerators, washing machines and computers, to intermediate products like steel, coal and cement. All told, some RMB 590 billion worth of goods or 19% of 1997 industrial output were still stockpiled in warehouses unsold. With such a general "lack of effective demand" in existence, the only credible source of growth stimulus for China's economy would therefore have to come from the "New-Deal" kind of increased investment demand.

In his report to the NPC, Minister of the State Planning Commission, Chen Jinhua proposed to increase China's fixed assets investment in 1998 by 10% to US$336 billion, which included US$156 billion for capital construction, US$57 billion for technical upgrading of industries, and

---

[13] In fact, the outgoing Finance Minister Liu Zhongli, in presenting his draft budget for 1998 to the NPC, took pride in announcing that the central government's deficit for 1998 would only be RMB 46 billion (US$5.6 billion), RMB 10 billion less than the actual figure for 1997. See "Report on Implementation of the Central and Local Government Budgets for 1997", *China Daily*, March 24, 1998.

[14] "Zhu Cuts Rates in Boost to Economy", *South China Morning Post*, March 25, 1998; and *Ming Pao* (Hong Kong, March 25, 1998).

US$43 billion for housing construction.[15] Subsequently, Central Bank Governor Dai Xianglong's and other policy makers argued for another 15% increase in order to sustain 8% growth.[16] It suffices to say that increasing fixed assets investment was, technically and financially speaking, the best way for China to prime pumping its economy at that time.

Strictly speaking, what Zhu had contemplated for boosting China's economic growth through increased capital investment was not exactly a "New Deal", which by definition was designed primarily to promote employment, even at the expense of economic efficiency. Furthermore, Zhu's original objectives were not just maintaining growth but also reforming SOEs amongst others.

Thus, he had to ensure that new financial resources were channelled into the right place for the right purpose. This was not easy because of China's "outdated investment system", which followed short-term market signals.[17] In any case, any large capital project would take time to plan, implement and yield its desired results. Technically, the economic effects of all large investment boosters would carry a time lag, and they might not even create the immediate multiplier effect to add to the 1998 gross national product (GNP). In short, it was far from certain that Zhu could achieve his 8% growth target for 1998.[18] But should this happen, Zhu would not be blamed for any under-performance.

Pushing to Complete the Unfinished Business of Reform

Actually Zhu had staked his reputation and prestige not on achieving the short-term goal of 8% growth, but on his long-term ambition of completing the reform that was initiated by Deng Xiaoping. The reform on the SOE

---

[15]"Report on Implementation of the 1997 Plan for National Economic and Social Development and the Draft 1998 Plan for National Economic and Social Development", *China Daily*, March 24, 1998.

[16]"Investment to Maintain Growth", *China Daily: Business Weekly*, March 8–14, 1998. See also, "Funds Sought for 'New Deal'", *China Daily: Business Weekly*, March 29–April 4, 1998.

[17]"Funds Sought for 'New Deal' — Outdated Investment System Requires Urgent Reform", *China Daily: Business Weekly*, March 29–April 1, 1998.

[18]However, Qiu Xiaohua, Chief Economist of the State Statistical Bureau, remained optimistic that China could achieve 8% growth in 1998. *China Economic News* (Beijing, No. 11, March 23, 1998).

sector had bogged down. Back in September 1997, Zhu declared in Hong Kong to the effect that he could "fix the SOE reform problem" in three years. He reiterated this commitment shortly after he became Premier, with a clarification as to why his original SOE reform goal would still be achievable.[19] Was Zhu then really in a better position to tackle the SOE reform?

First, as indicated earlier, one major reason for the past reform failure had been the lack of a strong political will to take hard decisions concerning the broader political and social ramifications of the reform. Zhu had shown his determination, and he had also been given a strong mandate for this task. Second, as also discussed earlier, he had assembled a team of able technocrats to assist him. Above all, he also pushed for the reform of the government structure at the same time, i.e., to improve governance. The expected administrative reorganization and retrenchment aimed at not just weeding out the incompetent bureaucrats and those who would have dragged their feet over the reform, but also cutting the umbilical cord between government departments and enterprises.

One should never underestimate the enormous administrative complexity of implementing a central government policy in a big country like China, as reflected in the oft-repeated aphorism: "For every policy from above, there is a counter-measure below". Of even greater importance, after such a shake-up, many inefficient SOEs would be exposed and subjected to hard budget constraints once they had lost the support of their *po-po* ("mother-in-law") patronage behind them.

Third, thanks to the experimentation with the SOE reform since 1994, China had accumulated a lot of useful experiences and in fact perfected the techniques of reforming SOE within China's specific institutional context. Without doubt, Zhu and his men had already grasped the main technicalities of how to go about reforming different categories of SOEs.

---

[19]At his first press conference as Premier, Zhu clarified what he said in Hong Kong about "solving the SOE problem in three years" actually meant, "extricating the large SOEs from their present financial difficulties". He also pointed out that China's SOE problem was actually not as bad as the foreign media had put it. When the past official statement mentioned 40% of SOEs having made a loss, it was referring to 40% of all the 79,000 industrial SOEs, which are mostly small in size. But in China, large SOEs are more important, with 500 large SOEs mainly responsible for delivering 85% of profits and taxes to the state. But for these large SOEs, only 10% or 50 of them were suffering losses. This means that the SOE problem is not really so hard to tackle from the long-term viewpoint. *China Daily*, March 20, 1998.

Fourth, Zhu's new SOE reform initiative was also bolstered by related supportive reforms. Previous SOE reform efforts were constrained by the absence of a new social safety net. Zhu was now pushing ahead with reform on housing and medical care. Indeed, he wanted to see the commercialization of housing for SOE workers in one year and that of their medical benefits in two years.[20] This better enabled individual SOEs to separate their economic functions from their traditional burdensome social welfare functions.

Of greater importance came from the reform of China's banking and finance, whose problems were also part of the SOE problem. The Asian financial crisis had precipitated Zhu to overhaul China's banking and financial sector. Plans were underway to strengthen the central banking functions of the People's Bank of China by restructuring it along the US Federal Reserve System. For the ailing state-owned commercial banks, the government had decided to inject a massive US$32.5 billion to re-capitalize them.[21]

In implementing the SOE reform, Zhu would not go for a "big bang" approach. Instead, he would be most likely to continue with the ongoing strategy of *Zhuada Fangxiao* or "Nurturing large SOEs (into modern conglomerates) while leaving smaller ones (to the market force)", which could better meet the Party's guideline of "balancing reform with development and stability", i.e., a gradualist approach. But Zhu might want to see more SOE to restructure, merge and corporatize. He could also be more resolute in shutting down the hopeless ones. It had later come to light that China in 1997 had actually made more progress in its SOE reform than was commonly realized.[22] Zhu, as a new Premier, must be seen to be doing even more.

---

[20]"Deadlines on Housing and Medical Reform", *South China Morning Post*, March 25, 1998. Specifically for housing reform, China would start from May 1998 abolished subsidized rented housing. State workers would now have to choose between buying their homes or paying market rents. "Reform Aim to End Subsidized Home Rents", *ibid.* March 31, 1998.

[21]"Financial System to Undergo Five Major Changes", *China Daily*, February 28, 1998; "US$32.5b Bond Plan to Bolster Key Banks", *China Daily*, March 2, 1998.

[22]According to Minister of the State Planning Commission, Chen Jinhua, by 1997, 1,989 out of 2,500 SOEs selected for the experiment, had been corporatized. Many SOEs had been formed into "enterprise groups" — the Chinese equivalent to the Korean *chaebols*, which increased to 120 from 57. Furthermore, 675 SOEs were closed down and 1022 had been

However, Zhu's SOE endeavour in 1998 was likely to be hampered by two unfavourable developments. First, as discussed earlier, China's slower economic growth had created a less conducive macroeconomic environment for any drastic reform measures. Secondly, as was widely reported in both Chinese and foreign media, China's rapidly growing urban unemployment could be potentially a real "minefield" for Zhu if he were to undertake a more radical approach.

Officially, China's urban unemployment in 1997 was only 3.1% (for the "registered unemployed" only). If the 12 million state sector workers who had been laid off under the disguise of *xiagang* (or "off post" with minimum benefits) were to be included, the unemployment rate would hit 7%. Subsequently, some 4 million or so civil servants would join the ranks of the *xiagang* workers if Zhu were to go ahead with the plan to downsize the government bureaucracy by half, not to mention the increasing stream of layoffs from the restructured SOEs.[23] According to the outgoing Minister of Labour Li Boyong, only a "5–6% unemployment rate would be acceptable to China based on its existing social and economic conditions."[24] In other words, China's *real* urban unemployment situation had already reached a dangerous level.

Hence, the great dilemma for Zhu. So far not much was known to the outside world about Zhu as a real politician. Now as Premier, Zhu had to take heed of the larger political interests of the Party, which remained very fearful of *luan* (disorder). His plans to downsize government and Party structures certainly pitted him against the many powerful interest groups.

Rationally, Zhu should have narrowed his battle front by not pushing the SOE reform too hard. If his reformist zeal were to get the better of

forced to merge with others, resulting in 1.7 million layoff ("Report on Implementation of the 1997 Plan for National Economic and Social Development and the Draft 1998 Plan for National Economic and Social Development" for the ninth NPC, *China Daily*, March 24, 1998). See also, Chang Xinze and Zhao Xiao, "On Several Problems of Further Reform of State-owned Enterprises", *Nankai Economic Studies* (Tianjin, No. 6, 1997).

[23]"Economist Predicts 28pc Jobless Figure by 2000", *South China Morning Post*, March 16, 1998. See also the interview with China's Vice Minister of Labour Lin Yongsan in *Ming Pao*, March 8, 1998.

[24]"Minister of Labour Said 6% Unemployment Rate is Acceptable to China", *Xinbao*, March 9, 1998.

him, prompting him to seek a more radical solution to the SOE problem, this could have well sparked off widespread social unrest that could have endangered the Party. Then the spectre of Zhu as China's potential Gorbachev would have come true.[25] In the circumstances, Jiang Zemin and Li Peng would have to rally all the conservative forces to depose him. Such would then be an equally unpalatable spectre of Zhu as another Zhao Ziyang.[26]

Zhu appeared to be increasingly aware of the high social cost associated with reforming China's SOEs at the time of China's economic slowdown. In his first tour of China's Northeastern provinces (the old industrial heartland with numerous ailing SOEs) as Premier, Zhu spoke of the government's "responsibility for ensuring the livelihood of laid-off workers" and urged local governments and enterprises to set up re-employment centres for those workers.[27] For the reforming SOEs, obviously, it was easier to keep those workers than find them new jobs, and hence a signal for these SOEs to go slow on reform and restructuring. A strong indication had thus emerged that Zhu, for reasons as discussed above, was not in a rush to attack the SOE reform head-on that year, despite his rhetoric of daring to "blaze trail".

Zhu had instead urged individual provincial governments to proceed with their SOE reform in accordance with their own conditions, realistically balancing their reform progress with their capacity to absorb the laid-off workers. In the meanwhile, he concentrated first on the other supportive reforms. In any case, administrative reorganization and improvement of governance were no less urgent. This would then enable him to build up the vital institutional framework for a more decisive attack on the SOE reform later when the socio-economic climate had improved. With such a smart tactic to balance reform with stability, Zhu could still accomplish a lot of what he had promised to do in following three years.

---

[25] Thomas Friedman of the *New York Times* argued that Zhu might just turn out to be the "Future Gorbachev of China", though Zhu publicly hated to be referred to as such ("Bet on Big Surprises from Zhu and Netanyahu", *International Herald Tribune*, March 30, 1998).

[26] Should this happen, Zhu would end up like another Zhao Ziyang, who was deposed by the Party conservatives led by Deng for supporting the student unrest at Tiananmen. See "Would Zhu become the Second Zhao Ziyang?" *Lianhe Zaobao* (Singapore, March 19, 1998).

[27] "Jobless Could Foil Zhu's Plans", *The Sunday Times* (Singapore, March 29, 1998).

3

WHY CHINA HAD NOT BEEN ASIA'S NEXT FINANCIAL DOMINO

Introduction

The Asian financial crisis started first in Thailand in the middle of 1997 and then quickly spread to other Asian economies in the region. This chapter was circulated to the Singapore government under the original title: "Will China be the Next Financial Domino?" on November 17, 1997, when the region was in the thick of the financial crisis, with international and regional media wildly speculating that China would possibly succumb to the region's financial turbulence and fall as the next domino.

The exchange rate of the Thai baht, like many other Asian currencies, was closely pegged to the US dollar, much like a fixed exchange-rate regime. At the same time, Thailand's central bank had maintained high domestic interest rates in order to shore up its currency. This encouraged many speculators to borrow from foreign banks and offshore markets to fund property speculation and other risky projects in Thailand — a situation known as "borrowing short and lending long". This in turn created a kind of "perfect storm" for the subsequent financial turmoil, as currency speculators, including the notorious George Soros, soon spotted the cracks in the system and mounted severe attack on the Thai baht in mid-May of 1997. On July 2, 1997, Thailand's central bank, having run out of its foreign exchange reserves, admitted defeat in defending the baht by putting it on a managed float. International speculation pressures were soon directed at the Philippines, Indonesia and Malaysia, all of which shared a lot of financial and monetary similarities with Thailand and hence their exchange rates also experienced sudden downward pressures. In late

July, the currencies of these three countries sharply plummeted with serious ramifications for their domestic financial institutions.

In the meanwhile, the contagion effect of the Thai crisis had continued to grow, spreading to South Korea, where many of its export-oriented industries were heavily leveraged with lot of external borrowings. So the Korean won had also collapsed. Taiwan and Singapore on account of their low exposure to external borrowings were only indirectly affected by this financial tsunami while Hong Kong, with the Hong Kong (HK) dollar directly pegged to the US dollar, would later be the next target for international currency speculators.

All this had prompted Malaysia's outspoken Prime Minister Mahathir Mohamad to openly point an accusing finger at "rogue speculators" and he specifically named the hedge fund operator George Soros as the major culprit. On August 20, 1997, the IMF approved the rescue package for Thailand. On September 20, Mahathir and Soros traded insults to each other at the IMF/World Bank Conference in Hong Kong, with Mahathir denouncing currency trading as "immoral" and Soros calling Mahathir "a menace to his own country". On October 8, Indonesia declared that it would seek IMF help, and a rescue package of US$38 billion was arranged in mid-November.

In the early phase of the crisis, it was commonly thought to be a currency crisis or a foreign exchange problem with impact mainly on the region's financial markets. In the early weeks of the crisis, Singapore's Prime Minister Goh Chok Tong had lightly dismissed it as only a "hiccup" in the region's financial development. Little did people at that time expect the currency crisis to develop into a full-blown financial crisis, which led to the collapse of not just the stock markets and property markets, but eventually economic growth. In fact, the financial crisis had given rise to a lingering economic crisis in the region, with many countries experiencing low economic growth for several years. The collapse of economic growth, in turn, gave rise to social instability. In the case of Indonesia, it led to the collapse of the Suharto government.

At the APEC summit in Vancouver in November 1997, President Jiang Zemin had similarly shrugged off the Asian financial crisis (*Yazhou jinrong fengbao*) as something that would not affect China when he was confronted by the international press. Prior to this, the region had already circulated a market rumour that Chinese Renminbi would soon be devalued even though. Zhu Rongji had repeatedly ruled out such a scenario. It subsequently came to light that the market rumours of the imminent devaluation the Renminbi were actually manufactured by the currency speculators who were then quietly preparing the market positions in Hong Kong in order to short the HK dollar, which was directly pegged to the US dollar.

On the eve of the Asian financial crisis, China's economy did display a number of worrisome signals, which included an overheated property sector in several cities and a banking sector that was saddled with a huge amount of bad loans (at 15% of China's GDP, compared to Mexico's 7–10%). Why did the Chinese leadership so smugly dismiss the potential contagion effect of the financial crisis to China? This is essentially what this chapter intends to explain.

To begin with, China's economy had fairly strong economic fundamentals, and its external economic balance looked stable and healthy. But what is most important was that China had not over-borrowed. Its major capital inflow came from foreign direct investment (FDI), not foreign loans as in Thailand and South Korea, and China's loans were essentially long-term, not short-term commercial borrowings. Hence, China's overall external debt burden was manageable in the context of its total exports and total foreign reserves.

What is most crucial is that the Renminbi was basically not convertible on the capital account. This means that the conventional trigger mechanism of international currency speculation could not be applied to China. With capital control, overseas currency speculators just cannot short the Renminbi in any significant amount. Also, China's two stock markets at that time were still small and were only selectively and indirectly open to foreign investors. In sum, it was not possible for China to be hit by an externally generated financial crisis. Nor was there reasonable ground for the outbreak of a domestic financial crisis, since both lenders (banks) and borrowers (state-owned enterprises (SOEs)) belonged to the state.

Looking back, China did successfully fend off the onslaught of the Asian financial crisis, which brought about many years of low growth for the region as a result of implementing various post-crisis economic retrenchment policies. Some of those deflationary policies were in fact mandated by the IMF as a "conditionality" for its rescue.

However, China still could not escape from the side effects of the crisis. China, too, also suffered from the overall effects of economic contraction, both regionally and domestically, as its economic growth went down from 9.3%

in 1997 to 7.8% in 1998, and further to 7.6% in 1999. In other words, the immediate aftermath of the crisis for China saw the sudden plummeting of high growth in its dynamic decade of double-digit rates of growth of the 1990s that was sparked off by Deng Xiaoping's Nanxun. The immediate aftermath of the crisis was the period when the Chinese economy was under strong pressure to maintain its growth at 8%, which was what Zhu Rongji called the bao-ba target.

Against such short-term pain like a dip in its economic growth, China had reaped some long-term gains at the peak of the crisis as several currencies in the region had collapsed and China's Renminbi was also under strong pressure to devalue in order to maintain its export competitiveness. But Zhu Rongji stood fast and kept his words by refusing to go for a "competitive devaluation" that would have certainly destabilized the region's financial situation further and devastated the suffering economies in Southeast Asia. For keeping the exchange rate of the Renminbi unchanged, China had paid a price as its export growth for 1998 plunged to 0.5% from 21% of 1997, hence contributing to its slower growth in 1998.

Thus, China remained an important pole of economic stability in this turbulent region. Its responsible behaviour in not devaluing the Renminbi during this episode has since been widely recognized. Subsequently, many commentators and several leaders from Association of Southeast Asian Nations (ASEAN) had openly praised the Chinese government for such positive contribution. China had indeed reaped some long-term political goodwill from the region that had subsequently proved useful for China to build up its buttressing relations with ASEAN.

Viewed from the domestic angle, the crisis had brought home to Zhu Rongji China's fragile banking and financial sector, which was highly vulnerable to a similar financial crisis if China were as economically open as the other Southeast Asian countries. As the word "crisis" in Chinese (also in Japanese) means "danger and opportunity", the Asian financial crisis had indeed driven the Chinese leadership to the urgent need of deepening the financial sector reform.

Thus, a high-level national conference on financial work was convened on November 17, 1997 under the auspices of the Party's Central Committee and the State Council, whose major objectives include careful examination of the accumulated problems in the financial sector and new measures to deepen financial reforms so as to guard against future financial risks.

Zhu was the key figure at this conference. He started off by pointing out that had he not persisted in his efforts to implement his policy of macroeconomic controls by suitably tightening fiscal and monetary policies prior to 1997, China would have already fallen prey to the similar "problems now occurring in Thailand". Hence, he used this as a good excuse for him to push forward a more vigorous and comprehensive package of reforms. The reform measures were contained in his keynote speech, "Deepen Financial Reforms and Guard Against Financial Risks", that has been published in Zhu Rongji's collected works.[1] In this sense, the Asian financial crisis had spurred China's efforts to reform its financial sector.

Asia's Financial Turmoil

The Asian financial crisis had grown and spread. It started first in Thailand on July 2, 1997, ironically a day after the smooth handover of Hong Kong's sovereignty to China. Within weeks, the ripple effect of the Thai financial crisis reached its neighbouring economies of the Philippines, Malaysia and Indonesia, causing their currencies and stock markets to plunge in tandem. Since these Southeast Asian "Tiger Economies" had long experienced strong growth, their policy makers and commentators alike initially dismissed the financial turmoil as a temporary structural adjustment problem in response to the overheating of their economies or the misalignment of their currencies.

The second phase of the crisis was marked by its spread into the East Asian "Dragon Economies", first Taiwan and subsequently Hong Kong. As the HK dollar's fixed peg with the US dollar came under attack by currency speculators on October 22, 1997, the Hang Seng stock index nosedived 24% in four trading days. For the first time, the sharp fall of the Hong Kong stock market reverberated through major capital markets in the developed world, with Dow Jones suffering its single biggest point loss ever on October 27.

In November 1997, the crisis further demonstrated its powerful contagion effect by bringing South Korea, the world's 11th largest industrial

---

[1] Zhu Rongji, *Zhu Rongji on the Record: The Road to Reform 1991–1997* (with Forewords by Henry Kissinger and Helmut Schmidt), Brookings Institution Press, pp. 418–436.

power, to its knees,[2] and driving Japan's fourth largest broking house, Yamaichi Securities, to bankruptcy. What started off as a national financial crisis in Thailand on account of its serious external economic imbalance had, in the short span of six months, developed into a serious regional financial crisis. In the modern financial world of globalization and instantaneous communications, the financial problem of one economy was apt to be easily transmitted to another.

Yet, China was the one country in the region, which had remained relatively unaffected by the existing financial turmoil. Was China's financial sector the next domino to fall? This chapter will address this question by examining its pros and cons together with their relevant backgrounds.

China's Apparent Immunity

When the financial crisis was brewing in Southeast Asia during the summer of 1997, China's economy was heading for a successful "soft landing". Growth for the first half of 1997 was 9.5%, while consumer inflation fell further to 3.5%. Strong economic growth, together with the smooth return of Hong Kong to China's sovereignty, had further boosted Jiang Zemin's leadership and enabled him to successfully conclude the crucial post-Deng Fifteenth Party Congress in September.[3] At the 1997 Asia-Pacific Economic Cooperation (APEC) meeting in Vancouver, Jiang "confidently shrugged off the economic crises gripping its two Asian neighbours (of Japan and South Korea)" and declared that the "situation in China today is excellent".[4]

---

[2] On December 4, South Korea accepted the IMF bailout package of US$55 billion together with tough structural adjustment conditions.

[3] For further discussion on the politics and economics of China before and after the Fifteenth Party Congress, see "*China after the Fifteenth Party Congress: New Initiatives*", *EAI Occasional Paper No. 1*, World Scientific and Singapore University Press, 1997.

[4] "Confident China Shrugs off Asian Economic Crisis", *Reuters*, November 24, 1997. At the APEC Summit, China's Foreign Ministry Spokesman Shen Guofang said, "China would not be affected by the contagion effect in neighbouring countries because its fiscal policies had carefully sought to avoid similar instability". "Mainland Claims Turmoil Immunity", *South China Morning Post*, November 25, 1997. See also "Defying Asian Gloom, Jiang says China Will Maintain Growth", *Associated Press*, 25, November 1997.

Zhu Rongji had even later reaffirmed that China would not devalue its *Renminbi*.[5]

Was the Chinese leadership over-confident in its ability to ride out the financial storm? Subsequently, international media had turned its attention to China as the next possible victim.[6] According to some Western commentators, a number of pre-crisis signals had also surfaced in China. To begin with, the financial woes in Southeast Asia had been attributed to the weak financial structures of these economies and their lack of transparency. In this regard, China's financial and banking system in terms of both management quality and supervision standard had been ranked the worst, next to Vietnam, in the region.[7] China was also by far less transparent than the Southeast Asian economies.[8] Hence, China *should* have had a lot to worry about.

One could also find some *prima facie* evidence to show China's susceptibility to the financial crisis. China's ailing SOE sector was sufficiently familiar. China was also developing its own sort of "property bubble", with an over-built and under-sold real estate sector in its major cities, especially Guangzhou, Shanghai and Beijing (for example, the estimated vacancy rate of commercial office buildings in Shanghai's Lujiazui was 60–80%, and 40% in Beijing[9]). More seriously, China's fragile banking sector looked

---

[5] "Zhu Insists Devaluation is Not On", *South China Morning Post*, December 1, 1997.

[6] See, e.g., "China's Domino", Editorial, *Asian Wall Street Journal*, November 11, 1997; "China Is Moving to Avert Spillover from Asian Crisis", *op cit.*, November 13, 1997; and "In Wake of Asian Crisis, China's Red-Hot Economy Appears to Cool", *International Herald Tribune*, December 1, 1997.

[7] In February 1997, the Hong Kong-based Political & Economic Risk Consultancy (PERC) ranked China as the second worst of all the 13 economies, with 7.44 point on a 10-point scale, much worse than Thailand (5.27), Malaysia (5.28), Philippines (5.69) and even Indonesia (6.49). *Asian Intelligence* (No. 470, February 12, 1997).

[8] Similarly PERC ranked China as the third least transparent economy in the group of 14: China's was at the high 8.2 point in the scale compared to 6.5 for Thailand and 7.4 for Indonesia. Singapore, with 4.4, was ranked as the region's most transparent economy. *Asian Intelligence* (No. 498, November 19, 1997).

[9] For Shanghai, see *Business China* (Economist Intelligence Unit, January 20, 1997); for Beijing, "Builders Do Battle for Beijing's Heart", *Asian Wall Street Journal*, December 5, 1997. Conditions in some smaller coastal cities were more serious, e.g., Haikou in Hainan.

precarious, with as much as one-third of the outstanding loans being non-performing. As pointed out by China expert Nicholas Lardy, even if China's banks could immediately recover half of their existing bad loans, their total financial losses would amount to 15% of China's GDP, compared to the USA's 2% from its savings and loans debacle and Mexico's 7–10% from its bank failure.[10] Was China's leadership just too smug?

In reality, the Chinese leadership, particularly Zhu Rongji, had been watching closely and perhaps, anxiously, on how the Asian crisis was unfolding and spreading. When the financial turmoil first hit Thailand and its neighbouring countries, China's leadership typically thought that the problem was temporary and could be localized though it might offer China a useful lesson for planning its future financial liberalization.[11] It was not until the crisis reached Hong Kong in late October that China started to get alarmed.

Apart from having committed to defend the HK dollar, Beijing had built up a huge commercial stake in the Hong Kong economy. It suffices to say that international currency speculators actually chose the day to mount their ferocious attack on the HK dollar when Beijing's largest public offer, the "China Telecom", was floated on the Hong Kong stock exchange. It was difficult to estimate the size of losses suffered by China's "Red Chip" companies and its established PRC firms in Hong Kong in the subsequent financial mayhem following the collapse of Hong Kong's stock and property markets. In this sense, China had already been indirectly hit by the Asian financial turmoil.

The crisis had prompted China to hold a "Financial Summit" in Beijing on November 18, 1997, attended by Jiang Zemin, Li Peng, Zhu Rongji and many high ranking central and provincial leaders. The official assessment of China's vulnerability to the Asian financial crisis had not been disclosed to

---

[10]Nicholas R. Lardy's statement of testimony before the "Committee on Banking and Financial Services", US House of Representatives, The Brookings Institution, 1996.

The real extent of bad loans in China's state banks could be overstated by Lardy. Even if the estimate of bad loans was right, China's GDP was seriously underestimated, especially for the purpose of international comparison. Hence, China's high proportion of bad loans in terms of GDP could be exaggerated.

[11]On August 20, 1997, China's official organ "People's Daily" carried an article "Will the Thai Baht Crisis Affect China?" It argued that China should be cautious in opening up its financial sector.

the outside world, as it was a closed-door meeting.[12] The post-summit official statement emphasized the need for China to build up a sound financial structure as well as to strengthen supervision and regulation of the financial sector activities.[13] More importantly, after the summit, a high-level "Central Financial Work Leading Group" (i.e., a financial task force) under Zhu Rongji was set up to monitor China's financial development. Thus, China had taken the necessary precautions. But was China hit by the crisis?

China's Vulnerability

As uncertainty was the very hallmark of the financial crisis, it would be extremely difficult to say for sure if China was the next domino. Much also depended on whether the Asian crisis was on its way to fizzle out or was gathering more momentum to eventually engulf Japan and some Western economies. If the crisis were to develop into a global financial meltdown, the question of whether China would have been spared would have no meaning.

At the inception of the crisis, many Southeast Asian officials might have been misled by their apparently strong "economic fundamentals" to become too complacent, and hence failed to look into their underlying financial and monetary problems. As shown in Table 1, most Asia-Pacific economies had indeed displayed strong "economic fundamentals" in terms of high growth and low inflation, with their growth sustained by rapid export expansion, as well as high levels of savings and investment. China, noticeably, was at the top of the league insofar as economic performance indicators were concerned.

Yet, many of these economies had succumbed to the financial crisis one after another. Clearly, such "economic fundamentals" were only meant to explain the long-term growth potential of the "real economy", rather than to reflect the symptoms and malaise of the "financial economy". To predict the financial vulnerability, especially in the short run, it would be more

---

[12]The national financial conference was originally a scheduled annual event. But the Asian financial crisis had obviously upgraded it to a kind of financial summit, presided personally be Jiang Zemin.

[13]For Jiang Zemin's speech at the meeting, see *Renmin Ribao* (*People's Daily*, November 21, 1997), and also its "Editorial". See also, "Summit Set to Change Face of Banking Sector," *South China Morning Post*, November 18, 1997.

Table 1.   Economic fundamentals of China and other Asia-Pacific economies.

Selected Economies of Asia-Pacific Region	GNP per capita, 1995 /US$	Economic Growth (%)					Consumer Price Inflation (%)		Annual Export Growth (%)			Gross Domestic Savings (As % of GDP)		Gross Domestic Investment (As % of GDP)	
		1980–1990	1994	1995	1996	1/21997	1996	1/21997	1990–1995	1995	1996	1981–1990	1995	1981–1990	1995
China	620	10.2	11.8	10.2	9.7	9.5	8.3	3.5	14.3	23.0	11.0	30.8	42.2	30.5	39.5
Japan	39,640	4.0	0.7	0.8	3.0	0.3	2.6	1.0	0.4	11.6	–7.3	N.A.	31.0	31.7	28.5
NIEs															
South Korea	9700	9.4	8.3	8.2	6.7	5.5	5.0	4.6	7.4	32.4	14.3	32.4	37.0	30.6	36.6
Taiwan	12,400	7.1	6.5	6.4	5.5	6.1	3.1	2.0	N.A.	20.5	13.8	32.9	26.3	22.8	24.5
Hong Kong	22,990	6.9	5.5	5.0	5.1	5.4	6.2	6.5	15.3	16.7	15.6	33.5	34.5	27.2	33.1
Singapore	26,730	6.4	10.1	8.2	7.0	6.1	1.4	2.0	12.2	15.5	13.0	41.8	55.6	41.7	33.9
ASEAN															
Indonesia	980	6.1	7.4	7.5	7.5	5.6	7.9	6.7	21.3	11.1	14.5	30.9	36.0	29.3	38.3
Malaysia	3890	5.2	8.5	9.2	8.5	6.8	3.7	4.5	12.9	26.6	18.5	33.2	37.2	30.6	40.6
Philippines	1050	1.0	4.3	5.5	5.5	5.5	8.4	7.2	10.2	28.9	25.0	22.2	14.7	22.0	22.3
Thailand	2740	7.6	8.5	8.8	6.5	0.9	5.9	10.4	21.6	24.5	17.0	27.2	34.2	30.7	40.0
Vietnam	240	N.A.	N.A.	8.5	9.0	N.A.	13.5	(14.0)	N.A.	45.0	32.2	N.A.	19.1	N.A.	27.6

Note: N.A. denotes "Not Applicable".
Sources: World Development Report 1997 (World Bank), *International Financial Statistics Yearbook 1997* (International Monetary Fund).

Table 2.   External economic vulnerabilities: China and other Asia-Pacific economies.

Selected Economies of Asia-Pacific Region	Total Trade, 1996 As % of GDP	Stock of Inward FDI, 1995		Current A/C Balance (As % of GDP)		External Debt, 1996			Gross International Reserves, 1997	
		Value (US$bn)	As % of GDP	1995	1996	Total External Debt (US$bn)	As % of Export	As % of GDP	As of	US$bn
China	29.3	129.0#	18.6#	0.2	0.9	124.0	89.7	15.3	August	130.3
Japan	16.5	17.8*	0.4*	2.2	0.5	Neg.	Neg.	Neg.	September	225.6
NIEs										
South Korea	55.2	12.5*	3.3*	−2.0	−4.8	111.0	85.6	22.1	September	30.4
Taiwan	82.1	14.2*	6.6*	1.9	3.8	Neg.	Neg.	Neg.	September	85.7
Hong Kong	245.9	68.3	49.1	−3.4	−1.0	Neg.	Neg.	Neg.	October	91.8
Singapore	266.1	53.7*	72.8*	17.7	15.0	Neg.	Neg.	Neg.	August	76.8
ASEAN										
Indonesia	41.8	46.3*	26.5*	−3.4	−3.4	109.0	220.2	54.7	October	19.1
Malaysia	164.2	32.7*	46.2*	−8.5	−4.9	36.4	46.8	42.5	June	26.6
Philippines	63.2	5.3*	8.8*	−4.4	−5.5	39.5	192.2	64.8	August	10.3
Thailand	70.0	14.5*	10.1*	−8.1	−8.0	88.6	158.9	54.9	October	30.7
Vietnam	63.3	0.3*	1.9*	−8.9	−8.9	6.5	100.0	24.2	December**	1.8

Notes: "Neg." denotes negligible.

*Figures refer to year 1994; **Figures refer to as of December 1996.

#Figures from China's State Statistical Bureau showed that as of end 1996, total stock of inward FDI reached approximately US$172 billion.

Sources: World Investment Report 1996: Trade and International Policy Arrangements (United Nations), *World Development Report 1997* (World Bank), *International Financial Statistics Yearbook 1997* (International Monetary Fund), *Asian Development Outlook 1996* and 1997, Union Bank of Switzerland, Bank of America, Country Risk Reports, Various Issues (Political & Economic Risk Consultancy Ltd.).

useful to examine the "external balance" of an economy.[14] As shown in Table 2, all the Asia-Pacific economies were, in varying degrees, open and outward looking in terms of their heavy dependence on foreign trade and foreign capital (direct investment and loans) for their economic growth. But the three economies of Thailand, Indonesia and South Korea, which had suffered the humiliation of having gone to the IMF for rescue, did show up their serious external economic imbalances in terms of high current account deficit and high external debt.

In contrast, China's external economic balance looked sufficiently healthy and robust, next only to Singapore, Hong Kong and Japan in the region. On account of its strong export growth and rising trade surplus, China had registered a small current account surplus. China had also been conspicuously successful in attracting FDI so that its external debt (US$124 billion) was relatively small in terms of its total exports (US$150 billion) and its total international reserves (US$130 billion). Clearly, China had not over-borrowed as Thailand and others had. China's external debt profile was by far much better than that of South Korea, which had a lot of short-term commercial loans. In 1995, China's long-term debt was 88.8% of its total external debt. In the context of these key external economic indicators, China did appear highly *invulnerable* to external financial shocks.

Furthermore, the currency crisis in Southeast Asia was triggered off by a broadly similar mechanism, which were simply not operable in China. It was well known that the Chinese *Renminbi* was only partially convertible on the current account. It was therefore not possible for international currency speculators to "sell short" on the *Renminbi* outside China, and even more difficult for them to collect a large amount of *Renminbi* outside China for delivery. Also, as *Renminbi* transaction was highly regulated on the capital account, such currency instability could not spark off massive capital outflow. Though it was still possible for a small-scale capital flight to occur

---

[14] Economists had developed a warning system to forecast currency crises, based on such variables as declining international reserves, currency appreciation, rising domestic inflation, declining trade balances, fiscal deficit and so on. These indicators served a useful but not necessarily a reliable guide because the financial crisis of a country is a product of its own complicated and often specific, economic and political problems. *IMF Survey* (Vol. 26, No. 16, August 18, 1997); and Garciela Kaminsky, Saul Lizondo and Garmen Reinhart, *Leading Indicators of Currency Crises* (IMF Working Paper, 97/79).

through various loopholes, a large part of China's external liabilities were in FDI or long-term loans, which were tied down for the long haul for industrial and commercial development and could not be easily repatriated at short notice.[15]

The currency crisis in Southeast Asia typically interacted with the region's stock markets, which were heavily property based. The property sector itself was also heavily leveraged, thereby also badly exposing the banking sector. In the event, all these fed on each other to create a confidence crisis in a downward spiral. By comparison, China's nascent stock markets, as shown in Table 3, were small in terms of total capitalization, and they were only selectively open to foreign investors — i.e., the "B shares", "H share" (for Hong Kong) and "N shares" (for New York).[16] On December 1, 1996 China accepted IMF's Article VIII to allow free transfers for only current international transactions, but not capital flow into the stock markets. The Shanghai and Shenzhen stock markets, being so small, produced no significant effect on the domestic "real economy" even if they were likely to crash.

The Asian financial turmoil had been aggravated in some cases by inept political leadership or misguided domestic politics. For China, the stability of Jiang–Zhu leadership had left no doubt as to the resolve of Beijing to defend the *Renminbi* and to protect China from the regional financial storm. One could hardly imagine the tough-minded Zhu Rongji, armed with a large war chest of US$130 billion foreign reserves, would allow the *Renminbi* to go down in a free fall like the Thai baht or the Korean won. In short, there were no compelling reasons to believe that an externally generated financial crisis could occur in China.

What about domestic financial crisis? The Chinese economy had just emerged from Zhu Rongji's three-year macro-control to achieve a "soft landing". China's macro economy had so far sent out no significant distress signals. True, the property markets in many cities had come down. But China's real estate sector as a whole was still small, and most of China's

---

[15]China had by then recorded a total of US$320 billion foreign capital, roughly dividing into $200 billion of FDI and $120 billion of foreign loans. "Exchange Rate Stays Stable", *China Daily*, December 5, 1997.

[16]For a good discussion of China's stock market, see Xiao Minjie, "The Stable Development of China's Stock Market", *JETRO China Newsletter* (Vol. 4, No. 129, 1997).

Table 3. Currencies and stock market fluctuations: China and other Asia-Pacific economies.

Selected Economies of Asia Pacific Region	Stock Market Capitalization (As of June 1996)		Stock Market Fluctuation of Leading Indices[A] July 1–December 8, 1997 (%)	New Equity Issue, 1996		Currency Fluctuations against US$ June 27–December 8, 1997 (%)
	Value (US$bn)	As % of GDP		No.	Value (US$ million)	
China						
Shenzhen	47[B]	7.5	−17.2[C]	38	2,428	Negligible
Shanghai			−14.1[D]			
Japan	3,667	77.0	−21.7	20	4,869	−14.0
NIEs						
South Korea	161	43.9	−44.3	11	1,261	−24.9
Taiwan	248	102.1	−7.0	43	2,051	−15.4
Hong Kong	311	204.6	−22.0	97	8,312	N.A.
Singapore	143	198.6	−11.8	52	3,545	−13.2
ASEAN						
Indonesia	81	48.2	−41.5	69	6,159	−51.3
Malaysia	249	341.1	−37.2	136	4,039	−48.0
Philippines	76	120.6	−30.3	33	1,893	−30.6
Thailand	139	106.9	−23.8	41	1,050	−56.1

Notes: (A) Changes in leading stock indices of Shanghai and Shenzhen Stock Exchanges are for period between June 27, 1997 and December 8, 1997.
(B) As of end 1996, total combined stock market capitalization of stock exchanges in Shenzhen and Shanghai reached RMB 984.2 billion, or 14.5% of China' s GDP. Approximately 13% of the total number of listed companies were B-shares.
(C) Shenzhen Stock Exchange: A-share sub index (−16.3%); B-share sub index (−36.4%).
(D) Shanghai Stock Exchange: A-share index (−8.4%); B-share index (−26.6%).
Sources: Xinhua News Agency, Dow Jones International News, South China Morning Post, The Asian Wall Street Journal, Morgan Stanley Capital International.

construction activities had been directed to infrastructural and industrial development. For instance, in the first half of 1996, property development accounted for only 14% of China's total fixed investment.[17] In other Asian countries, the collapse of their property markets had simply dragged down

---

[17] *China Investment White Paper* (Annual Report) (Beijing, International Cultural Publishing Corporation, 1996).

many banks. In China, such a "property bubble" would not be serious enough to create a financial crisis, simply because the bulk of the bank loans in China were committed to SOEs, with only a small portion going to property development.[18]

China's banking sector might look shaky on account of its huge amount of non-performing loans incurred by SOEs. But this would only pose a serious challenge to Zhu Rongji for his future banking reform efforts (such as how to write off bad loans and how to recapitalize the banks), and could not by itself touch off a full banking crisis. With both lenders (banks) and borrowers (enterprises) all belonging to the state sector, how was it possible for a banking crisis to be ignited? According to a high ranking Chinese technocrat, China's total state assets stood at RMB 6500 billion, in addition to a huge stock of public dormitories and quarters in the state sector at a total worth of RMB 3000 billion. There was, therefore, no question of liabilities exceeding assets in China's state sector.[19] In other words, there was no reasonable ground to expect any home-grown financial crisis in China.

China an Unintended Casualty

Though China was well able to fend off the regional financial crisis, it still could not escape from its side effects. Economic growth target of 9% for 1997 were be on course, as manifested in the major performance indicators for the past 10 months.[20] But needless to say, the external operating

---

[18]In September 1995, China's State Statistical Bureau and other agencies conducted a national survey on property development. In 1994, the peak year for property boom in China, a total of RMB 1428 billion was committed to real estate development from all sources, but only RMB 345 billion or 24% was actually invested. Of this amount, only 23.4% were domestic bank loans — for the rest, 15.3% being foreign capital. *Ibid.* p. 272.

In 1994, China's total domestic bank loans stood at RMB 4310 billion. This means that the actual amount of loans for property development in 1994 works out to be only 3.2% of total bank loans — hence a really small direct bank exposure to property development.

[19]This argument was put forth by Guo Shuqing, then Secretary-General of the State Commission for the Reform of the Economic Systems, at a London conference, "China and Britain: Partners for the 21st Century" in November 1997. See *Xinbao* (*Hong Kong Economic Journal*, November 26, 1997), p. 10.

[20]Export growth for the first 10 months was still very strong. More surprisingly, China still recorded actual foreign investment of US$42 billion for the first 10 months, up by 29%, even though pledged investment had declined. "Foreign Investment to Increase", *China Daily: Business Weekly*, December 7–13, 1997.

environment for China's economy in 1998 was likely to be much more difficult. China would have to scale down its projected growth for next year, and this depended on how bad the after-effects of the crisis on the Asia-Pacific region were.

The crisis could potentially spell an end to China's long running FDI boom, as the inflow of foreign investment in the following year was expected to be smaller due to the general deflationary effect of the crisis and the drying up of regional liquidity. Roughly, more than 70% of China's foreign investment originated from the economies which had been hit, in varying degrees, by 1997 financial turmoil.[21] China's exports would also face tougher competition as the *Renminbi* had become "overvalued" relative to those of its competitors. Just imagine how much a challenge to Chinese exporters it could be as they now would have to compete not just against the Thais, but also the Korean producers, whose currencies had plunged in external value! China had ruled out an outright devaluation of the *Renminbi* for fear of damaging the HK–US dollar's peg. But it was still likely that China might eventually let the *Renminbi* float down gradually once the crisis had settled so as to regain export competitiveness.

What would be the longer-term effect of the Asian financial crisis on China? An important starting point was to examine how the crisis would affect China's ongoing economic reform plans. China had certainly learnt a valuable lesson from the crisis and was stepping up its efforts for banking reforms, particularly through tightening up supervision of the financial sector activities.[22] To become a more effective regulator, the People's Bank of China was restructured along the US Federal Reserve System, setting up 10 branches to replace the provincial and municipal branches.[23] At the same time, the government became more cautious in further opening up its financial sector to the outside world. China's original plan for the full convertibility of the *Renminbi* by 2000 was shelved.

---

[21] See "Chinese Cabinet to Meet over Foreign Investments", *Business Times* (Singapore, November 27, 1997); Also, "Shanghai Briefing", *South China Morning Post*, November 28, 1997.

[22] China had at that time announced that it would set up a board of supervisors as the watchdog body to oversee the management and operation of China's big four state commercial banks. "New Body to Check Bank Assets", *South China Morning Post*, November 13, 1997.

[23] "China's Central Bank Plans Restructuring", *Asian Wall Street Journal*, December 2, 1997.

If China's financial sector were the gainer from the crisis, the loser would clearly be the SOEs. Slower economic growth would render the reform of SOEs more difficult. China might slow down the restructuring of its large SOEs should its exports and foreign investment inflow plummet. Some privatization schemes might also be shelved. The collapse of the region's capital markets had obviously derailed China's plans of using them to draw in foreign capital for the privatization of SOEs. Zhu Rongji had promised to "fix" China's SOE problem in three years. Could he still deliver? In some sense, China was also on the casualty list of the Asian financial turmoil.

4

CHINA'S ECONOMY 1999: BOTTOMING OUT FROM ASIAN FINANCIAL CRISIS LOW

Introduction

China's economy ended 1999 with 7.6% growth (revised from its preliminary figure of 7.1%), which was the worst growth performance in that decade since Deng Xiaoping's Nanxun in 1992. In fact, 1999 marked the lowest point of growth for China for almost two and a half decades from 1991 to 2013. The year 1999 also carried great historical significance in the sense that the Chinese economy experienced the critical bottoming-out process, starting to recover from the low point of the 1997 Asian financial crisis.

Low growth in 1999 was not entirely unanticipated. Deng's Nanxun sparked off an instant foreign direct investment (FDI) boom in South China, giving rise to four heady years of double-digit rates of growth. This in turn gave rise to serious economic overheating of hyperinflation — with consumer price index (CPI) over 20% for three consecutive years. In the circumstances, Vice Premier Zhu Rongji, who was then in charge of managing the economy, had to introduce tough macroeconomic control measures to rein in excessive investment and bring down inflation. Zhu's macroeconomic management tools included some draconian administrative control measures along with a credit crunch.

By 1997, Zhu had broken the bone of China's hyper-inflation with the CPI dropping to 2.8%, but at the same time, he had also brought down the economic growth momentum from its double-digit rates of expansion to a deceleration in growth for four successive years. Viewed from a different angle, Zhu's vigorous retrenchment programme had no doubt strengthened the immunity of the Chinese economy against the contagion effect of the Asian financial crisis. But it can also be argued that without this crisis, China's economic deceleration would have probably come to an end and be bottomed out in 1997.

As it had happened, the Asian financial crisis struck the region in July 1997, which had initially spared China, particularly on the real economy side. After wreaking havoc on the financial sectors of many countries in the region, the crisis actually brought about serious economic recession to most countries in the region. As regional demand sharply plummeted in 1998, China's exports also suffered. The Chinese economy inevitably experienced the chilling effects of this regional crisis.

It may be noted that Hong Kong's return to China's sovereignty took place exactly on the same day (July 1, 1997) as this regional crisis first broke out. The Hong Kong economy soon fell victim to the full-blown crisis, especially after August 1997 when the HK dollar (that was directly pegged to the US dollar) and its stock market came under fierce speculative attacks by several hedge funds, including George Soros' Quantum Fund. Though the Hong Kong government with its huge foreign reserves had successfully managed to fend off the attacks on the HK dollar, the financial crisis nonetheless brought down the Hong Kong Stock Exchange and along with it Hong Kong's booming property markets, the most vital sector of the Hong Kong economy. In the event, the Hong Kong economy suffered from a lingering recession for a few years, and the depressed Hong Kong economy had immediately spilled over to China's Pearl River Delta, which was one of China's most important growth post. In this sense, the Asian financial crisis had brought additional woes to China via Hong Kong.

By 1999, there were many positive signs to indicate that China's economic decline was bottoming out. The government was looking forward to an early rebound to a higher growth of about 7.5% for 2000. At the same time, the economy seemed to be in a peculiar state of "growth with deflation", marked by falling prices and over-production and over-capacity. For the first time in China's long history, its domestic market was glutted with consumer goods and consumer durables, an unusual phenomenon for a "socialist market economy". Over-production can be traced to the structural problem of the state-owned enterprise (SOE) sector. But it was also the after-effect of the Zhu Rongji's many years of efforts in retrenching the economy.

In terms of the sources of growth, for 1999, China's exports grew at 6% to US$195 billion, compared to the 0.6% growth for 1998. The export rebound was in part the result of the region's economic recovery.

For a huge economy like China, domestic demand (i.e., domestic consumption and investment) is much more crucial for its economic growth. However, domestic demand growth in 1999 was still quite mixed. Retail sales for the whole year increased at the reasonable rate 6.8% while fixed assets investment (FAI) growth was low by historical standard at only 7.8%. FAI, used to be the main source of China's economic growth, plunged from 15% in May to below zero in September.

Consumer confidence had remained low, partly due to the deflationary process and partly as a result of the government's efforts to deepen the SOE reform, with many state enterprises laying off many millions of redundant workers in a phenomenon called Xiagang (off-post). To encourage people to spend more and save less, the government removed a tax on interests earned from saving deposits.

For higher growth in 2000, the government had indicated that it would pursue a pro-active fiscal policy along with a more aggressive monetary policy. It had planned to issue more new bonds. China's 1999 budget deficit, though at record high, was only about 2% of its GDP while its accumulated public debt was less than 10% of GDP, quite low by any international standard. Further deficit financing to stimulate growth was clearly sustainable. But the main problem was how to channel the right funds to the right industries. This would point to the need for further SOE reform.

Thanks to its strong export growth, China's external sectors in 1999 had been considerably strengthened, despite a smaller trade surplus (about 25% less) and lower FDI inflows (about 10% less). Total foreign reserves hit US$154 billion. There were no longer rumours of a possible Renminbi devaluation in 1999.

Overall, the survey of the structure of growth in 1999 and its prospects for 2000 had brought to the fore one stark reality. China's economy by the end of the 1990s decade had run out of the "Nanxun effect of growth", which had brought boom and prosperity to the coastal region because of the market reform amidst a lot of ups and downs. Looking back, as the tumultuous decade of the 1990s was drawing to an end, Zhu must have been quite pleased with himself for the fact that he had successfully managed the economic reform according to "Deng's Way" while steering the economy back to prosperity through the boom-bust cycles. In the process, he had gained considerable experience and confidence as a highly competent manager of Deng's "socialist market economy" in this period.

On the other hand, Zhu was facing many new challenges as he was leading China's economy into the new millennium. The growth prospects for 2000 and beyond were highly uncertain, much depending on how China would continue with its unfinished business of market reform on the one hand and how China would manage its closer economic integration with the regional and global economy after China's accession to the WTO.

Among his many new initiatives, Zhu placed lots of hope on his new grand development strategy of "Go West", i.e., pushing development into China's new frontiers in its Northwest. He was confident that this would open up new sources of economic growth for China in terms of new investment opportunities while also exploiting the potential "WTO effect".

In a way, China's economy in 1999 was at crossroads, much like what it is today (2015), when further growth would need to open up a new growth path along with a new round of economic reform. However, it has taken almost a decade and a half for the "Go West" campaign to take off! Only in recent years had China's Northwest started to see real new opportunities for fast growth associated with such new development projects as high-speed rail and the new "One Belt One Road" scheme.

The Paradox of "Growth with Deflation"

Thanks to the improvement in external and domestic demand in the second half of the year, China's economy ended 1999 with 7.1% real growth, down from the 7.8% of 1998, but slightly above the original official forecast of 7%.[1] Though 1999 growth performance still ranked China as the third best performer after South Korea and Malaysia in the post-crisis Asia-Pacific region, it was China's worst growth record since 1991. As can be seen from Figure 1, China's economic growth had been declining for seven years in a row ever since hitting a peak of 14.2% in 1992. However, there were some turn-around signs in the 1999 performance to indicate that China's economic decline was bottoming out.

Growth prospects for 2000 depended critically on whether the recovery phase would be long or short. A long and drawn-out recovery would mean

---

[1]"GDP Grows at 7.1% in 1999", *China Daily*, December 30, 1999. Also, "China Fulfils its Expected Economic Targets this Year", *Xinhua News Agency*, December 30, 1999.

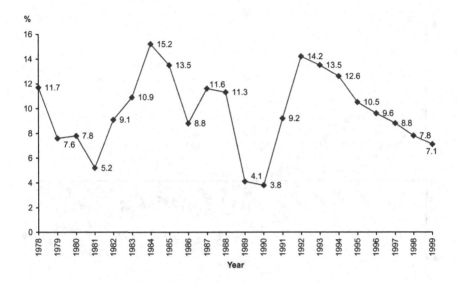

Figure 1.   China's economic growth 1978–1999.

Sources: State Statistical Bureau, *China Statistical Yearbook*, various editions, Beijing.

that the economy is mired in a structural deflation while an early rebound in 2000 would make it possible for the economy to recharge itself back to a higher growth momentum for the next three years.

Anyway, preventing the economy from its further slide was one thing, but recharging it back to higher growth was another. Exports were clearly emerging from the slump. However, domestic demand growth, which was more crucial for China's economic growth, remained mixed. On balance, there were positive signs in both external and domestic demands to warrant a more optimistic outlook, and China could look forward to a higher growth of about 7.5% for 2000.

Though China was not directly hit by the Asian financial turmoil, it did not escape from its indirect contagion effect. To ensure the fulfilment of its 8% growth target for 1998, the Chinese government had to undertake a kind of "New Deal" fiscal policy in the second half of 1998 for economic pump priming. However, such a Keynesian kind of spending spree based on deficit financing had apparently run out of steam by early 1999. Part of the reason was that the government found it difficult to implement its various fiscal stimulus packages effectively, i.e., by injecting the needed

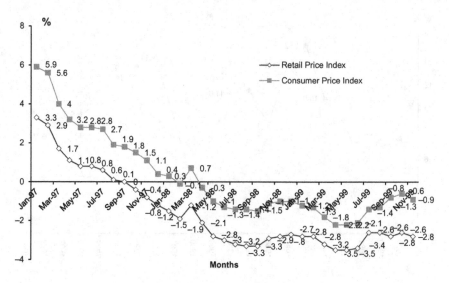

Figure 2.   Sliding into deflation.

Sources: The People's Bank of China, *Quarterly Statistical Bulletin*, various issues, Beijing.

funds into the needed industries because of serious over-capacity and over-production. Furthermore, the rise in FAI did not lead to a corresponding rise in effective demand, i.e., without the desired multiplier effect.

Following the 14.2% hyper-growth in 1992, China's economy started to overheat, and it took Premier Zhu Rongji (then only Vice Premier) several years of tough macroeconomic control measures to bring the economy to a "soft landing" in 1996. By the first half of 1997, as uncontrolled domestic demand had been effectively curbed while external demand slowed down due to the deterioration of the general international economic environment (which had also contributed to the Asian economic crisis), recessionary forces began to set in. As shown in Figure 2, the Chinese economy had since mid-1997 been quietly slipping into deflation, with the Retail Price Index (RPI) being in the negative for 27 months. In 1998, the government's expansionary fiscal policy, while artificially boosting growth, actually stoked deflation by aggravating over-investment and over-capacity. Consequently, China's economy in 1999 was plagued by over-production and under-consumption, amidst falling consumer confidence.

Scarcities of goods have long been a common hallmark of socialism, and the world has not forgotten the frequent sights of long consumer queues in the former Soviet Union. It is, therefore, a contradiction in terms to speak of China as a "socialist market economy" being plagued by a glut of consumer goods. Any Marxian economist would readily point out that over-production is only an endemic problem of the capitalist system of production. The fact nevertheless remains that the Chinese economy in 1999 had been historically the most productive.

For the first time in its long history, China's domestic market was flooded with an over-supply of consumer goods and consumer durables. Thanks to several years of bumper harvests, China had been enjoying a surplus in food production.[2] China in 1998 also topped the world in the production of coal (125 million tons), steel (116 million tons), colour TVs (35 million sets), and fridges (10.6 million).[3] The trouble is that all these industrial products were no longer the sinews of a modern economy.[4]

About 20 years ago, Deng Xiaoping was motivated to pursue economic reform in order to build up China's industrial capacity and to provide the Chinese people with a moderately adequate standard of living referred to as *Xiaokang*.[5] Does the state of "over-production" indicate the fulfilment of Deng's long-term goal? The answer is actually to the contrary. The Chinese economy then was in a peculiar state of "growth with deflation", which had its root cause in the country's unfinished economic reform.

First, the surplus production was the result of "an irrational supply structure", which had been created by excessive investment and overlapping production lines. Many products churned out by the SOEs were not of the

---

[2]China has all along been exporting rice and importing wheat. China annually exports about 4 to 5 million tons of corn and 2 million tons of rice. China used to import annually about 10 million tons of wheat; but the wheat import had been down to just over 1 million tons during that period because of good harvests at home. (US Department of Agriculture, *Grain: World Markets and Trade*, October 1999.)

[3]*A Statistical Survey of China 1999.*

[4]In fact, Beijing had called for the cutback of steel output by 12 million tons in 2000. *Renmin Ribao (People's Daily)*, December 23, 1999.

[5]See John Wong, "*Xiao-Kang*: Deng Xiaoping's Socio-Economic Development Target for China", *Journal of Contemporary China*, 7(17), 141–152, 1998.

required quality or the required diversity that were actually wanted by the increasingly demanding consumers.[6] Second, over-production existed alongside a situation of rising urban unemployment in the name of *Xiagang* (or disguised lay-offs). Both had contributed to the lack of effective demand.

To Premier Zhu Rongji, recharging China's economy back to higher growth this time around was more difficult than what he had done to slowing it down a few years ago. Zhu had precious few effective fiscal and monetary policy tools at his disposal. He could not simply reflate the economy with another stimulus package. He had to see to it that the economy would go through the much-needed structural adjustment first, which was closely linked to the progress of SOE reform. This explains why the issue of the SOE reform was back to the centre of the policy agenda at the Fourth Party Plenum in October 1999. The annual Economic Conference held in November 1999 had also harped on the same theme.

Growth Started to Pick Up

The Chinese economy, following its 7.8% growth in 1998, was widely expected to slow down in 1999, with the 1999 official growth target actually set at the moderate rate of 7%. But GDP growth in the first quarter of 1999 was 8.3%, then plummeted to 7.1% in the second quarter and further to 7% in the third, as the government's growth-inducing macroeconomic measures had worn out their effects. Apparently alarmed by the plunge, the government had introduced additional pro-active fiscal and monetary measures to boost both external and domestic demands. As a result, there were signs of picking up in the fourth quarter, which, however, ended with only 6.2% nominal growth. This was because growth in the last quarter of 1998 was at the exceptionally high 9.1% on account of the government's economic pump priming (Figure 3).

By most economic measures, China was then a full-fledged industrial economy, with the industrial sector (including building and construction) accounting for 49% of total GDP — compared to 18% for agriculture. Industrial growth therefore constituted the main engine of China's economic growth. In 1999, China's industrial value-added grew at 8.8% (Figure 4). This translated into 7.1% of GDP growth for the year.

---

[6]"Surplus an Inevitable Period of Economic Transition", *China Daily*, December 1, 1999.

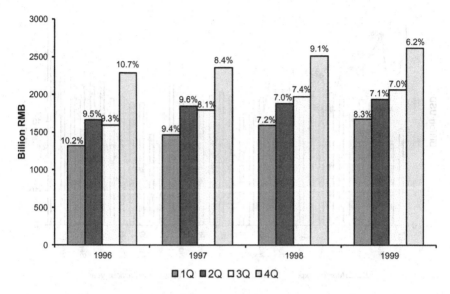

Figure 3. Quarterly GDP growth 1996–1999.

Sources: The People's Bank of China, *Quarterly Statistical Bulletin*, various editions, Beijing.

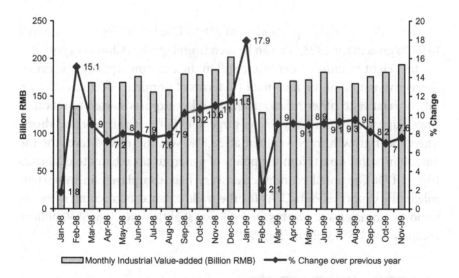

Figure 4. China's monthly industrial value-added 1998–1999.

Sources: State Statistical Bureau, *China Statistical Yearbook*, various editions, Beijing.

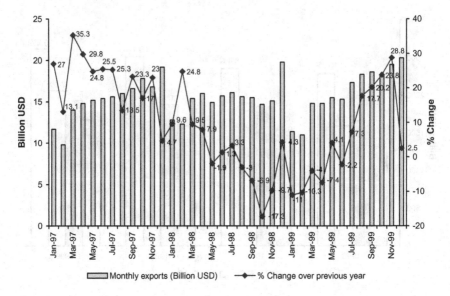

Figure 5.   China's monthly exports 1997–1999.

Sources: State Statistical Bureau, *China Statistical Yearbook,* various editions, Beijing.

For 1999, China's exports grew at 6% to US$195 billion, as compared to 0.6% growth for 1998.[7] As can be seen from Figure 5, China's exports for the first eight months of 1999 were still in the doldrums, partly because of the overvaluation of the *Renminbi* (in terms of nominal effective exchange rate or relative to other Asian currencies). But exports started to rebound since August, driven mainly by the surge of exports of garment and shoes. The export growth in November, at 28.8%, was the record level for the past 30 months. Apart from the policy of generous tax rebates to exporters (up to 17%), regional economic recovery had also played an important role in the export rebound.[8] As for the trade balance, on account of rising imports, China's trade surplus for 1999 was slightly down to US$30 billion, compared to US$43 billion for 1998.

---

[7] *Hong Kong Standard,* December 30, 1999. Also "Strong Growth of China's Foreign Trade in the First 11 months", *Xinhua News Agency,* December 15, 1999.

[8] "Beijing to Give Refunds on Tax", *South China Morning Post,* October 12, 1999.

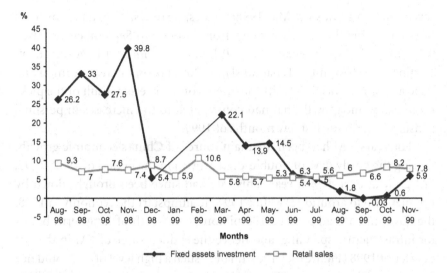

Figure 6. Slowdown in domestic investment and consumption.

Sources: State Statistical Bureau, *China Statistical Yearbook*, various editions, Beijing.

For a huge and still inward-looking economy like China, domestic demand roughly constituted about three quarters of its total GDP growth. This was the exact opposite of the Singapore and Hong Kong economies, where external demand accounted for about three-quarters of their GDP growth. Therefore, it was the rise of domestic consumption and domestic investment that was far more decisive for China's economic growth. For domestic consumption, retail sales for 1999 increased by 6.8%. This was a pretty good performance, given the state of continuing deflation.[9] FAI, however, grew at only 7.8%, compared to 14.1% in 1998.

As can be seen from Figure 6, retail sales after hitting the 10.6% peak in February (the Chinese New Year period) fell to 5–6% in the middle of the year. This was not surprising. With both the CPI and RPI (Figure 2) continuing to drift downward and stay in the negative territory throughout 1999, consumers did not rush to make purchases, especially since urban unemployment was also on the rise. To encourage people to spend more and save less, the People's Bank of China (the Central Bank) had cut interest rates

---

[9]"Mainland Retail Sales up 7.8pc", *South China Morning Post*, December 16, 1999.

seven times in a row since May 1996; but despite this, savings had continued to pile up. Total household savings from January to September increased 9.3% to 5,946 billion yuan (US$720 billion).[10] Finally, the government, starting from November 1, had to slam a 20% tax on interests from saving deposits. Still, it was the rise in consumer confidence as a result of the pick-up in economic growth that had contributed to the increases in personal consumption in the last few months of 1999.[11]

For years, FAI had been the main source of China's economic growth. During the heady days of double-digit growth in the period of 1992–1995, FAI grew at over 40% a year. This rate had since been brought down by Premier Zhu to around 15% after 1997. To jumpstart the economy in 1998, the government had to issue 100 billion yuan worth of long-term bonds for infrastructure spending, and hence the sudden surge of FAI in the last quarter of 1998 (Figure 6). Unfortunately, such a high level of FAI could not be sustained throughout 1999 even though the government issued 60 billion yuan worth of bonds in July and another 29 billion yuan in December.[12] In fact, the FAI growth rate plunged from 14.5% in May to below zero in September, indicating that China had stopped investing to create new industrial capacities.

The upshot clearly signified that the government's expansionary fiscal policy had not been very effective in bolstering growth. Actually, the basic constraint on the existing pro-active fiscal policy did not come from funding. Despite increased public spending, budget deficit for 1999 was expected to be only 2% of GDP.[13] This explains why the government was planning to issue more new bonds in 2000. According to Vice Finance Minister Lou Jiwei, further deficit financing would not pose a problem for China as its accumulated public debt amounts to only 800 billion yuan, or just about 10% of GDP, which was very low by international standards.[14] In short, there had been no lack of investible funds or new capital, but the problem came from the lack of investible opportunities or lack of absorptive

---

[10]The People's Bank of China, *Quarterly Statistical Bulletin* (No. 4, 1999).

[11]Household savings did start to decline from September. *Ibid.*

[12]"Additional Bond Issue of 100 billion yuan Next Year", *Singtao Daily*, December 9, 1999, and *Mingpao*, December 18, 1999.

[13]"China's Deficit a Top Concern for Minister", *Hong Kong Standard*, October 2, 1999.

[14]"The Government is Worried Over too Rapid Growth in Public Debt", *Mingpao*, December 9, 1999.

ability of the state sector, which was already saddled with over-capacity. For the expansionary fiscal policy to work effectively, the right funds must be channelled to the right industries. Hence, the root problem came from the ailing SOE sector.

As the pro-active fiscal policy did not produce its desired results, China's economists and planners looked to a more pro-active monetary policy as a supplement. In response to the criticism that the central bank was continuing with its over-cautious tight monetary policy of the mid-1990s, Governor Dai Xianglong promised a more aggressive monetary policy to boost growth.[15] But the fact remained that the growth of money supply as measured by the broad measure of M2 in November actually declined to its lowest level in 1999, at 14%.[16] The banks, overburdened with too many non-performing loans, were simply reluctant to lend out money. Hence the need to step up the financial sector reform.

Overall, China's external sector in 1999 had experienced a creditable performance, even though its total trade surplus had been reduced (by 25%) and its total FDI inflow lowered (by about 10%).[17] However, China's total foreign reserves at the end of November increased to US$154 billion (against its total external loans of about US$140 billion). This, along with the combined trends of a falling US dollar and a rising Japanese yen, should then ease the fears of a possible *Renminbi* devaluation in 2000. Based on China's economic fundamentals, there was no cogent economic logic to argue for the devaluation of the *Renminbi*, now or in the near future.[18] If anything, one might well see some pressures in 2000 for a slight upward revision of the *Renminbi* exchange rate.[19]

---

[15] See, e.g., "More Money for Reform", *Hong Kong Standard*, October 27, 1999; "Banks Urged to Better Utilize Deposit Surplus", *China Daily*, October 18, 1999; "Money Supply to be Increased", *South China Morning Post*, November 23, 1999.

[16] "Money Supply Growth Slows", *South China Morning Post*, December 11, 1999.

[17] Total FDI for the first 11 months of 1999 amounted to US$37 billion, down by 9.7% from the same period of 1998. "FDI in First 11 Months Down by 9.7%", *Mingpao*, December 22, 1999.

[18] Back in September 1999, IMF Regional Director Hubert Neiss stated: "The Chinese Government is in a Strong Enough Position to Keep the Yuan Stable" ("IMF: No Need to Devalue Yuan", *Hong Kong Standard*, September 2, 1999).

[19] "Experts' Views: Increasing Pressures for the *Renminbi* to Revalue", *Xinhua News Agency*, December 27, 1999.

New Growth Opportunities

As China's economy was bottoming out from lower growth in 1999, could it rebound quickly enough in 2000 so as to recharge itself to a higher growth momentum beyond 2000? This depended critically on whether it could capture the new opportunities for growth. Leaving aside the problem of reforming SOEs, a task which the government had repeatedly said it would tackle, two areas of new growth opportunities had cropped up for China to exploit in the years ahead: the potential WTO effect and the new frontiers in China's inland provinces.

China's much anticipated entry into the WTO in early 2000 was likely to re-ignite a new round of FDI boom, especially for FDI from North America and Europe related to telecommunications, banking and finance. Many multinational corporations (MNCs), which had hitherto been hesitant to invest in China, were now much more eager to come in so as to establish a foothold first. As for Asian sources, more Taiwanese FDI might return to China in force, especially for the electronics and the hi-tech sectors. China had passed a law to protect Taiwanese investments in China. Overall, FDI was not as important to China as a source of additional capital supply as much as a source of technology transfer and the export markets. For an economy hit by deflation, new FDI was particularly useful for providing the needed catalyst effect.

In 1999, Beijing was actively promoting the new concept of developing China's inland western regions as its new growth poles for the 21st century. Zhu was put in charge of mapping out a grand development plan for China's new frontiers. As discussed earlier, many industries in China's developed coastal region had become "over-invested". Accordingly, the marginal efficiency of investment in the new frontiers was much higher. Still lacking in infrastructure and human resources, China's inland western regions were not an immediate attraction to FDI. But they would certainly offer new opportunities for China's own domestic investment.

5

ANALYZING THE SOURCES OF CHINA'S HIGH ECONOMIC GROWTH

Introduction

The Chinese economy had, since the introduction of reform and the open-door policy by Deng Xiaoping in 1978, experienced phenomenal growth with an annual growth rate of 9.4%. High growth was basically unaffected by the 1997 Asian financial crisis and its aftermath. Indeed, despite the existing regional and global recession, China's economy ended 2002 with 9.1% growth, the highest since 1998. 2002 was the last year when the economy was under Zhu Rongji's watch, as he was due to hand over the Premiership to Wen Jiaobao in the spring of 2003.

At that point of time, it was also not known that China's economy had since registered double-digit rates of growth for the rest of the decade until the outbreak of the 2008 global financial crisis. Such sustained high growth has been attributed to the working of the "WTO effect", i.e., high growth due to greater economic efficiency arising from China's closer economic integration with the global economy through greater trade and foreign investment inflow after its accession to the World Trade Organization (WTO) in November 2001.

In 2002, many had attributed China's unexpected surge in growth to its rising exports. However, export growth had all along played only a marginal role in influencing China's overall growth performance. In fact, the 7.9% growth in the first three quarters of 2002 was mainly fuelled by a 21.8% increase in fixed investment in the same period.

This chapter is aimed at explaining the sources of China's economic growth. In running a systematic analysis of China's growth pattern up to 2002, it actually represents a pioneering effort of its kind well before the Chinese government started doing so. The National Bureau of Statistics (NBS) followed this approach only after 2007, probably for two reasons. First, China's economy in the first decade of reform of the 1980s was basically a half-reformed economy, not extensively market driven. Second, China's GDP (Y) accounting was not compiled strictly in accordance with the UN's System of National Accounts (SNA) until the early 2000s.

To begin with, economic growth for China, as for all other economies, essentially stems from two sources. The supply-side source of growth is mainly focussed on productivity growth. In simple terms, the growth of an economy on the supply side is just the sum total of its labour force increases plus labour productivity growth. As labour supply is not a problem for China and other developing economies, the key determinant here has been productivity growth. As a developing economy, China's major source of overall productivity growth is associated with the transfer of surplus labour from low-productivity agriculture to high-productivity manufacturing, much in line with the economic growth theory of the Nobel economist Arthur Lewis. This also explains why all developing countries have chalked up higher GDP growth once they started to industrialize. For China, industrialization-cum-urbanization has been a major source of growth.

Of course, China's productivity growth had also owed a lot to greater efficiency arising from implementing economic reform (e.g., greater marketization) and related institutional changes. This, in turn, yields the bigger concept called Total Factor Productivity (TFP), which simply registers the extra gains in output beyond the growth of the conventional inputs like capital and labour, i.e., the residual part of the production function, which has shifted as productivity has grown.

It suffices to say that TFP is conceptually and empirically difficult for economists to come up with accurate numbers. Nonetheless, the World Bank and many scholars from China have made many rough estimates of China's TFP growth in various post-reform periods, all of which show remarkable TFP increases since the start of economic reform. So much for the supply side analysis of economic growth.

For most market economies, the conventional analysis of growth is based on the demand-side approach. Thus, economic growth as increases in GDP (or Y) is the result of the rise in both domestic demand (domestic consumption or C plus investment or I) and external demand: i.e., exports minus imports or $X - M$. For most economies with few exceptions like Singapore and Hong Kong, domestic demand constitutes their major source of GDP growth. Within domestic demand, domestic consumption is usually much more important than domestic investment. Hence most economic growth, particularly in the USA, is basically consumption driven, as their final consumption (from household and government) usually makes up around 60–70% of their GDP.

Overall, this chapter, in examining the major drivers of China's growth, provides analytically the best systemic explanation of China's growth process and its pattern before 2002. In fact, the main features of this growth pattern have lasted to these days. First, China's economic growth has remained basically domestic-demand driven, almost the exact opposite of the highly open economies of Hong Kong and Singapore. In the 1980s, domestic demand accounted for over 90% of China's aggregate demand. Subsequently, this proportion still stood at about 80%, despite the surge in exports.

Second, in relation to domestic demand, for most years during 1980–2002, domestic consumption (household and government) had been the major source of growth, except for 1985 and 1993 when domestic investment took over as the main growth-driving force.

The regression analysis for 1980–2001 therefore yields a growth elasticity of 0.66 for consumption, 0.33 for investment, and only 0.02 for exports. This means that on average, every 1% increase in domestic consumption generates 0.66% more GDP; every 1% increase in domestic investment generates 0.33% more; but every 1% increase in net exports generates only 0.02% more.

Third, the contribution of external demand to growth appeared to be quite marginal. This was the case in 2002 as it is today. Not surprisingly, the Chinese economy in 2002 continued to experience high growth even though much of the global economy remained sluggish. This is because China's economy was (and still is today) domestic-demand driven.

This follows that the actual degree of the openness of China's economy is much smaller than what its gross export-GDP ratios would suggest. This marginal contribution by exports to growth can be explained by the fact that almost half of Chinese exports were actually "processing trade" associated with foreign-invested enterprises, whose output was also highly import-intensive; and as such, the domestic content or domestic value-added of exports remained necessarily low.

However, a caveat should be made here. China's export sector, usually regarded as a highly vibrant segment of the economy, is actually not as unimportant as this analysis has implied. In reality, the importance of exports to China's economy has all along been grossly underestimated in this kind of simple statistical analysis, which has clearly missed out the "spread effects" of the export growth. The export sector has actually created much greater total linkage effects than what has been captured in this "first-order" analysis. In other words, a lot of local service support and a lot of new investment linking to the export industries as well as the multiplier effect on the economy arising from the spending by the employees of the export sector have not been duly taken into account.

To sum up, China as a large continental-sized economy will continue to depend primarily on its internal dynamics for long-term growth. Up to 2002, domestic consumption had remained the major driving force of China's economic growth, with domestic investment providing a kind of "extra push" for additional growth.

Given that China cannot continue to rely indefinitely on increasing fixed investment to generate the major part of its growth, domestic consumption and external demand will have to take up the slack. Specifically for external demand, its contribution to growth will continue to be nominally small; and its future role will also remain quite uncertain. On the one hand, China's exports, hitherto mainly composed of many labour-intensive manufactured products, would eventually be losing their comparative advantage due to higher wages and rising costs. On the other hand, as China's economy is being upgraded and restructured towards more capital-intensive and technology-intensive activities, China's future exports would be made up of even higher domestic value-added products, and hence greater contribution to growth.

How do we look at the above analysis and its main conclusions from today's (2015) perspective, more than a decade later? To begin with, the analytical framework that was used in 2002 has remained very much valid today. In fact, China's NBS has since published yearly detailed analysis of how much the three major growth drivers of consumption, investment and exports has contributed to final GDP growth for a particular year.

Secondly, as can be seen from the following updated Table on China's changing sources of growth, whereas China's growth before 2002 had been mainly consumption driven, its double-digit rates of growth since 2002 have been strongly export-led and highly investment driven. As China's economic growth started to slow down in growth after 2012, from its previously double-digit rates of hyper growth to the more moderate medium rates of 7–8%, the government has also come to realize that such a pattern of growth is unsustainable.

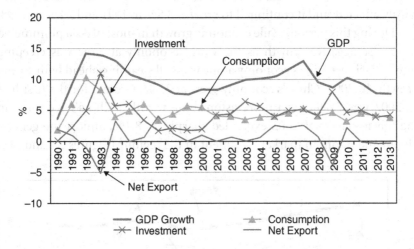

Figure 1.   Sources of China's economic growth 1990–2013.

Source: National Bureau of Statistics.

Accordingly, China's current leadership under Xi Jinping, at the Third Party Plenum in November 2013, called for a comprehensive reform, which, in the context of economic growth, included embracing the shift of development focus from maximizing growth in quantity terms to the more sustainable lower rates of growth geared to better quality. In terms of strategy, the new growth paradigm required a fundamental restructuring of GDP growth towards higher value-added activities as well as rebalancing the different sources of growth towards more domestic demand, particularly more domestic consumption driven.

In short, the economic growth analysis of this chapter and its main conclusion have turned out to be still relevant to today's new growth pattern that Xi Jinping has recently referred to as the "New Normal".

2002s Spurt of High Growth a Surprise*

China's economy had experienced spectacular growth for over two decades since the start of its economic reform in 1978. Real growth during 1978–2001 was at an annual rate of 9.4%.[1] The 1997 Asian financial crisis brought down many Asian economies. China's economy, however, was hardly affected, and it continued to grow at 8.8% in 1997 and 7.8% in 1998.

During this period, while economic growth in most of Asia plummeted to low or negative growth as the world economy at large was creeping into recession, China's economy alone was still steaming ahead with strong growth. In 2001, China's economy grew at 7.3%. Growth for the first half of 2002 was 7.8%. Even more astonishing was that China's economy in the third quarter of 2002 expanded sharply by 8.1%, amidst the general gloom and doom in market sentiment in the region[2] (Figures 2A and 2B).

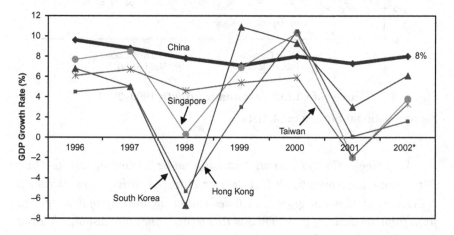

Figure 2A.   Economic performance of China *vis-à-vis* four Asian NIEs, 1996–2002.*

Note: *2002 growth forecast estimated by World Bank in its half-yearly report on East Asia. China's official growth rate for 2002 was estimated to be 8%. Singapore's preliminary official growth forecast for 2002 was 3% to 4%.

Sources: World Bank, *East Asia Regional Update: Making Progress in Uncertain Times*, November 6, 2002; *Asian Development Outlook 2002*.

---

*The original version of this chapter was jointly written with Miss Sarah Chan.
[1]"China Sees Extraordinary Economic Progress", *China Daily*, October 8, 2002.
[2] *China's Xinhua News Agency*, October 17, 2002.

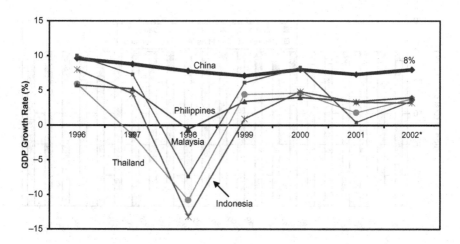

Figure 2B. Economic performance of China and the ASEAN-4, 1996–2002.*

Note: *2002 growth forecast estimated by World Bank in its half-yearly report on East Asia.

Sources: World Bank, *East Asia Regional Update: Making Progress in Uncertain Times*, November 6, 2002; *Asian Development Outlook 2002*.

For the whole of 2002, China's economic growth was expected to reach a robust 8%.[3]

Many foreign commentators had attributed China's unexpectedly high GDP growth of 7.9% in the first three quarters of 2002 to its high export performance, as indeed exports rose by 19.4% in this period.[4] This, however, should not be construed as saying that the Chinese economy had become so export-oriented that its growth was mainly fuelled by export expansion.

---

[3] According to the State Development Planning Commission, China's GDP was expected to exceed US$1,200 billion in 2002, up about 8% from 2001. "GDP to Grow 8% in 2002", *China Daily*, November 11, 2002.

[4] "China's Economy Expands Sharply as Exports Surge", *Asian Wall Street Journal*, October 17, 2002; and "Exports Help Power GDP Growth to 8.1pc", *South China Morning Post*, October 17, 2002. Why were Chinese exports immune to global recession? China's primary products accounted for only a modest share of total exports, which explains why China had not experienced the vagaries of volatile commodity prices. A wide variety of labour-intensive commodities produced by China were also globally cost competitive, with some necessity-type products like clothes or footwear which were income inelastic. As such, China was not so adversely affected by changes in the global economy.

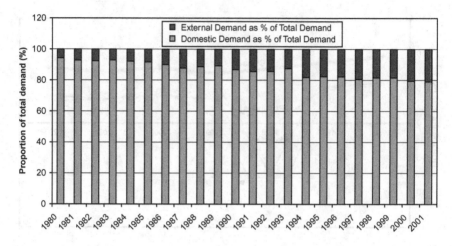

Figure 3.   China's source of economic growth, 1980–2001.

Note: Total or aggregate demand comprises domestic demand (i.e., consumption and investment of both private and public sectors, plus changes in inventories) and external demand (i.e., exports). Domestic demand accounted for 79% of total demand, while external demand accounted for 21% of total demand.

Source: Computed from data in *China Statistical Yearbook* (relevant years); *EIU*.

In fact, the opposite is true. China's economic growth remained highly domestic-demand driven, despite its rapidly rising exports over the years.

As shown in Figure 3 and Table 1, domestic demand was responsible for over 90% of China's total demand in the early and mid-1980s. In this period, exports continued to surge, domestic demand still stood at about 80%. This proportion was about the exact opposite of that of the highly open Singapore and Hong Kong economies, with their growth depending predominantly on external demand. In fact, China's 7.9% growth in the first three quarters of 2002 was basically fuelled by domestic investment, which actually increased 21.8% over the same period. This explains why China's economy continued to grow at high rates quite independent of the ebbs and flows of the international economy.

This chapter analyses the sources of China's economic growth over the past two decades, basically by examining the relative importance of domestic demand (i.e., domestic consumption and investment) and external demand (i.e., exports) in their contribution to GDP growth. In any economy, changes in these key macroeconomic variables, sometimes as

Table 1.   China's GDP by expenditure (various income components as a proportion of GDP, %).

Year	1980	1981	1982	1983	1984	1985	1986	1987	1988	1989	1990	1991	1992	1993	1994	1995	1996	1997	1998	1999	2000	2001
Private Consumption	51	53.1	52.4	52.3	51.1	52.2	51.2	50.5	51.9	51.7	49.9	48.5	48.2	45.4	44.5	46	46.9	46.6	46.4	47.4	46.9	47
Govt. Consumption	14.5	14.2	14.1	13.6	14.2	13.3	13.7	12.6	11.6	12.4	12.3	13.3	13.4	13.0	12.7	11.4	11.4	11.5	12.0	12.7	12.8	12.6
Gross Domestic Fixed Investment	28.9	25.7	27.2	28.2	29.8	30.1	30.7	31.9	31.4	26.3	25.8	28	32.1	37.6	36.1	34.7	34.1	33.6	35.4	35.6	36.5	37.4
Stock-Building	5.9	6.6	4.8	4.9	4.9	8.4	7.5	5.0	5.8	10.8	9.4	7.5	5.8	5.8	5.2	6.1	5.6	4.2	2.4	1.3	1.0	0.9
Domestic Demand	100.3	99.8	98.3	99.2	100	104.2	102.5	99.9	101	101.1	97.2	99.6	102	98.6	98.3	97.9	96.2	96.2	97.1	97.2	97.9	98
Exports of G&S	5.9	7.6	7.9	7.5	8.4	9.4	11.3	13.9	12.9	12.4	14.9	16.5	16.8	14.5	22	21	20.8	22.7	21.8	22.0	25.3	25.5
Domestic Demand as % of AD	94.4	92.9	92.5	93.0	92.2	91.8	90.1	87.9	88.8	89.4	86.9	85.7	85.8	87.6	81.8	82.4	82.3	80.6	81.7	81.7	79.4	79.1
External Demand as % of AD	5.6	7.1	7.5	7.0	7.8	8.2	9.9	12.1	11.2	10.6	13.1	14.3	14.2	12.4	18.2	17.6	17.7	19.4	18.3	18.3	20.6	20.9

Note: AD stands for aggregate or total demand.
Sources: Percentages calculated from data in *China Statistical Abstract 2002*; EIU.

a result of government's policy manipulation, will ultimately affect the final GDP growth. An analysis of the behaviour of these big macroeconomic components can thus help us understand better the pattern of China's future economic growth.

Domestic Demand as Major Driving Force

China's dynamic economic growth over the two decades of the 1980s and 1990s can be easily explained by simple economic theory. On the demand side, China's high growth stems from its high levels of domestic investment, being matched by equally high levels of domestic savings. In the 1980s, China's average gross domestic savings were consistently over 30% of its GDP. In the 1990s, domestic savings were above 40%. As in the East Asian newly industrialized economies (NIEs) of South Korea, Taiwan, Hong Kong and Singapore, the Chinese government was able to mobilize such huge pool of savings for infrastructural investment. And this easily translated into high GDP growth.

Such simple analysis, however, cannot explain China's growth fluctuations: Why is it that in some years growth could reach double-digit whereas in others, it dived? Upon departing from central planning after 1978, the growth of the Chinese economy was interspersed with ups and downs, as indeed there were several cycles in China's past economic growth (Figure 4). Chinese policy makers, from time to time, did intervene in the growth process by bringing it down when the economy overheated, and boosted it when it got depressed.

To better understand the pattern of growth and fluctuation, one needs to look closely into the sources of growth, i.e., to analyse the two key macroeconomic components of "domestic demand" (DD) and "external demand" (ED) that together constitute the "aggregate demand" (AD), as manifested in the simple macroeconomic identity: $Y = C+I+G+(X-M)$ (see Box 1).

Thus, China's economic growth (increases of Y or GDP by the expenditure approach) occurs when its AD goes up. AD goes up because its domestic demand (comprising personal and household consumption C, domestic investment I, and government spending G) and external demand (exports net of imports) goes up. Figure 5 shows how domestic demand and external demand interact with AD to generate the process of growth and

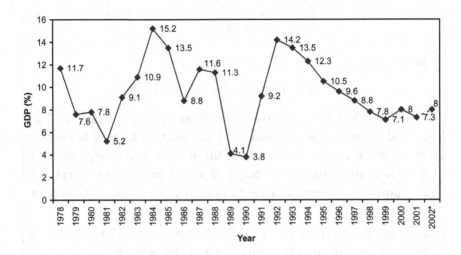

Figure 4. Fluctuation in China's economic growth, 1978–2002.

Sources: China Statistical Yearbook, relevant years. For 2002 GDP growth forecast, *China Daily,* November 11, 2002.

fluctuations. In other words, changes in the magnitude of domestic demand and external demand not only affects growth but also causes fluctuation.

For a large economy like China, domestic demand naturally constitutes the mainstay of its economic growth. Not just for growth, variation of the individual components of domestic demand (i.e., C, I, G), particularly for fixed investment I, has actually been the major source of China's growth fluctuations over the past two decades. Figure 6 shows how China's past economic growth process tended to "swing" with the ups and downs of consumption and investment, giving rise to a number of "reform cycles".[5]

The last upswing occurred in 1992 when Deng Xiaoping's *Nanxun* (tour of South China) touched off an explosion of domestic investment (over 50% increases) and subsequently, serious economic overheating. It took Premier Zhu Rongji strenuous efforts to cool down the economy by squeezing hard on fixed investment, and so eventually achieving a soft

---

[5]This happened in the half-reformed Chinese economy of the 1980s and early 1990s, which lacked a built-in self-adjusting macroeconomic mechanism. Thus, when too much investment ran into bottleneck of energy, transport and industrial raw materials, the government was forced to apply a severe credit crunch by bringing expansion into an abrupt halt.

BOX 1

The national income accounting identity is as follows:

$$Y = C + I + G + (X - M). \tag{1}$$

Y is GDP calculated using the expenditure approach, whereby $Y =$ *national income*, $C =$ *consumption*, $I =$ *investment*, $(X - M) =$ *net exports or NX*. It refers to total expenditure on final consumption, total capital formation (fixed assets acquired plus changes in inventory) and net export of goods and services by residents of a country in a certain period of time.

Economic growth increases in GDP or Y over time, i.e., dY/dt. Hence, differentiating Equation (1) with respect to time will give

$$\dot{Y} = \dot{C} + \dot{I} + \dot{G} + (\dot{X} - \dot{M}), \tag{2}$$

where $\dot{Y} = dY/dt$

$\dot{C} = dC/dt$ (change in C over time)

$\dot{I} = dI/dt$ (change in I over time)

$\dot{G} = dG/dt$ (change in G over time)

$N\dot{X} = d(X - M)/dt$ (change in NX over time)

From Equation (2), we can derive

$$\frac{\dot{Y}}{Y} = \frac{\dot{C}}{Y} + \frac{\dot{I}}{Y} + \frac{\dot{G}}{Y} + \frac{N\dot{X}}{Y}, \tag{3}$$

where economic growth rate is $\frac{\dot{Y}}{Y}$ while $\frac{\dot{C}}{Y}, \frac{\dot{I}}{Y}, \frac{\dot{G}}{Y}, \frac{N\dot{X}}{Y}$ are the respective contribution rates of C, I, G, NX to $\frac{\dot{Y}}{Y}$ (i.e., rate of growth of Y). Technically, $\frac{\dot{C}}{Y}, \frac{\dot{I}}{Y}, \frac{\dot{G}}{Y}, \frac{N\dot{X}}{Y}$ are also the respective weighted growth rates of C, I, G, NX as seen from the following equation:

$$\frac{\dot{Y}}{Y} = \frac{\dot{C}}{C}\frac{C}{Y} + \frac{\dot{I}}{I}\frac{I}{Y} + \frac{\dot{G}}{G}\frac{G}{Y} + \frac{N\dot{X}}{NX}\frac{NX}{Y}, \tag{4}$$

where $\frac{C}{Y}, \frac{I}{Y}, \frac{G}{Y}, \frac{NX}{Y}$ are the respective shares of C, I, G, NX in Y while $\frac{\dot{C}}{C}, \frac{\dot{I}}{I}, \frac{\dot{G}}{G}, \frac{N\dot{X}}{NX}$ are the respective growth rates of C, I, G and NX.

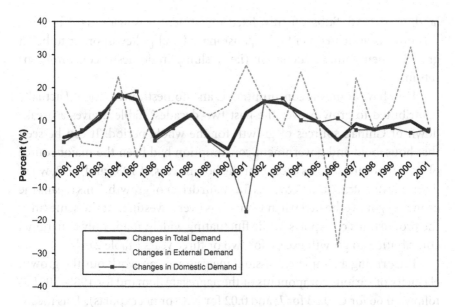

Figure 5. Changes in total (aggregate) demand at 1990 market prices, 1981–2001.

Sources: Computed from data in *China Statistical Abstract 2002* and *EIU*.

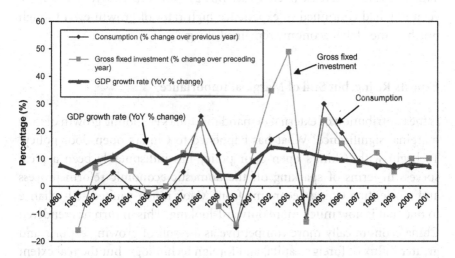

Figure 6. China's domestic demand and economic growth performance, 1980–2001.

Sources: Computed from data in *China Statistical Abstract 2002* and *EIU*.

landing in 1996. Subsequently, fixed investment was again used by Zhu, this time as an instrument of expansionary fiscal policy in order to boost growth when domestic deflation (i.e., a slump in domestic consumption) sets in.

How have domestic consumption C and domestic investment I actually contributed to growth over the past two decades? Table 2 gives a break-down of China's sources of growth for the whole period. It can be seen that household and government consumption had been the major source of growth for most years except for the boom years of 1985 and 1993, when domestic investment took over as the main driver of growth. This means the economy got overheated when China was over-investing. At the same time, the proportions of exports, while fluctuating widely, made only a marginal contribution to growth except for two or three years (Table 2).

Performing a simple regression analysis, we can work out the growth elasticity of various components of the aggregate demand for 1980–2001 as follows: 0.66 for C; 0.33 for I; and 0.02 for NX (or net exports). This means that on average, every 1% increase in domestic consumption brought about 0.66% increase in GDP; every 1% increase in investment brought about 0.33% increase in GDP; but every 1% increase in net exports brought about a meagre 0.02% increase in GDP (see Box 2). Not surprisingly, the Chinese economy had continued to experience high rates of growth even though much of the global economy remained sluggish.

Exports Rising, but Still of Marginal Importance

Is the contribution of external demand to China's economic growth of only marginal significance? What has happened to China's open-door policy? To begin with, China's open-door policy has indisputably been a great success in terms of sparking off the domestic economic reform process and reorienting China's economy from Mao's much-vaulted self-reliance to one that is now much more outward-looking. This in turn has rendered China economically more competitive as a result of growing exports and greater influx of foreign capital and foreign technology. But the real extent of China's economic openness has remained much misunderstood.

By conventional measure, as shown in Table 3, the Chinese economy was certainly quite "open", as its trade-GDP ratio rose from 15% in 1982 to

Table 2. Sources of aggregate demand in China, 1981–2000.

		Percentage Point Contribution to GDP Growth by Each Expenditure Category		
Year	GDP Growth Rate (%)	Consumption (%)	Gross Fixed Investment (%)	Net Exports (%)
1981	5.3	5.7	−1.0	0.6
1982	12.1	6.8	3.7	1.6
1983	9.6	6.2	4.1	−0.7
1984	12.4	7.5	5.7	−0.8
1985	11.3	7.6	8.4	−4.7
1986	10.2	5.5	3.3	1.4
1987	10.6	5.4	2.6	2.6
1988	11.3	7.6	4.9	−1.2
1989	2.9	2.3	0.7	−0.1
1990	5.2	1.2	0.03	4.0
1991	8.9	5.2	3.3	0.4
1992	12.7	7.7	6.7	−1.7
1993	16.5	6.4	13.4	−3.3
1994	13.9	7.3	3.1	3.5
1995	9.7	5.3	3.9	0.5
1996	10.2	7.1	2.5	0.6
1997	8.7	4.7	2.0	2
1998	8.0	5.3	2.4	0.3
1999	6.7	5.6	2.1	−1.0
2000	8.6	5.7	3.1	−0.2

Notes: (1) Consumption refers to personal or household consumption plus government consumption. Investment refers to investment by both the private and public sectors.

(2) Computed from data in *China Statistical Yearbook*, using 1978 as the base year (1978 = 100). GDP growth rates (listed in the table) differ from the official figures due to statistical discrepancies using the GDP by expenditure approach.

Source: Lin Yifu, "Export and Economic Growth in China: A Demand-Oriented Analysis", China Center for Economic Research, Peking University, Paper No. C2002002, May 23, 2002.

48% in 2000. Also, through the 1990s, China's foreign direct investment (FDI) had come to account for quite a substantial proportion of its overall domestic capital formation. In fact, on the basis of export–GDP ratio, China can be ranked economically more open than USA and Japan!

BOX 2

Based on the dataset which contains annual figures over the period 1980–2001, a multiple regression analysis is run to find out how much China's GDP or income will change given a unit change in the GDP components, namely consumption, investment and net exports.

Year	GDP (USD Billion)	Consumption* (USD Billion)	Gross Fixed Capital Investment Investment (USD Billion)	Net Exports (USD Billion)
1980	304	199	106	−1
1981	288	194	93	0
1982	290	193	93	4
1983	308	203	102	2
1984	309	202	107	−1
1985	299	196	115	−14
1986	293	190	112	−11
1987	317	200	117	1
1988	395	251	147	−4
1989	437	280	162	−4
1990	383	238	135	10
1991	400	247	142	12
1992	469	289	178	5
1993	599	350	260	−11
1994	542	310	224	7
1995	701	403	286	12
1996	825	481	327	18
1997	902	525	341	34
1998	961	561	363	36
1999	1005	604	371	30
2000	1080	645	405	30
2001	1159	691	444	25

Notes: (1) Consumption refers to both private and government consumption.
　　　(2) GFCI includes stock-building.
　　　(3) Net Exports = Total Exports minus imports.
Source: EIU.

(*Continued*)

BOX 2 *Continued*

Based on the above-mentioned data, the log-linear regression model is generated as follows. Assuming Y = GDP, C = consumption, GFCI = Gross Fixed Investment, NX = Net Exports,

$$\ln Y_t = 0.650041 + 0.663873 \ln C_t + 0.332125 \ln GFCI_t$$
$$+0.015076 \ln NX_t,$$
$$t = (9.284)^*(19.534)^*(12.701)^*(5.0695)^*, \quad (R^2 = 0.99961).$$

The significance of each variable in determining the GDP growth is shown in parenthesis. The t-statistics show that all variables are statistically significant at $\alpha = 0.05$ (5% significance), which indicates that the model is stable over the dataset period.

In the log-linear model, both the slope and the elasticity coefficients are the same. The elasticity values as found from the regression results are as follows:

Income elasticity of Y in relation to variables		
C	GFCI	NX
0.66	0.33	0.02

The results indicate that net exports over the past two decades played a very meagre role in increasing China's GDP. For every 1% increase in net exports, GDP on average was estimated to rise by 0.02%. For every 1% increase in consumption, holding other variables constant, China's GDP was estimated to rise by approximately 0.7%. Likewise for investment, every 1% increase in GFCI resulted in an increase of GDP by 0.3%.

Note: More results of the multiple regression can be found in the appendix.

(Figure 7). This is because China's nominal GDP tends to be downward-biased on account of its old socialist pricing structures whereas exports are denominated in US dollar terms.

Consequently, it is more realistic to express GDP in purchasing power parity (PPP) terms, and the ensuing export–GDP ratio results in a lower

Table 3.   Some indicators on the openness of the Chinese economy.

Year	Export of Goods and Services as % of GDP	Trade in Goods as % of GDP	Trade in Services as % of GDP	Trade in both Goods and Services as % of GDP	FDI Inflows as % of Gross Fixed Capital Formation
1982	7.9	13.1	1.6	14.5	0.5
1983	7.5	12.8	1.5	14.3	0.7
1984	8.4	15.5	1.8	17.2	1.4
1985	9.4	21.2	1.9	23.4	1.8
1986	11.3	20.7	2.1	26.3	2.1
1987	13.9	22.4	2.2	27.4	2.3
1988	12.9	22.1	2.1	26.8	2.6
1989	12.4	21.1	1.9	25.6	3.0
1990	14.9	24.5	2.7	27.2	3.5
1991	16.5	27.3	2.8	30.0	3.9
1992	16.8	28.6	4.0	32.6	7.4
1993	14.5	27.0	3.9	30.9	12.3
1994	22.0	36.5	6.1	42.6	17.2
1995	21.0	34.0	6.3	40.2	14.8
1996	21.0	34.4	5.3	39.7	14.3
1997	22.7	35.1	5.8	41.1	14.6
1998	21.8	33.6	5.3	39.8	12.9
1999	22.0	35.3	5.8	41.2	10.8
2000	25.3	42.9	6.1	47.8	9.2

Notes: (1) Nominal GDP at 2001 market prices.
(2) Data for years 1980 and 1981 are unavailable.
Sources: Data calculated from official figures in *China Statistical Yearbook, EIU database, IMF International Financial Statistics Yearbook 2001.*

ranking for China. It makes sense to say that China was economically less open than Japan and USA, and very much so compared to the four East Asian NIEs and ASEAN-4, as shown in Figure 8. A large economy, be it Japan, USA or China, tends to be more self-sufficient and therefore less dependent on trade. Naturally, China's per-capita trade turnover was also much smaller than that of the other economies.

It may be stressed that though China's exports (at US$266 billion in 2001) were nominally very large in absolute terms, making it the world's sixth largest exporting nation, the net value-added of its export trade remained relatively low. First, almost 50% of China's exports were generated by foreign enterprises. Second and more importantly, China's exports were

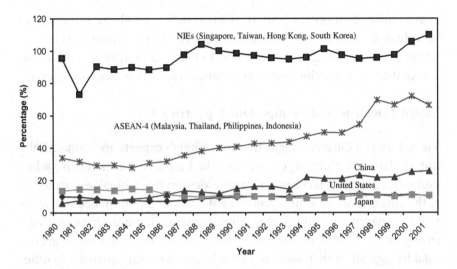

Figure 7.   Openness of the Chinese economy: Export–GDP (nominal) ratios.

Source: Export–GDP ratios calculated from data provided by *EIU*.

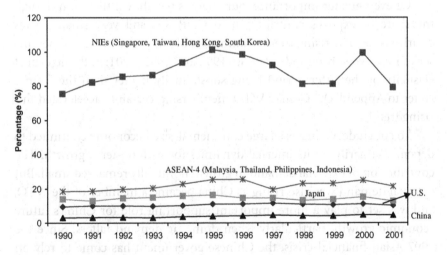

Figure 8.   Real openness of the Chinese economy: Export–GDP (PPP) ratios.

Source: Export–GDP (PPP) ratios calculated from data provided by *EIU*.

heavily dependent on the import of intermediate products, estimated to be as high as 50%. As the domestic content of China's exports was low, its domestic value-added or contribution to GDP necessarily remained low. Hence the small contribution of external demand to China's GDP growth.

External Demand Still an Important Supporting Role

Viewed from a different angle, however, China's exports are economically not all that unimportant, even if we take into account its relatively low domestic content. It is commonly acknowledged that China's export sector is the single most vibrant segment of the whole economy because of its better management and better technology. As such, it must have exerted a strong catalytic effect on the rest of the economy, creating a much greater total linkage effect than what is shown in our foregoing analysis. In other words, our limited exercise here has probably failed to capture all the "spread effects" of the export sector. A proper approach would need to trace all the multiplier effects of the foreign trade sector through a detailed input–output table.

Of even greater importance, our analysis has shown that even though the share of export's contribution to GDP was still very small, it was clearly rising. The rising trend is unmistakable when we break up the time series into two sub-periods of 1980–1992 and 1992–2001: with the export elasticity of the latter period being substantially higher than the former (refer to Appendix).[6] China's WTO membership certainly accelerated this rising trend.

To conclude, China as a large continental-sized economy continued to depend primarily on its internal dynamics for its long-term growth. The contribution of external demand to growth nominally remained small. But external demand was also rising as China became a member of the WTO, and was set to play a more important supporting role for China's future economic growth, particularly when domestic demand falters. Since the 1997 Asian financial crisis, the Chinese government has come to rely on increasing fixed investment to pump prime growth. Beijing will not be able to continue with this proactive fiscal policy for long without running into

---

[6]The elasticity coefficient for net exports in the post-*Nanxun* period was 0.02 as compared to 0.01 for the 1980–1992 period.

unacceptable levels of fiscal deficits.[7] External demand will have to come in to play an increasingly crucial role in supporting China's future economic growth.

Appendix

Further to the results shown in Box 1, another multiple regression analysis is run to find out how much GDP or income changed given a unit change in consumption, investment and total (or gross) exports.

Year	GDP (USD Billion)	Consumption* (USD Billion)	Gross Fixed Capital Investment	Total Exports (USD Billion)
1980	304	199	106	18
1981	288	194	93	22
1982	290	193	93	23
1983	308	203	102	23
1984	309	202	107	26
1985	299	196	115	28
1986	293	190	112	33
1987	317	200	117	44
1988	395	251	147	51
1989	437	280	162	54
1990	383	238	135	57
1991	400	247	142	66
1992	469	289	178	79
1993	599	350	260	87
1994	542	310	224	119
1995	701	403	286	147
1996	825	481	327	172
1997	902	525	341	201
1998	961	561	363	210
1999	1005	604	371	245
2000	1080	645	405	298
2001	1159	691	444	296

Notes: (1) *Consumption refers to both private and government consumption.
(2) GFCI includes stock-building.
Source: EIU.

---

[7]China's fiscal deficit/GDP ratio was only just within the "safety limit" of 3%, the Golden Rule for European Union (EU). But China cannot afford to play around with such proactive expansionary policy year after year. For further discussion of this subject, see Cui Zhiyuan, "How Serious is China's Fiscal Deficit? Applying EU's 'Golden Rule'", *EAI Background Brief, No. 127,* July 16, 2002.

Based on the above-mentioned data, the log-linear regression model is generated as follows. Assuming Y = GDP, C = consumption, GFCI = Gross Fixed Investment, X = Total Exports,

$$\ln Y_t = 0.661083 + 0.79880 \ln C_t + 0.151919 \ln GFCI_t + 0.047944 \ln X_t,$$
$$t = (5.056)^*(14.089)^*(3.0484)^*(2.9578)^*, \quad (R^2 = 0.99869).$$

*denotes that all variables are statistically significant at $\alpha = 0.05$ (5% significance), which indicates that the model is stable over the dataset period (1980–2001). The elasticity values as found from the regression results are contained in the table below:

Income elasticity of Y in relation to variables		
C	GFCI	X
0.79	0.15	0.05

It can be deduced from the results that for every 1% increase in consumption, China's GDP on average was estimated to increase by approximately 0.8%. For every 1% increase in investment, GDP was estimated to increase by 0.2%. And for every 1% increase in total or gross exports, GDP was estimated to rise by nearly 0.05%.

Breaking the data into two different periods and performing a regression analysis on the two separate time periods yield different results. Using data on GDP, consumption, investment and net exports,

Period 1980–1992:

Equation (1):

$$\ln Y_t = 0.35426 + 0.81491 \ln C_t + 0.2239 \ln GFCI_t + 0.01401 \ln NX_t,$$
$$t = (2.0689)^*(11.918)^*(4.693)^*(3.732)^*, \quad (R^2 = 0.99718).$$

Income elasticity of Y in relation to variables		
C	GFCI	NX
0.81	0.22	0.01

Period 1992–2001:

Equation (2):

$$\ln Y_t = 0.80938 + 0.654818 \ln C_t + 0.314286 \ln GFCI_t + 0.01572 \ln NX_t,$$
$$T = (11.992)^*(10.1202)^*(4.1333)^*(6.1274)^*, \quad (R^2 = 0.99984).$$

The t-statistics denoted by asterisk show that all independent variables are statistically significant at 0.05 significance level.

Income elasticity of Y in relation to variables		
C	GFCI	NX
0.65	0.31	0.02

From the results, it is found that in the early reform period of 1980–1992, China's GDP was estimated to increase by 0.01% given a 1% increase in net exports. In the post-*Nanxun* period (1992–2001) however, China's GDP was estimated to rise by 0.02% given a 1% rise in net exports.

6

GROWTH AND CHANGE OF CHINA'S SERVICE SECTOR

Introduction

China's service activities (officially called the "tertiary industry"), on account of their socialist legacies, were initially smaller and more backward than other developing countries. Regarded as an unproductive and highly regulated sector where private ownership was strictly prohibited, the service industry started to develop only after the government embarked on economic reform and the open-door policy.

The service sector had experienced high growth during 1979–2002, averaging at 17% and higher than the GDP growth rate in the same period. Nevertheless, China's service economy was still under-developed. In 1978, China's service sector accounted for only 24% of GDP. In 2002, it had increased by 10 percentage points to 34%. But this proportion was still much lower than the average level of 60–80% for the developed countries, and 50% for the developing countries.

However, China's service industry had been an important driver of employment growth. The employment in the service sector increased from 12% of the total in 1978 to 28% in 2001. Since 1994, service sector employment surpassed manufacturing employment. In the late 1990s and the early 2002, a growing service sector was an important source of non-farm employment, particularly for the large number of laid-off workers from the restructured state-owned enterprises (SOEs). In 2013, the service sector provided 38.5% of the country's total employment, compared to 30.1% for manufacturing.

Official estimates on the size of China's service sector in the early periods had been grossly understated. For instance, the economic activities of millions of migrant rural workers, who were engaged in various informal sectors in urban areas, were not properly accounted for in the national statistical coverage while certain social services performed by the SOEs were counted as part of manufacturing activities, thus further underestimating the relative size of the whole service sector. China's National Statistical Bureau had revised the GDP figures upward at least three times during the last two decades (the latest one being for 2013), and each revision exercise basically involved the recalculation of service activities.

The development of various service industries among different regions in China had been uneven. The service industries in the eastern coastal provinces were relatively more developed than those in the western or inland provinces. China's traditional service activities were primarily constituted by commercial services (retail and distribution) and postal and communications. As economic reform took hold, banking and finance activities had expanded rapidly while some new and knowledge-intensive industries like the Internet and e-commerce had also emerged.

As in other developing economies, most service activities in China were traditionally regarded as "non-tradable". But growing industrialization and globalization plus technological progress have rendered many service activities today tradable or exportable. With the Chinese economy increasingly integrated into the global trading system, China's service trade also grew rapidly. In 2001, China accounted for 2.3% of the world's total trade in services compared to a mere 0.8% in 1985. But China's 2.3% share in the world's service exports was small compared to its 4.4% share in the world's merchandise exports. Furthermore, service exports accounted for only 11% of China's total exports of goods and services, which was much lower than the world's average level of 19%. In 2013, China was the world's largest trading country and its global share for trade rose to 12%. Its global service trade increased to only about 8%.

While its merchandise trade for most years has been in surplus, China's trade in services has consistently been in deficit, i.e., being a net importer of services. Since the 1990s, China's deficit in service trade has been steadily rising. In 2001, China suffered a large deficit of US$6.4 billion in its service trade while its merchandise trade chalked up a surplus of US$12.5 billion. By 2013, China's deficit in service trade had widened to US$125 billion, in sharp contrast to the surplus of US$235 billion for its trade in goods.

In China's balance of payments account, sectors contributing to the deficit included transportation, insurance, royalty payments, business consultation, communication, and movies and audio–video products while tourism, computer and information, financial, advertisement and other commercial services enjoyed a trade surplus. On the whole, China's huge deficit in its service trade clearly indicates that the development of its service sector has remained weak and uncompetitive by international standards and its export capability for high value-added services remained limited.

Take the 2013 Balance of Payments account. The biggest source of service imports was overseas travels, with a deficit of US$77 billion for 2013, which was likely to be underestimated and the difference could be reflected on the "error and omission" items, which was US$78 billion for 2013.

Apart from tourism, the other most important item for China's import of services is education and schooling, which have not been properly accounted for. With China's outgoing tourism and the number of Chinese students going overseas to pursue further studies are on the rise year after year, as a result of rising incomes in China, these two sources of service deficits for China will get even larger in the years to come.

In 2014, the number of outbound tourists had surpassed the 100 million mark. According to the Ministry of Education, the number of students studying abroad in 2013 was 414,000 — the actual number is likely to be more, particularly for those students studying in high schools overseas. If the average spending of a Chinese student overseas was US$20,000 a year, the education deficits for China would amount to the hefty US$10 billion.

In 2001, less than one-third of China's FDI was channelled to the service sector, partly due to protectionist policies. For the first nine months of 2002, real estate accounted for nearly half of total FDI in the service sector while financial services accounted for a minuscule 0.5% due to restrictions still prevailing in the financial sector. But the situation was expected to improve as China had then just been acceded to the World Trade Organization (WTO). China would start to lift, on a gradual basis, restrictions in sectors like banking, insurance, securities and telecommunications.

In future, China's service sector would have to brace itself for increasing foreign competitions. To sustain its long-term economic growth, China would have to develop a more competitive service sector. A robust service sector holds *the key to China's future economic growth through the expansion of domestic demand, particularly as the Chinese economy matures.*

Indeed, the service sector will rapidly expand in future under the leadership of Xi Jinping, whose policies of accelerating urbanization on the one hand and further economic reform on the other, will operate to restructure the economy towards more service-oriented and less manufacturing-based. As China's economy is gradually being restructured and rebalanced, its growth path will inevitably change. For the past 10 years (2002–2012), domestic investment contributed on average 53.2% and domestic consumption only 45.1% to China's total GDP growth, with the share for external demand (exports minus imports) just about 2%. In other words, China's past dynamic growth was primarily investment driven. But this pattern of growth is clearly unsustainable. The main thrust of China's economic reform and rebalancing is to render China's future economic growth more consumption driven. This will, in turn, lead to more rapid expansion of its service sector.

In 2014, service accounted for 48.2% of GDP, compared to 42.6% for manufacturing and 9.2% for agriculture. Since 2006, with the exception of 2010, the service sector has contributed a larger share to overall GDP growth than manufacturing. This trend is likely to continue as the Chinese economy is being restructured to be more consumption oriented.

In February 2015, the State Council came out with a plan to boost China's long-term service exports. In 2013, China's total service trade amounted to only US$540, just about 25% of its total trade in goods. The government therefore set a target for trade in services to reach US$1 trillion in 2020, as a major shift of emphasis away from the export of goods. The future development efforts will focus more on increasing the international competitiveness of China's service exports by intensifying the development of its "tradable" service activities from financial services, communications and transportation to tourism and cultural exports, particularly service goods containing "core Chinese values".

The service sector is therefore set to grow larger and larger in future as the economy becomes more developed and per-capita GDP continues to grow. Domestically, apart from the effect of macroeconomic rebalancing, accelerated urbanization will certainly speed up further expansion of the service sector. All high-income economies will become "post-industrial societies", which are essentially service based.

Rapid Growth of Service Industries

A modern economy conventionally encompasses three main sectors based on the structure of its GDP: agriculture, industry (including manufacturing) and services. China, however, follows the outmoded classification of grouping its industries into three main sectors: "primary, secondary and tertiary", with primary industry referring to agriculture, secondary industry to mining, manufacturing and construction, and tertiary industry to comprise all the rest. What is called "service industry" in market economies specifically refers to "tertiary industry" in China.

China adopted this "primary–secondary–tertiary" classification basically to follow the Marxist prejudices against service activities. By the definition of an eminent pre-war economist Colin Clark,[1] tertiary industry was used as an ordinal concept to mark the final stage of economic development. But according to Nobel laureate Simon Kuznets,[2] services do not represent the final stage of industrialization since the expansion of both manufacturing and service industries corresponds with the decline of agriculture. To Kuznets, economic growth and structural change are the one and the same process. Modern economic growth (as marked by increases in GDP) typically does not let one group of industries grow first followed by others in a pre-determined order. Hence, all modern market economies follow this "structural classification" by grouping industries into three main sectors: agricultural, industrial and service.

Since 1979, China's tertiary industry has enjoyed explosive growth. Along with the rapid development of the economy, output of services soared from 87 billion yuan (US$56 billion) in 1979 to a hefty 3,453 billion yuan (US$418 billion) in 2002, growing at an annual average of 17% over the last two decades, higher than the country's GDP growth rate (near 10%) in the same period (Figure 1). In 1978, China's GDP was divided into three components: 28% for primary sector, 48% for secondary sector, and 24% for tertiary sector. By 2002, the proportion had changed respectively to 15:51:34 (Table 1, Figures 2 and 3). In other words, compared with 1978,

---

[1]C. Clark, *The Conditions of Economic Progress*, Macmillan & Co. Ltd., 1941.
[2]S. Kuznets, *Economic Growth of Nations: Total Output and Production Structure*, Harvard University Press, 1971.

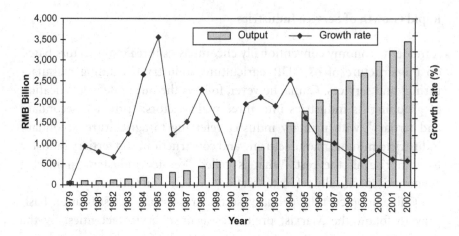

Figure 1.   Growth of China's tertiary industry, 1979–2002.

Sources: *China Statistical Yearbook*, 2002. *Statistical Communique*, 2002, National Bureau of Statistics of China.

the proportion of the tertiary industry in the national economy increased by 10 percentage points by 2002.

In terms of employment in the three sectors, structural change appeared even more remarkable. Employment in the tertiary industry increased from 12% in 1978 to 28% in 2001 (Table 2). In a dynamic perspective, as China's economy underwent extensive transformation and industrialization, employment in the primary sector had markedly declined while employment in the secondary and tertiary sector had correspondingly increased. Of even greater significance, by 1994, employment in the tertiary industry surpassed that of the secondary industry (Figure 4). This meant that China's employment structure was moving rapidly towards the pattern of the more developed economies where the service sector was the biggest employer.

The structural change in the Chinese economy was basically consistent with the pattern of evolution of the developed economies. The decline of the primary industry in the overall national economy was accompanied by an increase in the other two sectors, particularly since the mid-1980s. As shown in Figure 2, in terms of output, the proportion of the tertiary industry exceeded that of the primary industry in 1985, and the growth of the national economy since then was mainly driven by the secondary

Table 1. Composition of output in China's industries (value-added as % of GDP), 1978–2002.

Year	Primary	Secondary	Tertiary
1978	28.1	48.2	23.7
1979	31.2	47.4	21.4
1980	30.1	48.5	21.4
1981	31.8	46.4	21.8
1982	33.3	45.0	21.7
1983	33.0	44.6	22.4
1984	32.0	43.3	24.7
1985	28.4	43.1	28.5
1986	27.1	44.0	28.9
1987	26.8	43.9	29.3
1988	25.7	44.1	30.2
1989	25.0	43.0	32.0
1990	27.1	41.6	31.3
1991	24.5	42.1	33.4
1992	21.8	43.9	34.3
1993	19.9	47.4	32.7
1994	20.2	47.9	31.9
1995	20.5	48.8	30.7
1996	20.4	49.5	30.1
1997	19.1	50.0	30.9
1998	18.6	49.3	32.1
1999	17.6	49.4	33.0
2000	15.9	50.9	33.2
2001	15.2	51.1	33.6
2002	14.5	51.7	33.7

Sources: *China Statistical Yearbook*, various issues, 2002.

and tertiary industry instead of the primary and secondary industry.[3] For the period 1990–2001, of the 9.3% annual growth in GDP, 5.8% could be attributed to the secondary industry, 2.5% to the tertiary industry and the remaining 1% to the primary industry.[4]

---

[3]"China's Services Trade: Development and Experiences of Opening-Up", Report submitted to the WTO Council for Trade in Services (special session), Report No. TN/S/W/9, December 19, 2002.

[4]*Ibid.*

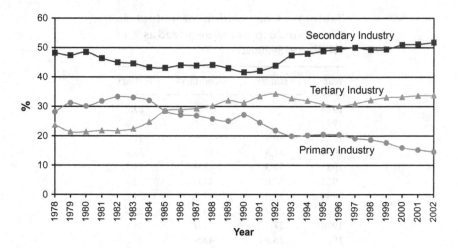

Figure 2. Composition of output in China's three industries (value-added as % of GDP), 1978–2002.

Sources: *China Statistical Yearbook*, 2002. *Statistical Communique*, 2002, National Bureau of Statistics of China.

Despite its rapid expansion, China's service sector remained relatively small by international standards. In 2001, for instance, China's service sector stood at only 34% of its GDP, which was lower than the average level of 60–80% for the developed countries and 50% for the developing countries. In many ways, China's economy was still at an underdeveloped stage. Prior to economic reform (1978), China's tertiary industry was largely neglected and became stagnant because the tertiary industry in a socialist economy was considered an unproductive sector. It was also highly regulated and private property ownership was strictly prohibited. This sector started to develop only after the Chinese economy began to move towards the market system.

Viewed from a different angle, the relatively small size of the service sector meant that it can be a new source of China's future economic growth. The expansion of service activities also created new employment opportunities. In short, the service sector held the key to resolving China's employment problem.

Service Sector Still Small

China's service activities, on account of their socialist legacies, were known to be more backward than other countries. Despite rapid growth over the

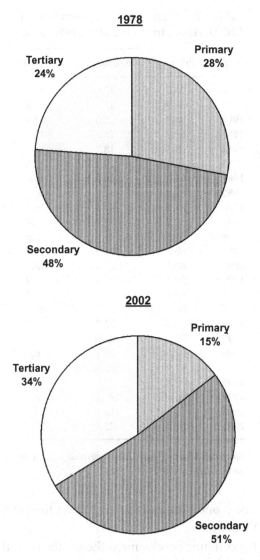

Figure 3.　Share of output in China's three industries, 1978–2002.

Source: *China Statistical Yearbook*, 2002.

past two decades, China's tertiary industry constituted only a relatively small part of its entire economy, especially when compared with industrialized countries and other developing countries in the world. As shown in Table 3, the share of China's service sector in 2001 was only 34% or half the average

Table 2. Share of employment in China's three industries (%), 1978–2001.

Year	Primary	Secondary	Tertiary
1978	70.7	17.6	11.7
1979	69.9	17.9	12.2
1980	68.9	18.5	12.6
1981	68.2	18.6	13.2
1982	68.3	18.7	13.0
1983	67.2	19.0	13.8
1984	64.2	20.2	15.6
1985	62.5	21.1	16.4
1986	61.1	22.1	16.8
1987	60.1	22.5	17.4
1988	59.5	22.6	17.9
1989	60.2	21.9	17.9
1990	60.1	21.4	18.5
1991	59.7	21.4	18.9
1992	58.5	21.7	19.8
1993	56.4	22.4	21.2
1994	54.3	22.7	23.0
1995	52.2	23.0	24.8
1996	50.5	23.5	26.0
1997	49.9	23.7	26.4
1998	49.8	23.5	26.7
1999	50.1	23.0	26.9
2000	50.0	22.5	27.5
2001	50.0	22.3	27.7

Sources: China Statistical Yearbook, various issues, 2002.

of the high income economies, and was even lower than that of Cambodia, Indonesia and Vietnam.

According to economic development theory, the output of a country's service industry should reach approximately 40% when its per capita GDP reaches US$500 and 50% when per capita income hits US$600.[5] China's per capita GDP had then already exceeded US$800, but its service sector still accounted for only one-third of the GDP.

---

[5] H.B. Chenery and M. Syrquin, *Patterns of Development 1950–1970,* Oxford University Press, 1975; S. Kuznets, *Modern Economic Growth,* Yale University Press, 1966.

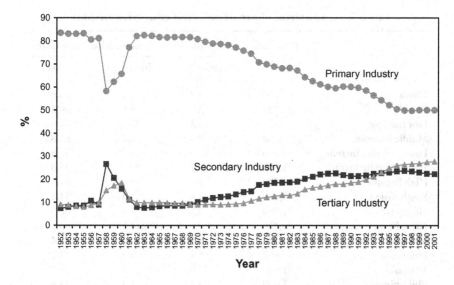

Figure 4. **Share of employment in China's three industries, 1952–2001.**
Source: China Statistical Yearbook, 2002.

Official estimates of China's service industry might well have under-stated its actual size. Under China's household registration system, "rural population" is classified as the agricultural (or primary) industry, no matter which occupation the rural workers are engaged in. There is a real possibility that many service activities produced below the township level had escaped the GDP accounting or been grouped under the "primary sector". The problem of underestimation was also present in the state-owned industrial sector (*qi ye ban she hui*), where SOEs not only had to engage in industrial production but also operated schools, hospitals and performed a wide array of other social services. Many of these service activities were considered part of SOE output and hence included in the secondary industry, not the tertiary sector.

In terms of composition, China's mainstream service industries consisted of commercial and traditional activities (for instance, retail and restaurants) and some infrastructural industries such as postal and communication industries.[6] This differed from the service sector of the

---

[6] *Ibid.*

Table 3.   Industrial share of selected countries in 2001.

	Per capita GNI (USD)	Composition of Value-added (% of GDP)		
		Agriculture	Industry	Services
China	890	15.2	51.1	33.6
World	5,120	3.9	29.8	66.3
Low Income	430	23.8	31.6	44.6
Middle Income	1,860	9.8	36.4	53.8
Lower Middle Income	1,230	12.5	39.7	47.6
Upper Middle Income	4,550	7.1	33.1	59.8
High Income	26,900	1.9	28.6	69.5
South Korea	9,460	4.4	41.4	54.1
Singapore	21,500	0.1	31.6	68.3
Hong Kong	25,330	0.1	14.3	85.6
Malaysia	3,330	8.5	49.1	42.4
Indonesia	690	16.4	46.5	37.1
Thailand	1,940	10.3	40.5	49.3
Philippines	1,030	15.2	31.2	53.6
Vietnam	410	23.6	37.8	38.6
Laos	300	50.9	23.4	25.7
Cambodia	270	36.9	21.9	41.2
Japan	35,610	1.4	31.8	66.8
USA	34,280	1.6	24.9	73.5
UK	25,120	1.0	27.4	71.6
Germany	23,560	1.3	31.0	67.7
France	22,730	2.9	25.6	71.5

Source: Data sourced from www.worldbank.org/data/countrydata/country data.html.

developed countries where mainstream industries were usually information technology (IT), business consulting, research and development (R&D), and banking and financial services.[7] In China, for instance, the vital services sectors like finance, insurance and real estate (FIRE), accounted for a mere 23% of total value-added generated by the service sector in 2000 (Figure 5). This paled in comparison to the US and Taiwan, where the ratio of value-added by FIRE was 54% and 45%, respectively. In terms of employment, in 2001, the number of workers employed in the transportation, wholesale

---

[7] *Ibid.*

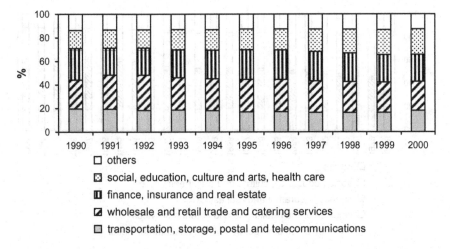

Figure 5. Share of value-added in China's tertiary industry (sectoral breakdown), 1999–2000.

Source: China Statistical Yearbook, 2002.

and retail sectors accounted for 59% of the total employed in China's service sector (Figure 6), compared to only 34% in the US.

Uneven Development of Service Industries among Regions

Due to unbalanced growth of China's provinces and cities, there were wide gaps in the development of the service industries among the various regions, e.g., those in the eastern coastal provinces were relatively more developed than those in the western inland provinces (Table 4). In fact, China's six richest coastal provinces and cities — Guangdong, Zhejiang, Jiangsu, Shanghai, Shandong and Liaoning — accounted for 45% of the output of services in the national economy (Figure 7).

Gearing up for WTO Challenges

Trade in Services

As discussed earlier, services are mostly regarded as non-tradable, either because of their nature or due to their high transportation costs per product unit, high tariffs or other restrictions. Traditionally, services are

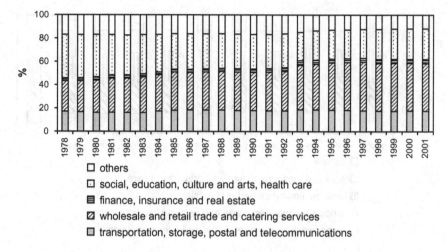

□ others

□ social, education, culture and arts, health care

▤ finance, insurance and real estate

▨ wholesale and retail trade and catering services

□ transportation, storage, postal and telecommunications

Figure 6.   Share of employment in China's tertiary industry (sectoral breakdown), 1978–2001.

Source: *China Statistical Yearbook*, 2002.

Table 4.   Proportions of tertiary industry in western, central and eastern China (%), 1978–2001.

Year	Proportion of Tertiary Industry (%)		
	Western	Central	Eastern
1978	18.8	18.1	19.5
1989	27.5	28.9	30.4
2001	38.3	35.4	40.2

Sources: *China Statistical Yearbook*, various issues.

considered "non-tradable" also because their activities, particularly those in the public sector, are not exportable. However, as the economy had developed, along with further globalization and technological progress, services have increasingly become tradable. Many large transnational firms were offering cross-national-border services previously regarded as non-tradable due to their ownership of such intangible assets as organizational skills and technological know-how. This was possible because of growing globalization and deregulation trends.

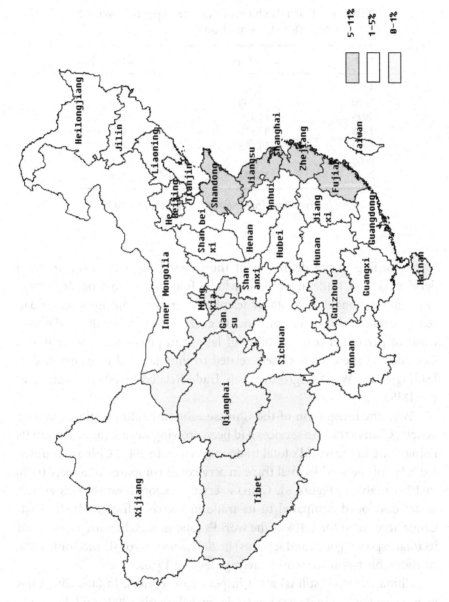

Figure 7.   Interprovincial share of tertiary output in China's economy, 2001.

Source: *China Statistical Yearbook*, 2002.

Table 5.   China's share of service exports in world total, 1985–2001 (US$ million).

Year	Service Export	World Share (%)
1985	2,925	0.77
1990	5,748	0.73
1995	18,430	1.55
1998	23,879	1.79
1999	26,165	1.90
2000	30,146	2.06
2001	32,903	2.26

Sources: International Trade Statistics, WTO, 2001, 2002.

According to the definition of the General Agreement on Trade in Service (GATS), trade in services includes four items: cross-border supply (e.g., international long distance telephone service), consumption abroad (e.g., tourism), commercial presence (e.g., multinational banks) and movement of personnel (e.g., mobility of labour in professional occupation). Commercial presence is closely related to international investment, thus leading to the WTO's Agreement on Trade-Related Investment Measures (TRIMS).

With the integration of the Chinese economy into the global trading system, China's trade in services had been growing steadily, as evident in its rising share in the world's total trade in services. In 2001, China accounted for 2.3% of the world's total trade in services as compared to a mere 0.8% in 1985 (Table 5, Figure 8). China's services export however was grossly under-developed compared to its trade in merchandise goods. In 2001, China accounted for 4.4% of the world's total in merchandise exports. Of its total exports (goods and services) in 2001, services constituted only 11%, considerably below the world's average level of 19%.

China was and (still is) a net importer of services. In fact, China has experienced deficit in its services trade since the early 1990s, and the deficit has increased steadily (Figure 9). In 2001, according to statistics provided by the State Administration of Foreign Exchange, China's services trade deficit amounted to US$6.4 billion (Table 6), as against its surplus of US$34

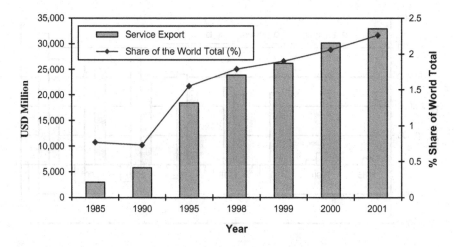

Figure 8.   Growth of China's export of services.

Sources: *International Trade Statistics*, WTO, 2001, 2002.

Table 6.   China's trade in services, 1985–2001 (US$ million).

Year	Exports	Imports	Trade Balance
1985	2925	2261	664
1990	5748	4113	1635
1995	18,430	24,635	−6205
1998	23,879	26,467	−2588
1999	26,165	30,967	−4802
2000	30,146	35,858	−5712
2001	32,903	39,260	−6357
2002* (January–June)	18,099	22,425	−4326

Source: WTO, 2002.
*China State Administration of Foreign Exchange, Balance of Payment Sheet.

billion in merchandise trade.[8] In 2013, deficit in service trade widened to US$118 billion.

---

[8]"China's Services Trade: Development and Experiences of Opening-Up", Report submitted to the WTO Council for Trade in Services (special session), Report No. TN/S/W/9, December 19, 2002.

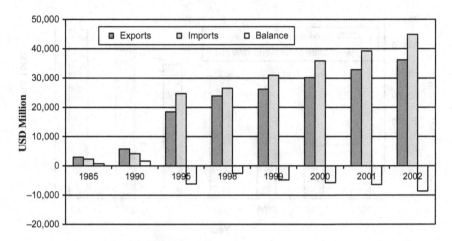

Figure 9.   China's trade in service.

Sources: WTO, 2002; China State Administration of Foreign Exchange, Balance of Payment Sheet. Data of 2002 is estimated based on the data collected in the first half.

As can be seen from China's balance of payments account (Table 7), the deficit exists for most items of the service trade. Transportation, insurance, royalty payments and business consultation (including legal and accounting services) were the areas in which China suffered the largest deficit while in communication, finance, advertising and movies and audio–video products, China could still maintain a narrow trade surplus or deficit because of its protectionist policies toward the service sector. Services that China enjoyed a strong export comparative advantage included tourism, some form of commercial services, and computer and information services.

Among the service industries with a trade surplus, tourism was the single most important service export for China, accounting for about half of its total service exports. Despite the "9/11 incident" in the US, China's tourism export still amounted to US$18 billion in 2001, up by 9.7% over the previous year and accounting for 53% of China's total service export, with a trade surplus of US$3.9 billion. Other commercial services, and computer and information services enjoyed a surplus of US$1.5 billion and US$0.1 billion, respectively, while the financial and advertisement sectors registered a respective trade surplus of US$22 million and US$19 million.

Table 7. China's export and import of services, 2001 (US$ million).

Item	Total Trade	Export of Services	Import of Services
Goods and Services	28,086	299,410	271,324
Service	−5931	33,335	39,266
Transportation	−6690	4635	11,324
Tourism	3883	17,792	13,909
Communication	−55	271	326
Construction	−17	830	847
Insurance	−2484	227	2711
Financial	22	100	77
Computer and Information	117	461	345
Fee for Patent or Royalty	−1828	111	1938
Consultation	−613	889	1502
Advertisement and Publicity	19	277	258
Movies and Audio–Video Products	−22	28	50
Other Commercial Services	1538	7282	5744
Government Services not Classified Elsewhere	198	433	235

Note: Negative sign denotes deficit.
Source: *China Statistical Yearbook*, 2002.

In sectors that registered a trade deficit, transportation (shipping and air freight) incurred a huge deficit of US$6.7 billion, which was more than the total deficit in the service trade. Insurance, patent and royalty and consultation sectors experienced a deficit of US$2.5 billion, US$1.8 billion and US$0.6 billion, respectively. In other sectors like communications, movie and audio–video product, the deficits incurred were US$55 million and US$22 million, respectively (Table 7).

On the whole, China's huge deficit in services trade clearly served to indicate that its service sector was weak and uncompetitive by international standards so that its export capability was rather limited. Given that China in future might not continue to chalk up trade surplus in its merchandise goods, its overall balance of payments situation could well deteriorate in the long term if its deficit in services trade were to persist.

FDI in Services

Foreign direct investment (FDI) in China's service sectors had been highly regulated from the outset of its reform. Prior to its accession to WTO, China had applied several restrictive measures in terms of the extent and conditions of market access for foreign service providers. These measures may be broadly classified into five types:

- Limitations on the sector in which foreign service suppliers were allowed to operate — e.g., no foreign firms were allowed to operate in the telecommunications sector.
- Limitations on the type of business allowed within each service sector — e.g., foreign accountancy firms were specifically barred from conducting auditing services.
- Limitations on the legal form of market entry — e.g., joint ventures (JVs) were generally a preferred form of market entry over wholly foreign-owned companies in many service sectors.
- Quantitative restrictions on market access in terms of, for instance, the number of service suppliers, the number of service operations, and the maximum share of foreign equity participation.
- Geographical restrictions, i.e., only selected "zones" and designated cities were open to foreign investment in service activities.[9]

In 2001, mainly due to protectionist measures, less than one-third of the FDI in China was channelled towards the service sector (Figure 10). This paled in comparison to the manufacturing sector, which absorbed the bulk of FDI. From January to September 2002, real estate accounted for

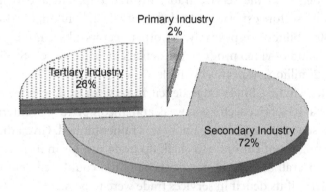

Figure 10.   Proportion of FDI in China by sectors, 2001.

Sources: Statistics on FDI, MOFTEC, 2002.

---

[9]"China's Unfinished Open-Economy Reforms: Liberalization of Services", OECE Development Centre, Technical papers, No. 147, April 1999.

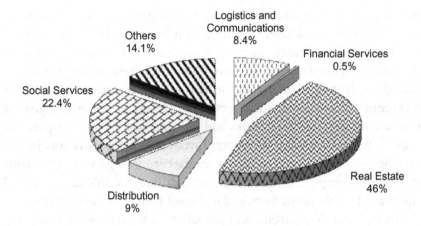

Figure 11. Share on FDI in China's tertiary industry, January–September 2002.

Source: Statistics on FDI, MOFTEC, 2002.

a hefty 47% of total FDI in the service sector while education, healthcare, recreation, etc. (grouped under "social services") accounted for 22%, with distribution, logistics and communications taking up 8% (Figure 11). What is noticeable is that the share of FDI in financial services (banking, insurance and securities) was a minuscule 0.5% due to the restrictions still prevailing in the financial activities. In the years to come, as China would gradually liberalize its service sector, new FDI in this sector was expected to increase to about 40% of China's overall FDI and with an annual growth of 10% to 15%.[10]

China's Service Sector after WTO

After its accession to the WTO in December 2001, China had to lift, on a gradual basis, most restrictions in sectors like banking, insurance, securities and telecoms. China relaxed its control on market access in other fields like legal consulting, accounting, engineering, medical, tourism, computer and other related services. China's service sector braced itself for increasing foreign competition. The situation could have been quite serious, as China's service industries were generally plagued by acute shortages of qualified and

---

[10]"FDI Patterns Set to Change", *China Daily*, May 28, 2003.

trained personnel. In terms of management experience, China's domestic service suppliers also lagged far behind their international counterparts.

To meet these challenges, China's service sector needed to undergo rapid reform and restructuring. Since China's WTO entry, the government had taken steps to liberalize the service market in accordance with its WTO commitments. In financial services like insurance and banking, some domestic insurers and local banks had implemented shareholding reform to allow the participation of foreign investors. Such a move was in line with the government's aim to strengthen the corporate governance systems of domestic companies. Introducing foreign shareholders also expanded capital assets of domestic firms and increased their operational efficiency.

To facilitate deregulation and reduction of governmental monopoly in certain service markets, the government had brought in a regulatory framework to ensure orderly developments in the market. In some sectors, laws had been enacted or were being drafted. In 2001, the Insurance Law was amended and the amendment of the Postal Law was near completion, while the drafting of the Telecommunication Law was under way. For a developing country like China, the enactment of law has never been an easy task, and the authorities had to make considerable efforts to ensure that the existing regulatory regime, while in line with the WTO rules, would not greatly impede or harm the development of its domestic service industries.

Services as the Key to Future Economic Growth

To sustain China's long-term economic growth, the government had to give higher priority to nurture its service sector, which remained the weakest link in the economy. Its failure to do so would undermine the competitiveness of China's export-oriented industries, which were heavily dependent on the efficiency of finance, transportation, distribution and similar business services at the other end of the value chain.

In fact, a robust service sector would hold the key to China's future economic growth through the expansion of domestic demand particularly as the Chinese economy was growing rapidly. Above all, it will always be an important source of employment, particularly for the massive number of laid-off workers from the restructured SOEs as well as the increasing number of rural migrant workers. In short, China's smooth transition to a domestic market-led economic growth crucially depended on the successful reform and restructuring of its service sector.

7

SPEEDING UP STATE-OWNED ENTERPRISE REFORM

Introduction

China's paramount leader Deng Xiaoping passed away in February 1997, and Jiang Zemin immediately succeeded him as the "core of the post-Deng leadership". Jiang's leadership position was formalized at the Fifteenth Party Congress on September 12, 1997, which carried the title "Holding High the Great Banner of Deng Xiaoping Theory for an All-round Advancement of the Cause of Building Socialism with Chinese Characteristics to the 21st Century". Jiang had obviously made use of this important meeting to bolster his leadership position in the Party by glorifying Deng's legacies. Jiang had indeed gone through the ritual of expounding the ideological basis of Deng's Theory.

In policy terms, the main agenda was to carry on with ("deepening") Deng's economic reform. The task for all this naturally fell on the shoulders of Zhu Rongji, who was formally confirmed as China's Premier to be in charge of the State Council, which was (and still so today) basically China's Economic Cabinet. It may be remembered that the economic reform was stalled after the Tiananmen event in 1989, but Deng re-ignited the reform process with fresh rigour as well as a new direction, by launching the Nanxun (Tour of South China) in 1992. Deng had made clear that the ultimate objective of his economic reform programme was to build a "socialist market economy with Chinese characteristics". In retrospect, the Nanxun had led to a great breakthrough in economic reform.

The main thrust of the post-Nanxun economic reform operation was the gradual "marketization" of the Chinese economy, which involved taking more and more commodities out of the price control list and subjecting them to the law of supply and demand. The price reform was a process, which started in the early 1980s, but the important "key" commodity items were liberalized (*fangkai*) only after the Nanxun. Zhu Rongji as the Executive Vice Premier was involved in the price liberalization. In particular, he played a key role in the 1994 reform of the taxation and foreign exchange systems. On the macroeconomic reform, he was also instrumental in perfecting China's macroeconomic control system. Thanks to these important reform breakthroughs, China's economy was able to withstand the onslaught of the 1997 Asian financial crisis.

However, one of the most important items in the unfinished business of economic reform had remained. This was about the state-owned enterprise (SOE) reform and, closely related to it, the financial sector reform or banking reform. Not surprisingly, the SOE reform was catapulted to the top economic reform agenda at the Fifteenth Party Congress. As Jiang Zemin put it, "To deepen the reform of state-owned enterprises is an important yet arduous task of the whole Party". For SOE reform, he called for measures that could corporatize large and medium state-owned enterprises according to the requirement of clearly established ownership, well-defined power and responsibility, separation of enterprise from administration.

The problems of Chinese SOEs (then over 100,000), particularly for their mounting losses and increasing indebtedness, were indeed a burning issue at that time. Many large SOEs in China used to operate like a "mini-welfare state" under Konai's "soft budget constraints", with the government always standing ready to subsidize their losses. But the previous government efforts of SOE reform based on the gradual improvement of enterprise governance had produced no significant results, partly because the Chinese leadership then did not have the required political will to carry the reform through.

With a confident and secure post-Deng political leadership under Jiang together with stable economic conditions as a result of strong economic growth (averaging 10% during 1995–1997), China was ready to renew its efforts to crack this daunting problem of SOE reform.

Apart from some broad principles as highlighted by Jiang at the Fifteenth Party Congress, the government then had not published detailed operational reform blueprint. There were also no new surprises in the policy announcement beyond the principle of "diverse public ownership" for legitimizing "partial" privatization", a term still ideologically, not wholly, acceptable at that time.

Strictly speaking, most of the proposed measures for SOE reform had either been tried out before or were already in practice. What is really new this time was the express political determination on the part of the leadership to confront the SOE problem head on.

From the outset, China had eschewed the "Big Bang" approach of SOE reform that was used by the former Soviet Union, which ended up in enriching a few and hence leading to the creation of the oligarchy in Russia. China dealt with the problem in a gradual manner. In terms of implementation, the basic Chinese strategy was to follow Zhuada fangxiao as the working guideline. For the large and medium SOEs, the emphasis was still on improving enterprise governance first with the view to transforming them into independent modern corporations with modern management. Such is the process of corporatization, and the government would provide the needed financial assistance.

For the numerous smaller SOEs controlled by provincial and municipal governments, they would be given more options to revitalize themselves, through restructuring and reorganization, mergers and takeovers, leasing and management contract, conversion into shareholding companies, or simply be sold off, particularly for the small and medium ones. More shake-ups and more layoffs would result in the process.

At that point of time, it looked very promising for China to "fix" its thorny SOE problem, particularly since Zhu Rongji was throwing his weight behind it. Indeed, Zhu had confidently stated that the SOE problem could be sorted out in about three years. There were sceptics at that time who considered Zhu a little too optimistic, for a lot of SOE problems defied simple technocratic solutions. The SOE reform everywhere was politically, economically and socially complicated. The reformed SOEs certainly needed a longer period of time to adjust to modern management culture, and to learn to behave as competitive business units.

In retrospect, Zhu did achieve a kind of breakthrough in the SOE reform. The major obstacle in restructuring the loss-making SOE is to retrench its redundant workers in the absence of a functioning social safety net. Any massive lay-off of workers would be politically and socially too drastic for China — all the more so ideologically, as China was ruled by the Communist Party which was supposed to take care of the interest of the workers. But Zhu had cleverly managed the problem of retrenchment through his innovative Xia Gang (or off-post) measures, i.e., many redundant workers in big SOEs were not dismissed outright but were gradually removed from their duty or simply pensioned off. For the many small and medium SOEs, which had to be closed down, open lay-off was inevitable. But China's strong economic growth all through these years had opened up new employment opportunities for the Xia-gang workers.

Overall, China's SOEs have since been radically transformed following the vigorous reform efforts by Premier Zhu Rongji. The state sector has also been drastically trimmed down, with SOEs generally becoming more market-oriented. The mainstay of China's state sector today is about those 120 or so centrally-owned SOEs (the yangqi) that are controlled by the State Assets Supervision and Administration Commission or SASAC. Thus, in 2011, SOEs made up only 5.3% of the total number of enterprises, but they accounted for 28% of the gross industrial profits and employed 20% of the industrial work force. Above all, 50% of the total industrial tax was paid by SOEs, which was about 4% of GDP. Indeed, SOEs have become important cash cows for the government.

Internationally, many large SOEs, especially "the yangqi," have expanded into overseas following the government's "going-out strategy", and they have built up strong presence in many countries. Of the 70 Chinese companies on the 2012 Fortune Global 500, 65 of them are SOEs, with about 10 of them being ranked as "world class enterprises". SOEs have, in fact, served as a useful vehicle for China to carry out its larger strategic and economic objectives overseas, especially in Africa and Southeast Asia, from natural resource acquisition to development assistance.

Viewed from a different angle, however, the average profit level of SOEs is still well below that of the private enterprises. Furthermore, many large SOEs are making profits out of their monopoly or semi-monopoly positions in the market. They also have easy access to cheap credit from the state banks. This is particularly true of the large yangqi connected with public utilities, basic infrastructure and natural resource acquisition. The yangqi are so big that they become natural monopolists. Their CEOs are directly appointed by the Party's Organization Department, holding ministerial or vice-ministerial ranks.

For years, it has been the government's policy to hold on to the important strategic industries while the private sector is given more room to grow and expand, thereby further shrinking the relatively smaller role of the state sector in the economy. The fact is that the state sector had also been expanding, especially after 2010. This had sparked off an outcry from liberal-minded economists about the potential threat of guojin mintui, i.e., a counter-SOE reform phenomenon with the state sector advancing at the expense of the private sector. And this has given rise to the new call for more SOE reform.

Furthermore, historically all the large yangqi have grown and developed under strong political patronage. Those related to the power sector, oil and gas, railway, telecommunications and shipping have continued to maintain their formal and informal political network. The case in point is the group of oil and gas SOEs belonging to the powerful "petroleum clique" headed by the deposed past Politburo Standing Committee member, Zhou Yongkang. With the downfall of Zhou, China's "Big Oil" was broken up and restructured.

Without doubt, the present China's political leadership under Xi Jinping has seized the opportunity to launch his new SOE reform initiative by combining further SOE reform with his anti-corruption drive. In fact, Xi has extended his anti-corruption campaign to clean up other 26 big SOEs such as the China Mobile and those connected with the power sector.

Economically speaking, Xi wants to see future SOEs more profitable so that more earnings from SOEs will be delivered to the government's revenue. Xi also wants SOEs to be more competitive, i.e., making profits through true market competition in a more level-playing field, not as a result of monopoly. This means that future SOEs will have to operate more like real private enterprises, more entrepreneurial and more profit-oriented. On the other hand, Xi does not want the full privatization of the SOEs. China is not ready for that yet. As the Chinese economy is still largely based on mixed ownership, the large strategic SOEs will also have to be on mixed ownership. In this sense, SOE reform in China is destined to be a continuing process along with the continuing evolution of the Chinese economy.

Zhu Rongji had made great strides in SOE reform, but there seemed to be always unfinished business. As long as the Party laid down certain ideological red line on outright privatization, the state sector will continue to exist. Thus, under the present political system, SOEs will remain an important pillar of the economy, and they will continue to evolve. There will also be new problems and new issues. But the evolution of SOEs in China, as elsewhere, cannot be divorced from the complex political and economic contexts in which SOEs are operating.

Coming to Grips with the SOE Problem

One of the most intractable problems for all reforming transitional economies is how to cope with their ailing SOEs. Chinese reformers, despite their eminent successful experience in their overall market reform efforts, had been similarly dogged by the same problem. In late 1993, China introduced a comprehensive economic reform programme to bring about a "socialist market economy", and it has generally achieved impressive results (e.g., reform of the tax and foreign exchange systems) except in the critical area of SOE reform, which was yet to experience an important breakthrough.[1]

Why had the SOE problem still eluded Chinese reformers? Lacking a favourable macroeconomic environment apart, fundamentally the Chinese leadership did not have the required political will to face up to the problems of the SOE reform.

In the Fifteenth National Party Congress (September 12–18, 1997), however, reform of SOEs was catapulted to the top of the economic agenda. The political and economic significance of this decisive move was obvious. Politically, Jiang Zemin must have felt sufficiently secure to tackle this daunting SOE problem.[2] Economically, the Chinese leadership had long realized that a bold, comprehensive attack on the SOE problem was needed in order to complete the unfinished business of economic reform. Without sorting out its SOE problem, China could not proceed to accomplish its much-needed financial sector reform. As long as these two critical areas remained in limbo, China would not complete its transition to a full market system and would continue to suffer from the inefficiency of a partially reformed economy. With the Chinese economy that continued its high

---

[1] For further discussion of China's past economic reform progress, see John Wong, "What Has China Accomplished in Economic Reform in 1994?", *IEAPE Background Brief No. 80*, December 13, 1994.

[2] Many China experts have been quite surprised by the ways in which Jiang had manoeuvred the other potential power contender, Qiao Shi, out of the Standing Committee of China's Politburo at the Fifteenth Party Congress. For a more detailed analysis of the post-Party Congress politics in China, see Zheng Yongnian, and Zou Ziying, "Power to Set Own Agenda: Jiang Zemin's New Political Initiative at China's Fifteenth Party Congress", *EAI Background Brief* No. 2, September 26, 1997.

growth and low inflation, it was indeed strategically the best time for China to come to grips with the SOE problem.[3]

SOE reform was an enormously difficult undertaking as it went beyond simple economics while involving many larger political and social issues. In fully committing itself to this difficult task, the technocratically-inclined Jiang leadership had clearly calculated the possible political and economic risks. As warned by the 1996 World Bank report, any mishandling of the SOE problem by the Chinese government could engender social instability in the urban areas and slow down China's economic growth. But the top leadership seemed quite upbeat about their ability to cope with the SOE reform problem, as they believed they already had a good grasp of the whole situation. In fact, at the 1997 IMF/World Bank meeting in Hong Kong, Zhu Rongji had confidently said that China could sort out the loss-making problem of its SOEs in about three years.

Was China able to succeed in reforming its problematic SOEs in a matter of a few years? The SOE issue, despite extensive media coverage and debates during the Fifteenth Party Congress, was surrounded by a great deal of public misconception. There was indeed considerable confusion, both inside and outside China, over the true state of affairs of China's SOEs in terms of their numbers, their actual conduct and performance, their linkages to the other sectors of the Chinese economy and so on. This chapter seeks to clarify China's SOE reform efforts and the related problems.

China's Unwieldy State Sector

SOEs or *guoyou qiye* are essentially products of socialism. In China, SOEs used to function primarily as socio-economic entities rather than as purely production units. The objective function of many large SOEs is not limited to making profits. Their operations include the provision of such social and welfare services normally considered "public goods" as education, medical services, housing, child care services and pensions.[4] Indeed, many

---

[3] For a succinct analysis of the then state of China's economy, see John Wong, "Good Political Arithmetick: China's Economy on the Eve of the Fifteenth Party Congress", *EAI Background Brief No. 1*, September 2, 1997.

[4] The Anshan Steel used to be the case where only about one-third of those on its pay roll were the "production people" directly linked to steel making, about one-third were service workers and the other one-third were pensioners.

large SOEs exist much like "mini-welfare states", and not surprisingly, they operate under "soft budget constraints", with the government always ready to subsidize their losses.

Chinese and foreign media added to the public confusion by using different sets of figures for the total number of SOEs and their different sizes. Official statistics from the *China Statistical Yearbook 1996* showed that China had about 320,000 SOEs, out of which some 240,000 were commonly classified as "small".[5] Of the 320,000 SOEs, only some 118,000 were engaged in industrial production, and about 16,000 were classified "large and medium".[6] There was considerable ambiguity as to how SOEs were exactly classified according to size, and how they were considered as "industrial" and "non-industrial".

Conceptually, all SOEs are supposed to come under the state's control, but was not clear how many SOEs actually reported to the central government, and how many were under the direct administrative control of the local governments of provinces, cities and counties. Further, there were even less published information regarding the SOEs run by the People's Liberation Army (PLA) and those controlled by the Commission of Science, Technology and Industry for National Defence as defence industry.

In 1978, SOEs accounted for 78% of China's total industrial output. By 1996 (as shown in Table 1), the share declined to 29%. But the lower output share of the state sector should not be misconstrued as its diminishing economic importance, since 108.5 million or 74% of the urban working population (*Zhi-gong* or "staff and workers") relied on the SOEs to provide them with some form of "cradle-to-grave" employment.[7] Furthermore, the state sector as a whole controlled approximately 61% of the total state assets and constituted some 55% of total domestic sales. In terms of foreign trade, about 67% of China's exports and 50% of imports in 1995 were conducted through the foreign trading arm of the state firms.

---

[5] See Premier Li Peng's "Government Work Report" presented at the National People's Congress in March 1997 (*Zhongguo gongshang shiba*, March 2, 1997).

[6] *China Statistical Yearbook, 1996.*

[7] This employment figure refers to the end of June 1997. (China Economic Information Service of the Xinhua News Agency, August 6, 1997.) China's employment statistics was confusing and misleading because of its peculiar definition of "unemployment" and complicated classification of "urban" and "rural" employment.

Table 1.   Gross industrial output in China, 1978–1996.

(RMB billion)

Year	Total Industrial Output	SOEs		Non-SOEs			
				Sector as a Whole		Of which: Collective-Owned Enterprises	
		Output	% Share*	Output^A	% Share*	Output^B	% Share*
1978	423.7	328.9	77.6	94.8	22.4	94.8	22.4
1980	515.4	391.6	76.0	123.8	24.0	121.3	23.5
1985	971.6	630.2	64.9	341.4	35.1	311.7	32.1
1986	1119.4	697.1	62.3	422.3	37.7	375.2	33.5
1987	1381.3	825.0	59.7	556.3	40.3	478.2	34.6
1988	1822.4	1035.1	56.8	787.3	43.2	658.8	36.2
1989	2201.7	1234.3	56.1	967.4	43.9	785.8	35.7
1990	2392.4	1306.4	54.6	1086.0	45.4	852.3	35.6
1991	2662.5	1495.5	56.2	1167.0	43.8	878.3	33.0
1992	3459.9	1782.4	51.5	1677.5	48.5	1213.5	35.1
1993	4840.2	2272.5	47.0	2567.7	53.0	1646.4	34.0
1994	7017.6	2620.1	37.3	4397.5	62.7	2647.2	37.7
1995	8229.7	2684.1	32.6	5545.6	67.4	2925.3	35.5
1996	9949.3	2868.3	28.8	7081.0	71.2	4016.7	40.4

Note: *denotes "as a percentage share of total industrial output".
Source: *The Statistical Survey of China* (Beijing, 1997).

From the standpoint of the government, the economic importance of the state sector in the Chinese economy was reflected in its traditional role as a major source of central government tax revenue (Table 2). Figure 1 shows that the non-state sector contributed less than half to total government revenue.

Viewed from a different angle, the relative decline of the SOE sector since the start of economic reform merely reflected the dynamic expansion of the non-state sector, particularly the township and village enterprises (TVEs) and various forms of individual enterprises and foreign ventures. In fact, SOEs were still predominant in the key areas of heavy industry such as iron and steel, coal, metallurgy, chemicals, energy production, and petroleum exploration, which operated on the economies of scale and were generally shunned by the TVEs or denied to foreign investors. Also,

Table 2.   Profits and taxes of state enterprises (1978–1994).

(RMB billion)

Year	Total Government Tax Revenue (A)	SOE Total Profits and Taxes		Ratio of C/A (%)
		Profits (B)	Taxes (C)	
1978	51.93	73.35	33.13	63.8
1980	57.17	66.92	38.24	66.9
1981	62.99	64.31	40.77	64.7
1982	70.00	63.15	43.88	62.7
1983	77.56	69.65	45.55	58.7
1984	94.74	78.89	51.47	54.3
1985	204.08	99.88	69.49	34.1
1986	209.07	79.51	74.52	35.6
1987	214.04	98.15	86.51	40.4
1988	239.05	116.49	105.06	43.9
1989	272.74	100.12	123.23	45.2
1990	282.19	49.15	123.10	43.6
1991	299.02	74.45	139.29	46.6
1992	329.69	95.52	155.54	47.2
1993	425.53	166.73	197.58	46.4
1994	512.69	160.80	223.63	43.6

Sources: 1. *The Statistical Survey of China* (Beijing, 1996).
2. *China Statistical Yearbook* 1996 (Beijing, 1996).

some 80% of China's basic industrial raw materials and a wide range of intermediate products continued to be produced by SOEs.

China had started publishing its own "Fortune 500", most of which were essentially SOEs, including the annual best performing "Top Three".[8] So were those "Red Chips" enterprises, which had been listed as "H shares" on the Hong Kong Stock Exchange and the "N shares" on the New York Stock Exchange. But this picture of China having many "viable SOEs" was

---

[8] For instance, in 1994, the "Top Three", in terms of profits and taxes, were the three largest iron and steel corporation of Baoshan, Shougang and Anshan. ("State Firms Still Play Major Role in Economy", *China Daily*, August 25, 1994.) In 1995, the Daqing Petroleum ranked first. (*Xinhua News Agency*, English Service, April 11, 1995.) China also compiled its top 500 Import and Export Firms in terms of turnovers, and virtually most of them were SOEs because until then the state had a monopoly in foreign trade. In 1996, all the top 10 were the former national trading corporations. (*China Economic News*, No. 6, August 11, 1997, Supplement.)

Figure 1.   Contribution to government revenue (1978–1995) in percentage terms.

misleading. In 1993, the Chinese government announced that about one-third of its SOEs were reported to have made losses, with another one-third just breaking even. The proportion of loss-making SOEs has since been increasing and by the first half of 1997, 47% of all SOEs reported losses.

It may be rather meaningless to speak of real "profit and losses" of any enterprise operating in China's then half-reformed economy without credible and transparent public accounting and auditing systems. Many SOEs did not function like profit-maximizing firms in market-oriented economy. Some made profits because of their monopoly position in a particular sector. Others had to incur losses for non-economic reasons (e.g., to carry out their socio-political mandate) or because of price controls (e.g., coal, gas, fertilizer and essential commodity items during the anti-inflationary period). Premier Li Peng, during his visit to Singapore in August 1997, pointed out that the extent of China's SOEs losses had been grossly exaggerated by foreign media. And Mr. Li was probably right.

Regardless of the real extent of the SOE losses and their real causes, it was widely acknowledged that the overall performance of China's SOEs had remained weak. It suffices to say that China's inefficient SOE sector posed three major economic problems: (1) a beleaguered SOE sector controlling a disproportionately large share of physical and human resources represented a clear case of massive misallocation of resources in the economy; (2) the continuing subsidy to cover SOE losses by the government had been a significant cause of China's chronic fiscal deficits; and (3) an unreformed SOE sector presented a major hindrance to the financial sector reform as state banks, under obligation to bail out ailing SOEs, had incurred huge amounts of bad debts and non-performing loans.[9]

Tardy Progress in SOE Reform

It is common knowledge that one fundamental economic solution to the SOE problem was to subject SOEs to real "hard budget constraints", i.e., closing down those which were financially not viable. In this regard, efforts were made to decouple the production function of SOEs from their non-production social obligations, which ultimately entailed breaking the traditional "three *irons*" guarantee — iron rice bowl, iron position and iron wages. But politically and socially, this was not a viable option for China until a new social safety net was well in place. Otherwise, it would run the risk of throwing tens of millions of workers into the streets. This could possibly explain why China's bankruptcy law, first introduced in 1986, had seldom been used as means to attack the SOE problem.

The other fundamental solution was to go for a wholesale privatization as it had been done in the former Soviet Union and other East European socialist states. But again, this was not a viable option for China as the Chinese Communist Party has remained, until this day, ideologically opposed to the idea of open privatization. In any case, such a "Big Bang" approach to economic reform (adopted by the East European socialists with dismal results) has never been the hallmark of China's style of economic reform, which was characterized by its cautious and gradualist approach based on "learning by doing".

Prior to 1993, the reform of SOEs in China was based mainly on improving enterprise governance with emphasis on progressive increase

---

[9]A Monetary Authority of Singapore (MAS) team made a fact-finding study trip to China to understand on the policy direction of SOE reforms and the contribution of the financial system to the latter. The study found that the proportion of SOEs making losses rose from 26% in 1992 to 44% to 1995, with debt-assets ratios as high as 85%. ("Recent Developments in China's State-owned Enterprise Reform and Financial Reform: Study Trip Report, July 28–31, 1997", External Economic Division, MAS.)

in managerial autonomy and accountability. Reform efforts in the early 1980s first started with the "profit retention scheme" (*lirun liucheng*) and the "contract responsibility system" (*zifu yinkui*), and subsequently, the introduction of "tax for profit system" (*li-gai-shui*). At the same time, urban price reform was slowly introduced along with measures taken to decentralize planning and increase reliance on market forces for price management, commodity and factor markets, investment financing, foreign trade and foreign exchange. The idea was to reduce the overall level of price distortion in the economy, which in turn would bring about a more conducive external macroeconomic environment for SOEs to operate closer to market conditions. Open privatization was, of course, not actively promoted as it would run into ideological conflict with the Party's orthodoxy, but "covert privatization" in the form of "shareholding companies" was quietly experimented, mainly by local-level SOEs.

Moving so gingerly, all these reform efforts had naturally achieved no substantive results. By the early 1990s, the basic socialistic *modus operandi* of China's SOEs, particularly for the large ones, remained unchanged. But new economic crises began to envelop the SOE sector. As a result of the government's post-Tiananmen credit crunch, many SOEs came into grief after having made heavy losses. Many more were trapped in a serious "Triangular Debt" involving both enterprises and state banks.[10] Apart from being a serious threat to the financial sector, these debt-ridden SOEs also imposed high fiscal burden on the government, which was obliged to subsidize their losses.[11] The Chinese leadership, therefore, had no choice but to renew its efforts to cope with the SOE problem.

---

[10]"Triangular Debt" refers to a situation whereby Firm A owes Firm B, Firm B owes Firm C, Firm C owes Firm D, and the chain runs on. The government had sought to end this vicious cycle by injecting large funds into the system but as soon as the old debt chain was eliminated, new ones started to appear. The "Triangular Debts" could have been possibly stopped if a "hard budget constraint" were imposed on the SOEs, allowing the inefficient ones to go bust. But this was politically impossible and socially disastrous in the absence of a social security net and welfare system to grapple with unemployment pressures.

[11]When SOEs made losses, the government had to subsidize their losses directly in the form of budget transfers, which amounted to 1.4% of GDP in 1994. But for those which had managed to break even, the government still had to provide them with implicit financial subsidies in the form of cheap loans and lax repayment, and this amounted to an additional 1.7% of GDP in 1994. Total subsidies were even higher before, e.g., 8% in 1987. See World Bank, *China: Reform of State-Owned Enterprises*, June 21, 1996.

Following Deng Xiaoping's tour of South China in 1992, China unleashed a new reform momentum in order to realize the so-called "socialist market economy". In the amended Constitution approved by the Eighth National People's Congress in March 1993, the name "state enterprise" or *guoying qiye* (literally, "state-run enterprise") was formally changed to *guoyou qiye* (literally, "state-owned enterprise"). This simple change in name was sufficiently significant as it sets out to make a distinction between enterprise ownership and enterprise management, a clear implication that the government is no longer under obligation to be administratively involved in direct enterprise management. SOEs are officially owned by the state but technically, they are to be managed by themselves, as in the case of Singapore's government-linked companies. In other words, SOEs can now incorporate various market-oriented systems.

During the period of 1993–1997, the main thrust of the SOE reform efforts had been directed towards the establishment of a "modern enterprise system", which was also incorporated into the comprehensive economic reform package adopted by the Third Party Plenum in November 1993. Specifically, apart from promoting further improvement in enterprise governance through "scientific" (modern) management, the government placed major emphasis on corporatization. Thus, SOEs were encouraged to develop into a profitable "modern enterprise system" by restructuring their internal operations and incentive structures, or to form into new enterprise groups or *qiye jituan* through mergers and acquisitions or other forms of integration. In the meanwhile, the experimentation of the shareholding system was also stepped up. In fact, Chinese reformers even looked into the Japanese *keiretsu* and South Korean *chaebols* for lessons of experience. Above all, the Company Law was enacted in July 1994 in order to provide a modern legal framework for the corporatization drive.

In early 1995, China's SOE reform efforts crystallized further into a more explicit strategy of *Zhuada Fangxiao* or "nurturing the big [into giant conglomerates] while letting go the small SOEs [to the forces of market mechanism]". The government had apparently taken the view that while they could "let go" the 240,000 or so small, mainly local-level SOEs, via various forms of restructuring including reorganization, mergers and takeover, leasing and management contract, conversion into shareholding companies, or even outright closure, they must and will retain the 1,000 large SOEs belonging to the central government, for obvious economic and social reasons. These key SOEs were still of strategic importance as they constituted the backbone of China's industrial economy in terms of total capitalization and employment. As mentioned earlier, some of these SOEs were not doing so badly. Socially, they were just too important to be allowed to go bust, for fear of widespread urban unemployment.

In his "Government Work Report" presented to the National People Congress in March 1997, Premier Li Peng confirmed that in 1996, of the 1,000 targeted SOEs, 300 of them had improved their performance after the injection of fresh state bank loans along with tighter financial control, and an additional 57 SOEs had formed into modern enterprise groups.[12] Year after year, the Chinese government had continued to provide huge financial resources to large SOEs just to ensure their survival and in the hope that they would eventually perform. What have been the results?

On the whole, the decade-long government efforts of grappling with the SOE reform problem had obviously produced no significant breakthrough. This was plainly evident from repeated official acknowledgement of mounting SOE losses and continuing indebtedness of SOEs. A survey conducted on 124,000 state enterprises showed that the asset–liability ratio of SOEs laid within the range of 71.5% to 83.3%.[13] Reasons for the persistent poor performance of SOEs were also plain enough. Basically, many large SOEs were still not operating entirely under "hard budget constraints". This was partly due to the sluggish progress in the social security reform. But many SOEs had not yet developed a modern, market-oriented management culture. Their management knew only too well that state banks are always on hand to bail them out if they ran into financial distress. At the local levels, the SOE reform suffered from a host of malpractice and corruption like "fake or fraudulent bankruptcy"[14] and

---

[12]"The 6-Measure of Promoting SOE Reform", *Zhongguo gong-sheng shibao* (*China Industrial and Commercial Times*, Beijing, March 2, 1997).

[13]"Workers Daily Says that State-Owned Firms are Bottomless Pits", *South China Morning Post*, August 30, 1997.

[14]Some firms had hidden agendas to rid themselves of debt and interest burdens by declaring themselves bankrupt, even though their financial situations might not have rendered such a drastic measure. State banks, on the other hand, were generally reluctant in pushing for more bankruptcies as this meant writing off huge debts from their balance sheets. In 1996,

the "three disorderliness (*san luan*)" — disorderly fee collection, disorderly levies and disorderly fund raising.

It may be stressed that China's top economic priority in this period was to cool its overheating economy. Therefore, the government did not really push ahead its SOE reform agenda very hard. Indeed, the various austerity measures introduced by Zhu Rongji since late 1993 for macroeconomic stabilization tended to "squeeze" many SOEs and actually aggravated their woes. Such continuing deterioration of the SOE financial conditions had, in retrospect, made both the government and the industry realize the urgent need for a more thorough-going reform of the SOE sector. Thus, on the eve of the Fifteenth Party Congress, the problem of SOE reform weighed heavily upon the Chinese leadership.

New Measures for Old Problems?

The timing for the decisive move on the SOE reform by the Chinese leadership was just right: (1) Politically, Jiang Zemin emerged as an unchallenged leader in the post-Deng power struggle. A secure and undivided top leadership was crucial for making hard reform decisions. (2) China's economy, having achieved a successful "soft landing", was heading for a new era of sustainable high growth with low inflation. Strong economic growth will generate more resources for the authorities to cope with the troubled SOEs. Specifically in the context of China, this also means that the non-state sector will continue to expand, thereby cushioning the adverse impact of the SOE reform. (3) Apart from a confident political leadership and strong economic fundamentals, Chinese reformers had more or less grasped the full technicality of their SOE reform problem, thanks to their bold experimentation on a wide front over the past few years.

Indeed, Jiang had been preparing the political and ideological ground for the new SOE reform strategy well ahead of the Fifteenth Party Congress. As noted earlier, it had been an ideological taboo in China to openly advocate "private ownership", which immediately evoked strong reaction from the conservative Party ideologues and sparked off the old debate on the relative virtues of socialism and capitalism — the so-called "Mr.

---

out of the total number of bankruptcy cases accredited, less than 2% (72 cases out of 6,232) were initiated by banks. (*Jingji Cankaobao*, Beijing , January 28, 1997.)

Socialist vs. Mr. Capitalist" debate. This explains why the past SOE reform strategy had deliberately avoided a direct attack on the "state ownership" issue by playing down the "privatization" aspects of the reform, so as not to cross such ideological off-limits. Jiang had to soften such ideological opposition beforehand. What Jiang did, in simple terms, was essentially to urge Chinese people to put aside futile debates over the "public vs. private ownership" by calling for "the third liberalization of thought",[15] and to remind his leftist critic that China was still in the transitional "primary stage of socialism", which would therefore warrant having "diverse forms of ownership to develop side by side" and "diverse economic sectors to develop side by side".[16] This implied flexibility in changing the ownership structure of SOEs, thus filling an important gap in the previous reform efforts, which encountered difficulty in coping with SOEs' weak internal incentive mechanism associated with ownership and controls.

Jiang's proposed reform package presented at the Fifteenth Party Congress was based on a multi-pronged approach. What was really new? China had not yet published the detailed SOE reform blueprint, which would probably be revealed at the next National People's Congress in early 1998. But judging from Jiang's Party Congress speech, there was actually not much that was new in terms of policy initiative, except for the principle of "diversification of public ownership", (which would facilitate SOEs to privatize parts of their operations and assets). In terms of actual implementation, the basic strategy was much like the *Zhuada Fangxiao*.

---

[15] In the weeks of run-up to the Party Congress, the Party's Propaganda Department had urged cadres to seriously study Jiang's speech on the "third liberalization of thought, based on seeking truth from facts", delivered at the Central Party School in May 1997. The "first liberalization" was advocated by Deng Xiaoping in 1978 calling for a more flexible interpretation of Mao's thoughts in order to prepare China for economic reform and the open-door policy. The second liberalization" was again advocated by Deng in 1992 during his "tour of South China", urging people to put behind the futile debate over "Socialism vs. Capitalism" so that China could move into a "socialist market economy". This time, Jiang, in calling for the "third liberalization", asked the Chinese people to forget about the debate on "public vs. private ownership", so that he can go ahead with his SOE reform plans. *Xinbao* (*Hong Kong Economic Journal*, August 15, 1997).

[16] Jiang Zemin's Report to the Fifteenth Party Congress on September 12, 1997 entitled "Hold High the Great Banner of Deng Xiaoping Theory for an All-round Advancement of the Cause of Building Socialism with Chinese Characteristics to the 21st Century".

For the large and medium SOEs, the reform was still on improving enterprise governance but the emphasis was on "corporatization" or transforming SOEs into independent modern corporations based on "scientific" (modern) management. In this regard, more than 500 SOEs were earmarked for corporatization and another 120 SOEs were formed into enterprise groups by 1997, and RMB 30 billion were set aside to recapitalize these firms. Thus, some merged, some broke up, some sought foreign partnership, and some sought listing on the stock exchanges in Shanghai, Shenzhen, Hong Kong and possibly, Singapore.

For the numerous smaller SOEs, the main reform strategy remained pretty much the same. But the government was much more willing to "let go", virtually allowing them to pick whichever way that best revitalized themselves — through restructuring and reorganization, mergers and takeovers, leasing and management contract, conversion into shareholding companies or just a sell-off. Since private ownership was no longer such an ideological minefield, certainly more SOEs were converted into shareholding companies at that time. It was also easier for firms to declare bankruptcy and be sold out, even to foreign partners.

These smaller SOEs were given more options and greater flexibility to choose their reform paths. Many of them were already engaged in potentially competitive activities that do not really need the presence of the state. The "dynamics" of the reform was more likely to be felt at the provincial and municipal SOEs than at the large ones controlled by the central government. At the same time, unlike those larger SOEs earmarked for priority government assistance in finance and technological upgrading, reform of smaller SOEs obviously experienced more drastic shake-up, and hence potentially more lay-offs and retrenchment of workers, either openly or disguised in the name of *Xiagang*. Jiang had already warned about such inevitability.

In the pre-Congress debate on the SOE reform, a lot of discussion had been focussed on the shareholding system (particularly the kind of "shareholding cooperatives"), which, technically speaking, is the Chinese form of "privatization in disguise". The shareholding scheme can address the crucial state ownership issue more effectively, i.e., without owning a stake in the enterprise, its workers and management do not have the inherent incentive to perform well. However, in Jiang's speech, the shareholding system was not singled out for special attention, probably because the authorities were yet to sort out the technicalities associated with large-scale promotion of the shareholding system, especially the "shareholding cooperatives".[17]

In summary, there were precious few real surprises in Jiang's new SOE reform package as presented at the recent Fifteenth Party Congress. Virtually, all the major proposed measures had either been tried out before or were already in practice. What was really new was the new political will on the part of China's top leadership along with declining social resistance to confront the SOE problem head on, which was conspicuously absent in the previous reform efforts.

Zhu Might Just Pull it Off

Jiang had adroitly used Deng's reform achievements ("Holding high the great banner of Deng Xiaoping Theory) to legitimize his new reform initiatives and allay possible public anxiety over future reform risks. Deng has been called the "architect of China's economic reform" for having initiated the reform process. Now Jiang was left to complete the rest, which was politically and technically more difficult to manage. Jiang handed the job to Zhu Rongji.

Zhu had to carefully calculate the ensuing risks and costs. The *Xia gang* problem was getting more widespread in the urban areas. Will Zhu still vigorously push ahead with more drastic restructuring and retrenchment of SOEs in the absence of an adequate social security system and a viable

---

[17] Many standard technical issues remained to be dealt with, e.g., how a shareholding company values its assets and how it will divide up the shares for allotment among the state or local government, the enterprise's own employees, and such legal entities as banks, pension funds, etc. At that time, the controversial issue was on whether or not each worker was allowed to vote as one shareholder regardless of the number of shares he holds, and how he can buy and sell his shares on the secondary market. Particularly for the "shareholding cooperative", some legal scholars had argued that it is "neither a horse nor a mule", as it displays a contradictory mixture of the capitalist element of shareholding along with the socialist element of a cooperative.

See, "Shareholding Cooperatives are in Urgent Need of Proper Legal Rulings", *Xinbao* (*Hong Kong Economic Journal*, August 30, 1997).

retraining programme?[18] According to China's Labour Ministry, 3.7 million workers would lose their jobs by the end of 1997 as a result of SOE reform, alongside with the annual new entrants to the labour force of about 14 million.[19] The total number of redundant workers in SOEs as estimated by the World Bank at that time was about 15 million, which could be a potentially explosive problem in terms of visible urban unemployment and the related high social security burdens.[20] Hence, a great challenge for Jiang.

Zhu was fortunate to have Deng's well-tried reform strategy as his guide. By avoiding the bureaucratic approach by issuing a highly structured reform programme with declared targets to fulfil, Zhu's reform strategy was basically in line with the old trial and error practice of "crossing the river by touching the stone". In other words, if the reform at any moment should run into strong resistance in some sectors or some areas, the reform process would simply slow down to avail itself of the next opportunity. Such was also Deng's adage of "Taking two steps forward and (if in trouble) one step back".

It was also in the nature of the Chinese past reform practice for the central government to provide only a clear mandate with broad guidelines.

---

[18] The "*Xia Gang*" phenomenon was in itself an innovative way by the Chinese government to grapple with unemployment pressures. Despite suffering from many flaws, laid-off SOE employees were still ensured a minimal level retrenchment benefits by their former employer until they were redeployed. As the SOE reform gained momentum, it was plausible to anticipate the emergence of a shrinking state sector, with concomitant expansion of the non-state sector and a robust tertiary industry. While the state concentrated on a few selected industry giants, the non-state sector (consisting of collectives, individuals and those with foreign investment) would gain importance in terms of its contribution to China's economic growth and job creation. Some cities such as Shanghai, Chongqing and municipals of Guangdong province have been quite successful in solving the problem of surplus workers. It was probably less problematic for regions with high foreign investment and a flourishing service sector which were channels of reemployment opportunities. In the case of Shanghai, its unemployment rate was controlled within 2 to 3%, with some 150,000 to 200,000 officially classified as "unemployed". In 1996, some 230,000 workers were made redundant but all of them were re-employed. In Chongqing, some 30% of its retrenched SOE employees were absorbed into the private sector in the last two years (Promising Re-employment Project", *Beijing Review*, August 1997.)

[19] *Dentusche Presse-Agentur*, September 22, 1997 (Dow Jones News/Retrieval.)

[20] A source had pointed out that the total number of laid-off workers resulting from SOE reforms would be 8 million by 2002, and their employment benefits would cost the state RMB160-billion.

See "Big Talk, Little Progress", *China Trade Report* (April 1996).

This was then picked up by local authorities to start reforming on their own initiative and in accordance with their specific local conditions. In this way, local governments created their own reform momentum. As to be expected, the more marketized coastal cities and coastal provinces would quickly seize the favourable reform climate and start their own innovative solution to the SOE problem. Overall, Jiang was fortunate to have with him the highly competent and determined Zhu Rongji as Premier, who was in charge of the implementation.

Specifically for implementation, Zhu Rongji had once declared that he could possibly "sort things out" in about three years. Zhu might have sounded a little too optimistic. He had probably reckoned that with the Chinese economy expecting to grow at an annual average rate of 8% up to 2010, the economic costs of the SOE reform could be easily absorbed. What was more needed for his reform efforts was continuing political and social consensus, which was steadily taking root. Looking forward, China might just be able to "fix" its SOE problem, perhaps not in a matter of a few years, but more likely in 10 years.

Given the current dominance of the state sector, in terms of physical, financial and human resources, and its social responsibilities and contribution to government revenue, it would certainly need a much longer time for the reform process to reap visible and real benefits for both the firms and the economy. China's SOEs at that time were plagued not merely by "hard problems", such as capital shortage and outdated technology and equipment, but also by a host of equally serious "soft problems", such as corruption, nepotism, and socialistic style of management and work habit, which could defy simple technocratic solutions. Furthermore, China would need to put in place a functioning legal framework. It would also take time for the reformed SOEs to learn to behave as competitive business units. Therefore, SOE reform is destined to be "a long drawn-out process."

8

BANKING REFORM AND FINANCIAL
LIBERALIZATION AS UNFINISHED BUSINESS

Introduction

Prior to 1978, when China's economy was under central planning, China operated a "monobank system", with the People's Bank of China (PBOC) functioning both as a central bank and a commercial bank. International business was handled by the Bank of China (BOC), which served as the foreign exchange arm of the PBOC. Under the mono-banking system, government and enterprise financing needs were fulfilled by the annual budget and annual credit plans, which regulated the direct allocation of financial resources. Government and enterprise transactions were reflected as book entries of the PBOC, which functioned much like the government's cashier. Under central planning, there was no need for financial intermediation, nor was there debt financing. Interest rates and money supply were fixed administratively in accordance with the state plan. Monetary policy was essentially an adjunct of the fiscal policy.

After 1979, with the start of market reform, the financing of enterprises began to shift from direct state allocation to loans, and a greater range of financial services was now required. First, in 1979 the Agricultural Bank of China (ABC), BOC, and the Construction Bank of China (CBC) were established as independent entities. Then, in 1984, the PBOC gradually developed its central bank function while its deposit-taking and lending functions were taken over by the then newly-created Industrial and Commercial Bank of China (ICBC). These four state commercial banks — the ICBC, ABC, BOC and CBC — have since been the main pillar of China's banking system.

Deng Xiaoping's Nanxun in 1992 sparked off a new economic reform momentum towards a "socialist market economy". As many new economic reform initiatives were undertaken, the need also arose for China to develop a modern and more market-oriented banking sector, not only to facilitate the financial sector development but also for the proper operation of its monetary policy. In 1994, Zhu Rongji introduced a comprehensive economic reform programme, which was remarkably successful in several areas, such as the reform of foreign exchange and taxation systems. Banking reform was also high on the agenda.

However, progress in respect of state-owned enterprise (SOE) reform throughout the 1990s had been slow and tardy because of many real political and social obstacles (e.g., shutting down some inefficient state enterprises and retrenching redundant labour in the absence of an adequate social safety net). SOE reform and banking reform were actually interrelated, and their reform basically involved exposing them increasingly to the working of market forces. Without significant breakthrough in the SOE reform, banking reform through the 1990s had also fallen short of its targets, bearing in mind that the many state banks were themselves out and out SOEs.

Zhu was an open-minded but also pragmatic Premier. Despite official rhetoric, he would only proceed with banking reform and financial liberalization slowly and cautiously. Thus, his efforts in the financial sector reform included making the exchange rate more flexible, expanding the interbank money supply, streamlining the bond and stock markets, opening the banking sector to more competition, and liberalizing interest rates.

Still, with a strong central planning mindset, Zhu would need to keep a tight rein on the banking sector as part of his macroeconomic control apparatus, particularly since the Chinese economy was facing high inflationary pressures through most of the 1990s. He would never let go the state control of the banking sector and the financial system. He would listen to important market signals, but would not let interest rate be completely guided by the market. In this way, the state could regulate the money supply directly to control inflation. Externally, he had also tightly managed the exchange rates of the Renminbi as well as the capital account. Both would insulate China's financial sector from international financial instability.

In retrospect, Zhu's success in restoring domestic macroeconomic stability and his steadfast belief in maintaining the stability of the Renminbi exchange *rate as well as tight capital controls had paid off during the 1997 Asian financial crisis. China's economy, alone in the region, was not directly affected by this regional financial crisis, which had ravaged many economies in the region.*

Subsequently, as Zhu was preparing China for the World Trade Organization (WTO) membership, he had to deepen banking reform and further open up China's financial sector in line with such international requirements. Again, Zhu's approach was cautious. Officially, all state banks were supposed to be commercialized, but they remained state-owned, operating with a lot of monopoly power rather than in accordance with market competition. In 1996, the government started with the gradual liberalization of interest rates. By 2013, interest rates had not been completely freed up.

Basically, China's financial system is still typically akin to what American economists Edward Shaw and Ronald Mckinnon called "financial repression". Among 20 or so China's large banks today, except for a few like Ping An Bank and Minsheng Bank, they are all state-owned banks. Interest rates for deposits are capped while other interest rates including bond yields money market rates and banking lending rates are mostly determined by market forces. The resulting spread between loans and deposits has created huge profits for the state banks, which will in turn channel the funds back to the government or certain SOEs. All these naturally go against the efficient allocation of capital.

Similarly for the exchange rates, which have not yet been floated in accordance with market forces. The Renminbi in recent years has also been rapidly and extensively internationalized, but its capital-account convertibility is still tightly controlled. The government has apparently taken the view that any abrupt, as opposed to gradual, liberalization of capital controls could open the floodgates to uncontrolled capital movements and expose the economy to the volatility of the international financial markets, which could in turn create pro-cyclical financial shocks.

Such are the conservative banking and financial reform policies that can partly be attributed to Zhu's legacies of sticking to a highly cautious approach to the financial sector reform. It suffices to say that the Chinese leadership had all along approached reform in all areas gradually and slowly. Stability was the utmost priority in all reform policies. As such, efficiency comes second. But for this, China had to suffer the loss of efficiency in terms of misallocation of financial resources. More seriously, on account of its failure to complete the thorough-going market reform, China's banking system had to from time to time deal with the problem of debts and non-performing loans, which became very serious on the eve of China's accession to the WTO.

It may be further added that today, over a decade later after undergoing various market reforms, China's banking system still has to face the problem of local government debt and shadow banking problems. This explains why Xi Jinping and Li Keqiang have recently called for a new round of reform with the market playing a "decisive" role, as opposed to the hitherto "basic role". To further deepen and broaden the financial sector reform, the government in September 2013 established the China (Shanghai) Pilot Free Trade Zone. In short, almost two decades later, banking reform and financial liberalization have remained as the unfinished business!

Viewed from a different angle, China's banking sector, though still largely regulated, has since grown and developed by leaps and bounds, along with the rapid growth of China's economy. In 2000, China counted only 104 commercial banks plus three state policy banks. By 2012, China had 2,617 banks, in addition to a large number of non-bank financial institutions. Domestically, the four state commercial banks: ICBC, CBC, ABC and BOC have remained the pillars of the China's banking system. Internationally, these "Big Four" have all become the world's 10 largest banks by assets and by capitalization, with the ICBC being the world's No. 1. Chinese banks had not been affected by the 1997 Asian financial crisis, or by the 2008 global financial crisis. Both events had brought many banks and financial houses in other countries to grief.

In 2000, there were only 163 foreign bank branches in China. As a sign of China's growing financial internationalization, the total number of foreign bank branches in China increased to 412 in 2012, with about 10% of them having been locally incorporated. China is set to further step up its regulatory reforms. This, along with the rapid internationalization of the Renminbi, would also internationalize China's banking and financial sector.

Reform and Growth

The main thrust of the banking reform in 1994 was directed to (1) setting up a strong and independent central bank, with the primary responsibility of maintaining monetary and exchange rate stability, and (2) commercializing the banking system in which the state-owned specialized banks would operate on a commercial basis, leaving unprofitable "policy lending" to the three newly-created "policy banks": the State Development Bank of China, the Agricultural Development Bank of China and the China Import and Export Bank. This sparked off the process of transforming the four state banks into commercial banks. In 1995, China enacted the Central Banking Law to confirm the status of the PBOC as the central bank of China. This was shortly followed by the promulgation of the Commercial Bank Law, the Negotiable Instrument Law and the Insurance Law, which together provided the rudimentary legal framework for financial supervision and the proper functioning of the financial sector.

In the meanwhile, competition had been gradually introduced into the banking system, and increased competition had in turn stepped up China's financial sector development. Broadly speaking, this was done in several ways. To begin with, the division of business among the four state banks was at first quite blurred. The four state banks were established originally for different business areas and they were not allowed to compete head on with each other. For example, foreign exchange business was once monopolized by the BOC. Subsequently, however, the other three state banks, along with the newly-established banks, and trust and investment companies (TICs), have since been permitted to conduct foreign exchange business. The increased competition thus reduced the foreign exchange business share of BOC from virtually 100% in 1979 to about 40% by 1996.

Since the mid-1980s, many banks and TICs have been established, starting with the setting up of the China International Trust and Investment Corporation (CITIC) Industrial Bank. Other new national banks include the Bank of Communications, the Everbright Bank, the Huaxia Bank and the Minsheng Bank (China's first non-state-owned bank). Large regional banks include the Guangdong Development Bank, the Shenzhen Development Bank, the Merchants Bank, the Fujian Industrial Bank, the Shanghai Pudong Development Bank, the Yantai Housing Savings Bank, the Bengbu Housing Savings Bank and the Hainan Development Bank. The entry of new financial institutions had thus created a more level playing field for all financial institutions, both state and non-state.

Furthermore, some regional banks had over the years expanded rapidly beyond their original regional characteristics. The Shenzhen-based Merchants Bank and Shanghai Pudong Development Bank, for example, established branches outside Shenzhen and Shanghai, respectively. Many urban cooperatives had also been converted into urban cooperative banks. Of greater significance, banks had started to become more consumer-oriented, offering consumer loans for automobile hire purchases and mortgages for state-owned housing schemes. The big state banks had taken steps to promote e-banking. In particular, the ICBC (China's largest commercial bank with 8.1 million enterprise accounts) had started to spread its online banking business to enterprises throughout China, and soon started online personal banking.

Above all, the banking sector had been gradually opened up to foreign banks. Initially, in the 1980s, a few foreign financial institutions were allowed to set up branches only in the Special Economic Zones. In 1990, Shanghai became the first coastal city to open to foreign banks. In 1996, several foreign banks in Shanghai were granted licenses to conduct *Renminbi* business on a limited basis. In 1998, more such licenses were issued. In 1999, both operational and geographical restrictions were further relaxed, so as to allow foreign banks to engage in domestic currency business in more cities and more provinces.

As a result of the gradual process of reform, along with the dynamic growth of China's economy and foreign trade, China's financial sector had experienced remarkable growth in the 1990s. By the end of 1999, China indeed boasted a fairly comprehensive banking and financial structure. It consisted of 4 wholly state-owned commercial banks, 3 policy banks, 10 joint-equity commercial banks, 90 city commercial banks, 836 urban credit cooperatives, 41,755 rural credit cooperatives, 230 (previously, 240) trust and investment corporations, 70 finance companies, and 15 leasing companies (Figure 1).

Figure 2 shows the assets distribution of China's banks and credit cooperatives. It can be seen that by the end of 1999, the four state banks accounted for 67% of the total banking assets while the three policy banks, 10%. Figure 3 is for their loan distribution, which shows that 65% of the total loans in 1999 came from the "big four" and 14% from the three policy banks.

As for foreign participation, at the end of 1999, there were altogether 177 foreign banking institutions operating in 23 cities and Hainan province. This included 157 foreign bank branches, 13 locally incorporated banks (6 foreign owned and 7 joint ventures) and 7 foreign finance companies

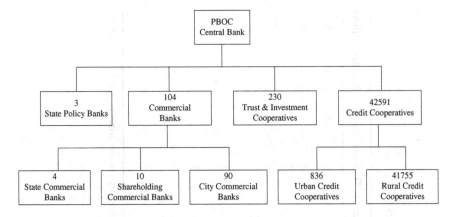

Figure 1. China's banking system, 2000.

Source: The People's Bank of China, *2000 China Financial Outlook*, Beijing.

(Table 1). The number of foreign banks allowed to conduct *Renminbi* business had reached 25 — 19 in Shanghai and 6 in Shenzhen. In addition, there were 248 representative offices of foreign banks in various cities of China.

At that time, foreign banks in China were playing only a modest role. Their total assets in 1999 amounted to only US$32 billion, or 1.5% of China's total financial assets. Their foreign currency loans amounted to US$22 billion, accounting for 12.8% of the total foreign exchange loans in China. The *Renminbi* business of foreign banks was even more limited: their *Renminbi* assets in 1999 totalled only 11 billion yuan, loans at 7 billion yuan, and deposits at 5 billion yuan.[1]

Impact of the Asian Financial Crisis

China was the one economy in the region which had been left basically unaffected by the 1997 Asian financial crisis. As the Asian currencies were plummeting one after another, Chinese *Renminbi* had stood its ground, despite repeated rumours by international speculators and fund managers about its imminent devaluation. At the height of the crisis, Premier Zhu Rongji had declared to the world that China would stand fast over the

---

[1] The People's Bank of China, *2000: China Financial Outlook* (Beijing, 2000).

Table 1.   Foreign bank branches in China, 2000.

	Total	Japan	HK	UK	France	USA	Singapore	Germany	South Korea	Netherlands	Thailand	Canada	Belgium	Others
Total	163	29	28	19	17	14	12	8	8	8	5	4	3	8
Shanghai	51	10	4	4	5	5	5	5	2	4	1			
Shenzhen	24	3	9	2	3	1	1	1		2	1		1	5
Beijing	18	3	1	2	1	4	1	1	1	1		1	1	
Guangzhou	15	1	3	1	3	2	1	1				2	1	2
Tianjin	14	3		2	3	1			4					
Dalian	10	6	2	1					1					
Xiamen	10		2	2	1	1	2			1	1			
Qingdao	3	1	1	1	1									
Shantou	3		2								1			
Zhuhai	3	1		1										1
Haikou	2		1	1										
Wuhan	2			1			1					1		
Others	8	2	2	1					1		1			

Note: In addition, there were other operational foreign institutions in China: seven joint ventures, six foreign banks and seven foreign finance companies.

Source: The People's Bank of China, *2000 China Financial Outlook*, Beijing.

☑ State-Owned Commercial Banks
☒ Policy Banks
☐ Joint-Equity Commercial Banks
☐ City Commercial Banks
■ Prefecture-Level Urban Credit Cooperatives
☐ Rural Credit Cooperatives

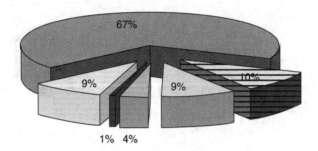

Figure 2.   Assets distribution of China's banks and credit cooperatives in 1999 (%). (Total assets: 15.49 trillion yuan.)

Source: The People's Bank of China, *2000 China Financial Outlook*, Beijing.

exchange stability of the *Renminbi*. China's efforts during the regional currency crisis had won the praise of many Asian governments. In the words of US Treasury Secretary Robert Rubin, China "has been an important island of stability in a turbulent region".[2]

In retrospect, it is actually quite easy to explain why China had successfully staved off the regional financial crisis. The Chinese economy in 1997, having gone through a three-year austerity drive, had just achieved a successful "soft-landing". Its macroeconomic fundamentals were far stronger than Asian economies in terms of higher growth and lower inflation. Essentially, what had made China different from those crisis-ridden Asian economies was China's healthy and stable external economic position. On account of its strong export performance and rising trade surplus, China did not have current account deficits. It had also been highly successful in attracting foreign direct investment so that its external debt was relatively small (US$124 billion in 1997, basically long-term loans),

---

[2]"Remarks for Opening Plenary, China–US Joint Economic Committee — Eleventh Session", May 26, 1998 (USIA, Washington, DC).

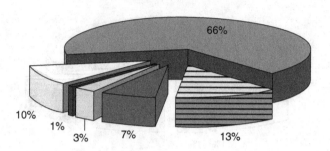

□ State-Owned Commercial Banks
◨ Policy Banks
▨ Joint-Equity Commercial Banks
□ City Commercial Banks
▪ Prefecture-Level Urban Credit Cooperatives
□ Rural Credit Cooperatives

Figure 3.   Loan distribution of China's banks and credit cooperatives in 1999 (%). (Total loan: 9.49 trillion yuan.)

Source: The People's Bank of China, *2000 China Financial Outlook*, Beijing.

especially in terms of its exports (US$180 billion in 1997) and its existing foreign reserves (US$140 in 1997). Clearly, China had not over-borrowed as Thailand or South Korea had.[3]

However, what had rendered China largely immune to the regional financial crisis was mainly due to the high degree of government intervention in the financial system because of capital controls.[4] In December 1996, China accepted International Monetary Fund's (IMF) Article VIII to allow free transfers for only current account transactions. But the *Renminbi* was not easily convertible for capital transactions. China's equity market was also small, and foreign investors were effectively segmented off in the US and HK dollar-denominated "B shares" market. In other words, because of such tight capital account control, it was not possible for international currency speculators to "sell short" on the *Renminbi* outside China, because

---

[3] See John Wong, "China's Economy in 1998: Maintaining Growth and Staving off the Asian Contagion", *EAI Occasional Paper No. 15*, World Scientific and Singapore University Press, 1999.

[4] For a detailed discussion of the impact of capital controls on the Asian financial crisis, see IMF, *Country Experiences with the Use and Liberalization of Capital Controls* (2000).

they just could not deliver the currency. Nor was it possible for outside panic to spark off a massive capital flight from China.

Though China had successfully warded off the regional financial crisis, China still could not escape from its many side-effects. China's economic growth slowed from 8.9% for 1997 to 7.1% for 1999. Furthermore, the regional financial crisis has set back China's original plans for full exchange convertibility by 2000.

Actually, China's capital controls were not really very water-tight, as the mechanism did not entirely block capital flight during the crisis years. Officially, capital flight could be hidden in the large "net errors and omissions" in China's balance of payments account, which amounted to US$48 billion for the three years 1997–1999. It could also be done by false invoicing of fake imports. According to a study by Peking University, total capital flight during 1997–1999 was estimated to be a staggering US$98 billion, because of smuggling, corruption and government inefficiency in the foreign exchange administration.[5] So China did pay a toll for having survived the regional financial crisis.

On the other hand, the regional financial crisis had also prompted the Chinese government to take several positive measures to strengthen its banking sector. This included restructuring the central bank along the lines of the US Federal Reserves system by merging PBOC's 31 provincial branches into 9 regional branches, and increasing the capital adequacy ratio of the "big four" with a view to meeting the Basle standard of 8%.[6] China had certainly taken some positive steps towards better banking supervision and greater financial prudence.[7]

When the Guangdong International Trust and Investment Corporation (GITIC) got into trouble, regulators in Beijing surprised foreign observers by taking prompt and drastic action to shut it down in October 1998, along with Guangzhou's GZITIC.[8] In fact, prior to the GITIC closure, the government had taken steps to liquidate the Hainan Development Bank

---

[5] "Capital Flight Worries Ease", *South China Morning Post*, July 12, 2000.
[6] The average capital adequacy ratio of the "big four" in 1999 was about 5–6%. It was 8% for the Bank of China, but only 5.4% for the Construction Bank. See "Beijing Presses for Better Capital-Adequacy Ratios", *South China Morning Post*, August 3, 2000.
[7] "China's Central Bank Tightens Oversight", *Asian Wall Street Journal*, November 17, 1998.
[8] *Business Times* (Singapore), October 30, 1998.

(June 1998) and two TICs. Subsequently, 21 urban credit cooperatives and 18 rural credit cooperatives were also closed as part of the government efforts to prevent contagion and maintain public confidence in the financial system.[9] In August 2000, the debt-ridden "ITIC," China Education, Science and Technology Trust and Investment Corporation (CESTTIC), was closed down.[10]

Need to Deepen Reform and Broaden Liberalization

Though China had fended off the Asian financial crisis, it still needed to continue with its banking sector reform, for several obvious reasons. First, as a result of the rapid expansion of China's banking sector, various problems and risks, especially in connection with the four state commercial banks, had cropped up. Some of these problems were new while others were systemic in nature. But they all needed to be addressed without delay. Secondly, banking reform was at the heart of China's remaining economic reform endeavour, particularly in respect to the crucial SOE reform, as mentioned earlier. Thirdly, as China's accession to the WTO was imminent, China had to urgently build up a modern financial architecture in preparation for the further opening-up of its financial markets as required by the WTO.

The starting point for reforming China's banking sector was to restructure the four state commercial banks. Prior to the 1994 reform, these "big four" were not run as truly commercial banks. They inherited a bureaucratic management style whereby, much like other industrial SOEs, bank branches were under the dual leadership of the bank headquarters and the local government. The banks were pressurized to make loans to loss-making SOEs, not based purely on commercial principles. Although such pressures had been reduced with the establishment of the three policy banks that were responsible for making policy loans, the "big four" were still occasionally pushed by the government to make unprofitable loans.

There was also a lack of proper incentive structure that rewards good performances and penalizes laggards. The management of the banks and their branches were mostly political appointees (i.e., the Party cadres) who

---

[9] *2000: China Financial Outlook.*
[10] "ITICs Face Shakeup", *China Daily*, August 8, 2000.

were not held directly responsible for the banks' commercial performance. Although the banks were all over-staffed, there was an acute shortage of well-trained professional staff. In short, the state commercial banks were no different from their cousins in the SOEs of the industrial sector. They all shared the common problems that had long plagued China's SOEs, such as weak internal control and poor discipline, low profitability, excessive employment, outdated technology and low product quality. For financial institutions, these problems would manifest themselves in their high non-performing loan ratio and poor assets quality.

Coping with non-performing loans

Indeed, the most pressing problem of China's banking sector at the time was how to deal with its non-performing loans (NPLs). There was considerable disagreement among experts over the exact proportion of bad loans that had been incurred over the years by the "big four". Some foreign experts believed that as much as 40% of China's total bank loans could be NPLs.[11] Official estimates from China, however, were much lower. The PBOC disclosed that "problem loans" in 1997 stood at 1.5 trillion yuan (US$180 billion), or 20–25% of the total bank loans. Of the "problem loans", a third was bad debts. This means that total NPLs accounted for about 8–9% of the total loans of the commercial banks.[12]

The difference in the estimation arises at least in part from the fact that China's loan classification scheme was far more lax than the common international standard. China's scheme was based on payment status of outstanding loans rather than on risk assessment; it was also based on repayment of principal rather than interest.[13] Indeed, as China gradually adopted international standards for banking supervision, particularly those required by the Basle Committee, the non-performing loan problem was bound to loom much greater than what is officially recognized.

---

[11] For example, James Dorn, an American economist, claimed that as much as 40% of all bank loans in China and that the four large state commercial banks were close to or at the stage of insolvency. See, "China's Financial Future", by James Dorn, *ChinaOnline* (http://www.chinaonline.com/commentary_analysis/ c909136e.asp).

[12] *China Overseas News Agency*, January 20, 2000.

[13] For a more detailed discussion, see Nicholas Lardy, *China's Unfinished Economic Revolution*, The Brookings Institution Press, 1998.

To recover NPLs that these four banks had made to loss-making SOEs in the past years, China in 1999 set up four Asset Management Companies (AMCs): Cinda, Huarong, Great Wall and Oriental, each with paid-in capital of 10 billion yuan provided by the Ministry of Finance. According to the so-called debt-to-equity swap scheme, the AMCs would purchase the problem loans of their respective banks in exchange for a stake in the debtor firms. The plan was for the AMCs to take control of debtor companies and initiate business restructuring. Eventually, the AMCs would hope to sell their shares either to domestic or foreign investors in order to repay the state commercial banks. The government's objective was to recover about 30% of the NPLs within 10 years.[14]

By the end of 1999, 73 enterprises had signed debt-to-equity agreements with the China Development Bank and the four AMCs, amounting to 95 billion yuan.[15] However, their implementation had been slow. There were three reasons for the delay. First, the AMCs and banks had failed to reach an exit agreement. The AMCs insisted on having the option of returning unsold equity shares to the original firm. Secondly, the two sides were divided over the issue of asset valuation and over the extent of control of the indebted firms by the AMCs after the swap. Thirdly, restructuring would inevitably result in drastic asset stripping and then more layoffs, which the government (especially at the local level) and the management were against. Despite these unsettled issues, the government was determined to proceed with the programme. It was seen as a major step towards revitalizing SOEs as well as improving the balance sheets of the state commercial banks. Indeed, the State Economic and Trade Commission had recommended more than 600 SOEs as possible candidates for debt-to-equity swaps.

Many economists, however, were still sceptical about the effectiveness of the debt-to-equity swap scheme. The first concern was that it appeared as merely an accounting gimmick, bringing about no substantial changes. In theory, the swaps would benefit both SOEs, by reducing their interest payment burdens, and the state commercial banks, by removing their NPLs

---

[14]"Mixed Views on Loan Recovery Bid", South *China Morning Post*, July 10, 2000.

[15]*2000: China Financial Outlook*. See also, "Debt-Equity Can Mean Debt Amnesty in China, Expert", *ChinaOnline*, January 6, 2000. The four state commercial banks had transferred 350 billion yuan in problem loans to the AMCs by the end of 1999. See, "Dai Xianglong: China's Commercial Banks Should Write off 9% of Loans", *ChinaOnline*, January 24, 2000.

at one stroke. In reality, the huge amount of NPLs was just transferred to the AMCs as a book entry. If no fundamental changes were subsequently introduced into the reforming state commercial banks and the involved SOEs, the scheme virtually amounted to a debt amnesty. It might even create a kind of moral hazard by encouraging debt repudiation on the part of debtor companies and hence undermine the credit culture. In the end, the state could be left with an even bigger bill to foot.

True, as noted earlier, the idea behind the debt-to-equity scheme was for the AMCs to force the SOEs to go through a painful revamp. This gave rise to the second concern: Were the AMCs in a position to enforce such restructuring? How would AMCs turn around ailing SOEs? It should be remembered that the AMCs were themselves also state-owned and therefore subject to similar sets of economic and political constraints as faced by many SOEs. This means that factors (such as redundancy layoffs) that had been holding back SOE reforms were also likely to bear down on the reform initiatives proposed by AMCs. This, in fact, was the underlying reason as to why the swap scheme had not met with conspicuous success.

It suffices to say that the debt-to-equity swap scheme offered little in way of reforming China's SOEs. But it seemed a necessary first step to reform state commercial banks. It allowed the state banks to unload their NPLs and start lending again. But before this, the banks had to be adequately recapitalized. Between them, the four state commercial banks eventually had to write off some 1.7 to 2 trillion yuan or 20–25% of their total loans. This was a huge but still manageable sum. China's debt to GDP ratio was about 20%, relatively low by international standards. There was room for government debt-financed recapitalization. In 1998, the government issued 270 billion yuan worth of special bond earmarked for recapitalizing the four state commercial banks. However, still more capital was needed to be injected for them to meet the 8% capital adequacy requirement.[16]

Recapitalizing the state banks was one thing, while preventing new NPLs from forming was quite another. Thus, the equally important second step was for banks to adopt modern bank management practices and for the government to set up a prudent supervision system. Progress was made

---

[16] For further discussion, see Liu Zhiqiang, "Progress in China's Banking Sector Reform", *EAI Background Brief No. 62*, May 9, 2000.

in these areas during that period. For instance, in 1999, China adopted a new asset classification system, under which loans were classified into five categories: pass, special mention, substandard doubtful and loss. Compared with the old loan classification scheme based on the repayment of principal, the new system reflected more accurately the level of real risks for the bank loans. This enabled banks to improve their asset management on the one hand, and the government to better monitor bank operations on the other. Now, the four state commercial banks were required to publish their balance sheet and the ratio of non-performing loans on a quarterly basis.

Finally, it may be pointed out that some NPLs were not only the outcome of bad economics or mismanagement but also bad politics. It was well known that some bad loans in China were simply corruption cases, which involved the illegal siphoning off of state assets to individuals. It was therefore not easy for the government to clean up all the NPLs in the short run. PBOC governor Dai Xianglong had stated that his immediate aim was to limit the proportion of NPLs of the state commercial banks to 20%.[17] (This topic will be discussed in greater detail in the following chapter.)

Facing the WTO challenge

With the passing of the "China Trade Bill" by the US Congress on May 25, 2000, China's accession to the WTO had become a foregone conclusion. The WTO membership would commit China to opening-up its economy further to foreign participation and greater international competition. Hence, China was under increasing pressures to put its financial house in order by stepping up reform and liberalization.

Dai Xianglong had outlined the steps China would take towards financial liberalization in preparation for its entry to WTO. This included (1) putting forward the agenda of capital account convertibility for the *Renminbi*, initially by improving the managed float of the exchange rate regime, (2) liberalizing domestic interest rates, first for money market rates and then for loan interest rates, and (3) encouraging the state commercial banks to seek listing on the stock market, i.e., moving towards privatization.

---

[17] *Mingpao* (Hong Kong, July 20, 2000).

For foreign financial institutions, restrictions would gradually be removed so that foreign banks could eventually enjoy resident status.[18]

According to the SINO-US Trade Accord signed in November 1999, US banks were allowed to conduct local currency business with Chinese companies (i.e., corporate banking) two years after China's accession to the WTO, and with Chinese individuals (i.e., retail banking) five years after accession. China had also undertaken to lift geographic restrictions on US banks five years after the accession.[19] Hence, there was an urgency for China's banking sector to overhaul itself.

Needless to say, foreign banks were generally more vibrant and more competitive than China's commercial banks. Foreign banks conducted business according to international rules and were free from government intervention, unlike their Chinese counterparts. Some foreign banks were also much bigger and with better-trained staff, more adequate capital and wider business scope. They also used more advanced technology and management system, and, above all, longer experience operating in the international financial markets. By comparison, domestic banks were generally weak in all these areas. Thus, there were considerable opportunities for foreign banks in China, particularly for consumer banking.

However, for the foreseeable future, foreign banks should not expect plain sailing for the China business because of the residual restrictions and the absence of a level playing field.[20] First, domestic banks would always enjoy home ground advantage, with extensive banking networks that had taken years to build, particularly for the established state banks like ICBC. Secondly, Chinese state banks had five years after WTO to gear up to foreign competition. The five-year grace period might still not be long enough for China to upgrade all its banks on a par with world-class

---

[18]"Banking System Reforms Continue", *China Daily*, June 16, 2000; and "Banks Told to go Public", *China Daily*, July 20, 2000. But Dai Xianglong said that China had not set a specific timetable for the free trading of its currency and that restrictions on *Renminbi* would be gradually eased over the next five years.

[19]For discussions about the potential impact of the WTO membership on the Chinese economy, see John Wong, "The Sino-US Trade Accord (I): Implications", *EAI Background Brief No. 49*, 1999; and Mai Yinhua, and Luo Qi, "The Sino-US Trade Accord (II): Analyses", *EAI Background Brief No. 50*, 1999.

[20]"Beijing Blocks the Banks", *Asian Wall Street Journal*, July 20, 2000.

banks. But this should be sufficient time for domestic banks to improve their competitiveness through such measures as merger or forming strategic alliance. The Bank of Communications and the BOC had already taken this move, and more would follow. More importantly, Chinese state banks had at that time stepped up their structural reform to pave the way for their public listing, possibly within three years.[21] That no doubt strengthened the competitiveness of Chinese banks.

It was certain that the entry of foreign banks would raise the demand for local talents in banking and finance. In the short run, foreign banks would pluck better-trained bank staff and managerial personnel from local banks by offering higher pay, and thus further aggravated the staffing problem in local banks. Such poaching of local talents by foreign banks has occurred in many developing countries in their early stages of opening up to foreign financial institutions. But over time, a lot of local talent, having acquired the experience, would flow back to local institutions. Viewed in this way, the presence of foreign competition was actually conducive to the long-term human resource development of China's banking sector.

Ultimately, how China faced WTO challenges depended in large part on its success in the SOE reform and in overhauling its banking system — the two being closely interrelated. A great deal of progress had been made, but much more was still needed to be done. The WTO membership might provide both the government and the banks just the needed impetus to speed up the whole reform process. The final outcome would then be a win–win situation.

---

[21]"State Banks to go Public", *China Daily*, August 7, 2000.

9

A LOOMING DEBT CRISIS
FOR THE STATE BANKS

Introduction

As discussed in early chapters, one of Zhu Rongji's major achievements in domestic economic policy were his determination to reform the country's state-owned enterprises (SOEs) and the related issue of financial sector reform. Thanks to his strong political will to undertake the reform task, he had achieved some significant breakthroughs. But at the same time, it had soon come to light that the SOE reform was not a one-off solution. SOEs were just part and parcel of the country's operating political and social systems, and the SOE problem had therefore remained as an unfinished business of economic reform that is actually lasting to these days.

This is particularly so for the state banks. During the last years of Zhu's premiership, the state banks had accumulated a lot of non-performing loans (NPLs) that threatened to bring down the banking system. A looming banking crisis was flying in the face of Zhu as he was preparing China for accession into the World Trade Organization (WTO). The problem, if remained unresolved, would not only blemish Zhu's past achievements but also increase risk to China's efforts of opening up the financial sector after the WTO.

Nobody in 2001 really knew the exact level of China's NPLs, which ranged variously from the official estimate of 24% of total loans to Moody's estimate of 40% of China's GDP and Standard & Poor's 50%. If the official figure were re-classified based on the internationally accepted criteria and by including the bad assets that had been transferred to the four Asset Management Companies (AMCs) for disposal, total NPL level would be close to Moody's estimate of 40%.

217

In quantitative terms, the NPLs in the whole banking system would amount to a staggering US$500 billion, or slightly over 40% of China's existing GDP, which was close to the level of Thailand on the eve of the 1997 Asian financial crisis, bearing in mind that this crisis first broke out in Thailand in mid-1997. Hence, a sufficiently serious situation for China at that time.

It should be stressed that this was not China's first debt crisis since it started the market reform in 1978. Nor was it China's last. Under central planning, all state enterprises received their working capital directly from the state's budgetary appropriation. With market reform, state enterprises would have to depend on loans from state banks for their working capital. This gave rise to an informal credit system, which was not strictly regulated. China's Bankruptcy Law was legislated in 1986 and officially became effective in 1988. But this economic law was hardly used even through the 1990s, simply because all the players involved, from creditors to debtors, were state entities.

There were obvious systemic risks from such a pattern of credit relationship. To begin with, all SOEs are explicitly or implicitly operating on a soft budget constraint, without any need to worry about their financial bottom-line for any of their commercial endeavour. They all tend to be highly leveraged, invariably ending up with high debt-asset ratios. State-owned banks on the other side of the spectrum similarly have also poor market discipline as well as weak risk aversion orientation, often giving out credit not on the basis of proper risk management guidelines. Worst still, the financial costs of any reorganization or reform of SOEs would invariably shift to the state banks. Hence, all state banks are debt prone.

As it had happened through most of the 1980s and the 1990s, whenever the government started to tighten credit, most enterprises would face a credit crunch, with many being caught in a debt chain that was commonly known as "triangular debt". The situation arises when one state enterprise would forestall meeting their payables on the excuse of lacking cash due to unpaid receivables from another state enterprise. Even those enterprises with adequate financial resources would sometimes choose not to pay their bills in favour of other demands on their capital, e.g., financing business expansion. Such is the culture of delay, if not default, that was quite common. Creditors basically had no effective recourse, simply because all parties are in one way or another related to the state.

It suffices to say that the phenomenon of the "triangular debt" became more acute in the late 1980s and again in the early and later parts of the 1990s, mostly at times of economic downturn. The debt problem in the early 1990s was absorbed by the economic boom in the mid-1990s. But Zhu's efforts in reforming SOEs towards the end of the 1990s had in some ways aggravated the debt situation of the state banks. This is because the closing down of some SOEs or their reorganization had actually brought the hidden debt into the open or simply transferred their liabilities to the state banks. In this way, the enterprise debt crisis eventually ended up as a potential banking crisis.

Furthermore, as it has turned out, the 2002 debt crisis was not China's last one. Today, some 15 years later, unbeknown to anyone then, China's economy is once again gripped by a serious debt crisis. In response to the external shock of the global financial crisis in 2008 that brought down China's economic growth, Premier Wen Jiabao hastily put up a huge stimulus package of 4 trillion yuan to pump-prime the economy. The fiscal stimulus, in shoring up economic growth, had led to excessive credit expansion (officially called "total social financing") in the following few years. This, in turn, led to an explosion of local government debts and the rapid expansion of banks' off-balance sheet commonly known as "shadow banking".

China's total debt in mid-2015, combining government, household and enterprise, stood at about 230% of its GDP. Such a debt-GDP ratio is historically the highest for China but still lower than that of Japan and USA, or just comparable to many other countries. The total bad loans or NPLs of China's 10 largest state banks had indeed increased a lot since 2008. However, the NPLs as a ratio to total loans in all China big banks still accounted for just a little over 1%. Officially, the financial situation of all China's big banks, as appeared on their books, is sound. In fact, China's banks are also well capitalized and they are making good profits every year, with its biggest bank, the ICBC, being also the world's biggest bank in terms of total assets.

What is the most serious for China's state banks is that their NPL problem is disguised in their "off-balance sheet" as part of the so-called "shadow banking", which comprised mainly wealth-management products and trust companies. In 2014, the size of such shadow banking was estimated to be about 70% of GDP. Not all of the shadow banking activities would end up as NPLs, but they are mostly unregulated lending and they are therefore potentially highly risky, particularly at the time when China's economic growth has slowed down.

In short, China has experienced three waves of debt crisis over the past three decades since the start of its market reform. All the three debt crises share a great deal of structural similarities. They seem to be repeatable, and hence also an endemic problem for China's financial sector. Why is this so?

As it is already quite obvious from the foregoing discussion, we can simply summarize the explanations into two categories. First, the institutional source of China's debt crisis has been very much associated with its socialist legacies and the working of a transitional or a half-reformed economy in which too many actors from creditors to debtors are connected with the state sector, with their activities and behaviour being not fully in line with proper market behaviour. Secondly and the structural cause of the frequent occurrence of debt is the fact that China's economic growth is mainly investment-driven, with most economic activities basically financed by bank loans and credit emanating from the state. Hence, the debt problem would come to the fore once the government starts squeezing credit and liquidity.

Viewed from a different angle, China's debt crises, past and present, are all manageable, unlikely to blow up as a Thailand-type of financial crisis in 1997. This is because China's debt is basically borrowing from itself as in Japan, much like a domestic affair, in sharp contrast to many European countries like Greece and Portugal where 80% of the debt were borrowings from foreigners. And China's debt was mostly incurred for investment and production purposes, not for consumption. More importantly, China debt crises had all along been cushioned by strong macroeconomic fundamentals, i.e., China's high domestic savings, relatively small external debt, a consistent current account surplus as well as its huge foreign exchange reserves.

Therefore, any potential banking crisis in China would have to be domestically generated. But this seems most unlikely, then and now, as most bank loans came from huge domestic savings deposits (some US$1.2 trillion in 2001, surpassing China's total GDP) with state banks, which enjoyed blanket government guarantee, while most of the NPLs were incurred by SOEs. As most NPLs were basically SOEs' debts owed to state banks, they practically became debts of the state. Hence, there was no real trigger to spark off a banking crisis in China.

Nonetheless, China's huge NPLs in 2001 had to be tackled. Without resolving the NPL problem, China's banking sector remains fragile and uncompetitive. In particular, China's big four state banks would urgently need to sort out their assets and restructure into "true commercial banks" in order to face foreign competition within five years of China's WTO membership.

The leadership under Hu Jintao and Wen Jiabao immediately set out to take measures to dispose of the NPLs, basically by indirectly bailing out the banks. This was done by transferring the NPLs to the four AMCs as debt-for-equity swaps. Should the AMCs fail to dispose of the NPLs within 10 years, the Finance Ministry would have to ultimately "pick up the bills". Hu and Wen were also quick to recognize that an effective banking reform was the long-term solution of the NPL problem. This involves measures to strengthen the governance of banks as well as tighten credit control. In this way, China had muddled through the second debt crisis.

Over a decade later, the Xi Jinping leadership today is even more emphatic in attacking the root causes of the NPL problem as it comes to deal with the "third wave" of China's debt crisis. To Xi, China's debt crisis and its solution is basically a reform problem. It is not just about banking reform, but also the deepening of the financial sector reform. The reform is confined not just to the financial sector, but also China's public finance system involving the central government and local governments as well as China's SOEs.

Furthermore, Xi wants not just a more thorough-going reform of various sectors, but also a stronger embrace of the market principles, with a view of putting the market at the centre of all economic activities. In short, Xi is trying to put an end to the recurrence of debt crisis for China once for all.

Bad Loans Stoke Fears of a Banking Crisis*

In the wake of the 1997 Asian financial crisis (which actually did not affect China much[1]), China stepped up efforts to reform its banking structure. Banking reform is an inherently difficult process because of its institutional complexities as well as its structural relationship with other sectors of the economy. For China, though its banking reform had made impressive progress under the impetus of its WTO membership, it has not effectively come to grips with its NPLs problem, which was crying out for attention.

---

*The original version of this chapter was jointly written with Professor Chen Chien-Hsun.
[1] For a study on China and the Asian financial crisis, see John Wong, "Will China be the Next Financial Domino?" *EAI Background Brief No. 4*, December 11, 1997. See also Chapter 3.

By the late 2002, the international financial community started to take alarm at China's persistently high levels of NPLs, which ranged from the official estimate of 26% (24% in early 2003[2]) of the total loan portfolio to Moody's 40% and Standard & Poor's 50%. China's NPL ratios were widely seen to be close to or have exceeded the levels of many Southeast Asian economies on the eve of the outbreak of their financial crisis. International media therefore raised the alarm that a serious banking crisis was looming in China. To quote some: "China's banking troubles cast a long shadow" (*International Herald Tribune*)[3]; "Banking: On the Road to Ruin" (*Far Eastern Economic Review*)[4]; "China's NPLs: Ticking Time Bomb" (*Asia Times*)[5]; and "Caught in Quicksand?" (*Business Week*).[6]

How bad was China's NPL situation at that time? Strictly speaking, nobody really knows the exact level of China's NPLs, not even the People's Bank of China (PBOC), as this involves complicated accounting exercise and auditing practice. Prior to 1998, Chinese banks used to classify its NPLs into three categories of "overdue, doubtful and bad".[7] Such a classification understated the true NPL level as it did not include highly risky bank loans that were still paying interests and were not yet overdue.[8]

Since July 1999, China followed an internationally accepted loan rating system by reclassifying its NPLs into five categories: Normal (pass), special mention, substandard, doubtful and loss (unrecoverable). The new

---

[2] See *China Daily*, May 30, 2003.

[3] William Peserk Jr., "China's Banking Troubles Cast a Long Shadow", *International Herald Tribune*, December 20, 2002. Also, Keith Bradsher, "Bad Loans in China Raise Fears", *International Herald Tribune*, May 11–12, 2002.

[4] David Lague, "China Banking: On the Road to Ruin", *Far Eastern Economic Review*, November 14, 2002.

[5] Dinkar Ayilavarapu, "China's NPLs: Ticking Time Bomb", *Asia Times*, December 7, 2002. Also, Antoaneta Bezlova, "Bad Loans Dim China's Rising Star", *Asia Times*, November 27, 2002.

[6] "Caught in Quicksand? Bad Loans Could Cripple China's Banking System — And the Economy", *Business Week* (New York, November 25, 2002).

[7] "Loans overdue" refers to loans due but not repaid after the due date has been extended. "Doubtful loans" refers to those loans which were overdue for more than two years. "Bad loans" are truly bad debts as they remain unpaid after the borrowers have gone bankrupt. See John Bartel and Yiping Huang, "Dealing with the Bad Loans of the Chinese Banks", *APEC Study Center Discussion Paper No. 13*, July 2002 (Columbia University).

[8] Nicholas R. Lardy, *China's Unfinished Economic Revolution*, Brooking Institution and Institute for International Economics, 1998.

loan classification required all banks to categorize their loans according to the repayment ability of the borrowers.[9] The more stringent loan categorization thus brought about a more realistic picture of China's actual loan performance. On March 24, 2003, China's Central Bank Governor, Dai Xianglong, put the total NPLs of China's state banks at the end of 2002 as 25.4% by the four-category classification or 29.6% by the five-category classification. Dai further stressed that he not only believed the figure to be true but also that China's NPL level had bottomed out.[10]

However, Dai's figure did not take into account the 1.4 trillion yuan (US$169 billion) of bad assets that had been transferred to the four AMCs, which were set up in early 1999 to relieve the debt burden of the state banks through the equity-swap scheme.[11] Thus, the total NPL for the whole banking system in 2002 would work out to be quite close to Moody's estimated level of 40% after the inclusion of the transferred loans to AMCs. In absolute terms, China's total NPLs would then amount to about US$500 billion — as compared to the even higher estimate of US$600 billion by Standard & Poor's.[12] This works out to be slightly over 40% of China's existing GDP, compared to Japan's 10%.[13] Given the fact that Thailand's NPLs, on the eve of its financial crisis, stood at 38% while South Korea's at 21%, China's staggering 40% level should therefore be reaching crisis proportions. Furthermore, China's banks were plagued by low capital ratios and inadequate provisions for bad debt, suggesting that some banks were, by international standards, already technically insolvent. Viewed in this context, some foreign commentators came to believe that a serious banking crisis in China was imminent.

Was China's banking sector heading for a meltdown? Was China's dynamic economic growth at that time really built on the basis of financial quicksand? To argue that what had happened in Thailand would inevitably recur in China is to ignore China's special institutional conditions as

---

[9] See *China Daily*, December 25, 2001.

[10] "Dai Xianglong: NPL Ratio has Bottomed Out", *Xinbao* (Hong Kong, March 25, 2003).

[11] "Bad Debt Burden", *China Daily* (Beijing, December 5, 2002).

[12] "Bad Debt to Cost US$600b", *The Standard* (Hong Kong, October 30, 2002).

[13] *Ibid.* See also, "On the Road to Ruin", *Far Eastern Economic Review*, November 14, 2002. It should be noted that not all of the 1.4 trillion yuan assets that were taken up by the four AMCs were bad loans. In fact, 171 billion yuan had already been recovered.

well as the nature and structure of Chinese NPLs. Apart from its strong external economic balances (i.e., persistent balance of payments surplus, huge foreign reserves and low external debt), China's relatively isolated capital market and capital control mechanism (i.e., the inconvertibility of the *Renminbi*) would be sufficient to insulate China from any externally transmitted financial crisis. It may be remembered that the 1997 Asian financial crisis was basically triggered off by external shocks, particularly because the seriously affected countries like Thailand, Indonesia and South Korea were already heavy short-term borrowers in the international financial markets.

This means that any potential banking crisis in China would have to be domestically generated. But such a domestic financial crisis was clearly inconceivable under the circumstances. This was because most bank loans in China came from its huge domestic saving deposits (9.8 trillion yuan or US$1.2 trillion in 2002) in state banks which enjoyed blanket state guarantee, while most of the NPLs were incurred by SOEs. In other words, the debts of SOEs owed to state banks practically became the debts of the state.[14] Under the circumstances, there was no real trigger to spark off a nationwide financial crisis, except under the highly unlikely scenario where people completely lost confidence in the state. The reverse, in fact, had occurred. The Chinese people, instead of losing confidence in the state banks, had actually stashed away their personal savings with the state banks year after year. As noted by Moody's report: "While China's banking system may technically be insolvent, abundant levels of liquidity act as a cushion against stress ... The strong deposit levels further reflect public trust in the state banks, despite their problems."[15]

Nor was China likely to face the Japan type of financial woes, even though China's NPL level was much higher than that in Japan, mainly because the Japanese economy had lost its growth momentum for almost a

---

[14] Fan Gang, "How to View the Problems in China's Economy? — In Response to the Notion of 'Coming Collapse of China'", *China & World Economy* (No. 5, 2002). Thus Fan Gang argues: "The bad debts of Chinese banks are, in a certain sense, debts of the state. Why? Because they are debts owned by SOEs to state-owned banks, which, in most cases, were formed with the intervention of the government," p. 7.

[15] Quoted from David Lague, "On the Road to Ruin", *Far Eastern Economic Review*, November 14, 2002, p. 34.

whole decade. For China, as long as it can sustain high economic growth of around 8%, its overall lending portfolio will also correspondingly expand. This, by default or by design, will eventually bring down the NPL ratio over time. In fact, that was exactly what Dai Xianglong had in mind when he confidently predicted that China's overall NPL ratio for the state banks would decline a few percentage points a year to reach 15% level by 2005.[16]

While the dynamic economic growth may have helped keep the banking crisis at bay and may have even helped digest some of the outstanding loans, the staggering amount of NPLs were needed to be tackled and banking reform still needed to be accelerated.[17] Apart from long-term risks, debt-ridden banks cannot effectively function as a financial organization. After China's entry into the WTO, the quest for a solution to the NPL problem had assumed even greater urgency with domestic banks having to gear up for competition with foreign banks.[18] China's leadership under Hu Jintao appeared to have recognized this serious challenge. Premier Wen Jiabao also emphasized that a banking reform was the key to resolving the problem of high NPLs in state banks.[19] A long-term solution does not merely involve the proper disposal of the NPLs, but also an effective reform of the banking system, including measures to strengthen the governance of banks and to tighten credit control.

Falling into a Debt Trap

Most NPLs in China's banking system are the product of China's past centrally planned economy legacies. Before economic reform, all SOEs received direct fund allocation from the state budget. In 1984, direct grant to SOEs was replaced by loans, thereby shifting the budgetary burden of SOEs to the state-owned banks, leading to a sharp rise in SOEs' debt to equity ratio. Since the effective interest rates on bank loans were very low, SOEs were encouraged to over-borrow for unprofitable activities. In 1994, the "Big Four" (Bank of China, Industrial and Commercial Bank of China, China Construction Bank and Agricultural Bank of China) bore more than

---

[16]"Will a Financial Crisis Break Out?", *Beijing Review*, January 16, 2003.

[17]"Mounting Debt Sparks Debate", *Asian Wall Street Journal*, January 20, 2003.

[18]The NPLs Problem is Banking System's Achilles Heel. See *Economist*, February 8, 2003.

[19]"Premier Wen Says Reform is Key to Resolving NPL Problem" (http://english.people-daily.com.cn/200303/18/eng20030318_113496.shtml).

75% of the debts incurred by the nation's 124,000 or so SOEs. As all SOEs operated on soft budget constraints with little incentive to make profits, indiscriminate lending from state banks eventually ended up as bad loans, particularly after the onset of the SOE reform in the second part of the 1990s. By subjecting SOEs to market pressures, many SOEs were forced to fold up, resulting in the further growth of bad debts with the Big Four.

China's economic growth has been essentially investment-driven. Loans were also incurred for long-term fixed investment called "policy lending", and state banks were required by administrative order to provide loans to support long-term development projects such as infrastructure building or technical upgrading of large SOEs. In 1991, more than 38% of loans (amounting to 700 billion yuan) from the Big Four were "policy loans". In 1994, when China introduced its first banking reform with the setting up of three policy banks (the State Development Bank, Export-Import Bank and Agriculture Development Bank), policy loans still accounted for about a third of total loans from the four state banks.[20] As it turned out, many policy loans for development projects were not commercially viable, as they were largely based on political rather than on strict market criteria.

Viewed from a different angle, however, a lot of NPLs were practically government subsidies to loss-making SOEs, disbursed in the form of loans from China's Big Four. Over the years, the NPL problem was also aggravated by the following factors: (i) The reform of SOEs that was vigorously pushed by Premier Zhu Rongji, had proved to be a slow and difficult process, because it required strong political will as well as putting in place an effective social safety net[21]; (ii) The weak fiscal position of the central government rendered it very difficult for the state to provide sufficient financial resources to recapitalize the state banks; (iii) Many local government authorities continued to interfere in bank lending; (iv) State-owned commercial banks continued to carry substantial burden of policy lending.[22]

Furthermore, China's four state commercial banks were not operating strictly in accordance with commercial principles. Apart from their overall

---

[20] Shen Gang, "Bad-Debt Burden", *China Daily*, December 5, 2002.
[21] For more detailed discussion of this subject, see John Wong, "Reforming China's State-Owned Enterprises: Problems and Prospects", *EAI Background Brief No. 3*, October 10, 1997.
[22] See Liu Xiliang and Luo Dezhi, "The Sources of Non-Performing Assets in China's Banking Industry" *Jinrong Yanjiu* (*Journal of Financial Research*), 10, 50–59, 2001.

poor governance, the banks lacked proper credit control mechanism and risk management. Bank officers were inexperienced with no proper training for project evaluation and credit analysis. Some loans, especially at local branches, were granted through corrupt practices. Worse still, as part of the socialist legacies, China was slow to develop a proper "credit culture". Many SOEs and activities supported by the state had, from the very start, harboured the idea of "borrowing with no intention of paying back". This led to the formation of many debt chains commonly known as "Triangular debt" — a debtor has refused to pay off its creditor on the excuse that its own debtor has not paid him. All this has added to the steady accumulation of NPLs in the banking system until it had reached an alarming proportion during that period.

No one seems to know the exact amount of NPLs within China's banking system, as the PBOC did not regularly release accurate loan data for fear of undermining public confidence. Table 1 provides some estimates of the size of NPLs in China's Big Four on the basis of the international five category classification. Thus, the ratio of NPLs for the Big Four rose from 28% in 1999 to 31% in 2001 and then fell to 26% in 2002[23] and 24% in early 2003. As to be expected, foreign estimates were much higher, varying from 34% (Ernst & Young) and 40% (Moody) to 50% (Standard & Poor's).[24]

The ratio of NPLs in individual state banks in 2002 varied from 22.4% for the Bank of China, 25.5% for the Industrial and Commercial Bank of China to 15.4% for the China Construction Bank.[25] Furthermore, the NPLs

Table 1.   China's NPLs ratio.

	1999	2000	2001	2002	2003 Qtr 1	2005 (Target Value)
NPLs Ratio (as % of total loans)	27.6	29.2	31.0	26.1	24.1	15

Sources: Jinrong Shibao, April 19, 2002; *China Daily*, December 2, 2002 and May 30, 2003; *Zhongguo Zhengquanbao*, February 21, 2003.

---

[23] See *Zhongguo Zhengquanbao*, February 21, 2003.
[24] See *The Standard*, October 30, 2002; *International Herald Tribune*, October 30, 2002.
[25] See *People's Daily*, November 3, 2002: *China Daily*, January 23, 2003.

were not distributed evenly across China. The NPL were not particularly high in the underdeveloped areas while Guangdong province had the highest provincial GDP and highest NPLs.[26] At the end of 2002, the PBOC set an ambitious target for the Big Four to reduce their NPL ratios of 2% or 3% a year to 15% by 2005.[27]

Creating Asset Management Companies

As the NPL level continued to mount, the Chinese government started to get worried, particularly after the outbreak of the 1997 Asian financial crisis. To address the NPLs problem, China followed two policy options, one was the recapitalization of the state banks and the other was the dilution of the proportion of bad loans. In 1998, the Ministry of Finance issued 270 billion yuan of special treasury bonds for the recapitalization of the four state banks, which were also encouraged to attract deposits and to invest those funds in government bonds or sound projects.[28] However, the recapitalization move had one snag as it tended to encourage state banks to rely more on government handouts while doing little to improve lending practices. Such was the so-called moral hazard problem.

China then tried out another approach in 1999. To bring about a more fundamental solution to the NPL problem, China established, along the US' Resolution Trust Corp. (RTC) model, four AMCs, namely, Cinda, Huarong, Great Wall and Orient. They were supposed to be independent corporate entities wholly owned by the Ministry of Finance with total paid-in capital of 10 billion yuan. Their main function was to purchase, manage and dispose of the banks' NPL assets, while seeking to maintain the value of the assets and keep losses to a minimum. Thus, Cinda, Huarong, Great Wall and Orient took over the NPL assets, respectively, from the China Construction Bank, the Industrial and Commercial Bank of China, the Agricultural Bank of China and the Bank of China.

By August 2000, the four AMCs had taken over a total of 1.4 trillion yuan (US$169 billion) worth of NPL assets, with Huarong alone acquiring

---

[26] See *Finance Asia*, September 30, 2002.

[27] See *China Daily*, December 5, 2002.

[28] See D.D. Li, "Beating the Trap of Financial Repression in China", *Cato Journal*, 21(1), 77–90, 2001.

Table 2. China's asset management companies.

Related Bank	Cinda	Orient	Great Wall	Huarong
	China Construction Bank	Bank of China	Agricultural Bank of China	Industrial and Commercial Bank of China
Establishment Date	April 20, 1999	October 15, 1999	October 18, 1999	October 19, 1999
Paid-in Capital (billion yuan)	10	10	10	10
Transferred NPL by August 2000 (billion yuan)	375.6	264.1	345.8	407.7
Share of Transferred NPL (%)	26.8	19.2	24.8	29.2
Disposal of NPL-2000 (billion yuan)	50.0	38.1	22.0	15.1
Disposal of NPL-2001 (billion yuan)	29.9	18.3	53.1	23.2
Disposal of NPL-2002 (billion yuan)	86.8	45.4	106.0	63.2

Sources: *Almanac of China's Finance and Banking, 2001*; see Ma Guonan, and Ben S. C. Fung, "China's Asset Management Corporation", *BIS Working Paper No. 115*, Bank for International Settlements, 2002; *PBOC website*, January 24, 2003.

408 billion yuan of NPLs from the Industrial and Commercial Bank of China; Great Wall 346 billion yuan from the Agricultural Bank of China; Orient taking over 264 billion yuan from the Bank of China, and Cinda 376 billion yuan from the China Construction Bank (see Table 2). This amounts to about 10–20% of the total NPLs in the China's banking system.

The AMCs were given special benefits to facilitate their disposal of the non-performing assets. For example, they were exempted from business registration fees and all taxes relating to the purchase of companies, and the acquisition and disposal of assets. They were also allowed to use a wide variety of methods and financing channels to dispose of assets, which include asset conversion, transfer and sale, debt repackaging, corporate reorganization and securitization. They could also issue bonds and commercial papers, secure loans from financial institutions, and apply to the central bank for refinancing.

While the common methods used in other countries for dealing with non-performing assets included sale, reorganization and securitization, China's AMCs relied heavily on the conversion of debt to equity.[29] This required an AMC to convert the commercial bank's non-performing assets into equity of the enterprise in question and then try selling it or listing it on the stock market. The idea was not just to get rid of the non-performing asset for the bank but at the same time to help the enterprise increase its capitalization and reduce its asset-liability ratio.[30]

As shown in Table 2, in 2001, the four AMCs disposed of 125 billion yuan of NPLs. Among them, Cinda's new disposals totalled 30 billion yuan. The total amount of assets disposed of by Great Wall was 53 billion yuan, of which 3.7 billion yuan was in cash. Huarong disposed of 13 billion yuan of NPL assets through international tender (with Morgan Stanley), but settlement had yet to be completed. Huarong also disposed of a total of 23 billion yuan in assets through debt restructuring, recourse, transfer, repackaging, auction, equity realization and offsetting of capital against debt, 8 billion yuan of which was in cash. Furthermore, by the end of 2002, the four AMCs had disposed of more than 301 billion yuan of NPLs (exclusive of debt-equity swaps), over 10% of which were dealt with through the participation of foreign capital while 101 billion yuan of assets were recovered (a recovery rate of 33.6%), with 68 billion yuan being in cash and at a recovery rate of 22.4%.[31]

The biggest problem with the AMC operation in China was the absence of a functioning financial market that could be used by AMCs to dispose of their acquired assets. Other problems included lack of information, unrealistic prices for the debt-equity conversion, a potential risk of debt repudiation, and unwarranted interferences from local governments.[32] Not unsurprisingly, participation by foreign institutional investors has not been entirely satisfactory. With both the banks and enterprises being owned by

---

[29] See Wu Yue, "The Preliminary Work in the Establishment of a Financial Asset Management System has Been Completed", *Zhongguo Jinrong (China Finance)*, 1, 23, 2000.

[30] See R. Smyth and Q. Zhai, "Equity for Debt Swaps in China's State-owned Enterprises: A Property Rights Perspective", *China Information*, 16(1), 1–24, 2002.

[31] See *PBOC website*, January 24, 2003; *Xinhua News Agency*, January 1, 2003.

[32] See E. Steinfeld, "China's Program of Debt-Equity Swaps: Government Failure or Market Failure?", *Working Paper*, Department of Political Science, MIT, 2001.

the state, some potential new investors tended to view AMCs as just another way to salvage the crumbling SOEs.[33]

It seemed clear that since China's capital market was still in its primitive state, AMCs probably would have to hold the NPLs for a rather long period. While the formation of AMCs served to relieve the NPL burden of state banks, the AMCs needed to develop an effective secondary market to unload their acquired NPL assets.[34] If the AMCs could not get rid of all the NPLs by the end of the 10-year duration, the Ministry of Finance would have to either write off the NPLs or take over the nominal equity.[35] "At the end of the day," said China's renowned economist Wu Jinglian, "The Finance Ministry would have to pick up the bills."[36]

However, as can be seen from Table 3, based on past international experience, the job of cleaning up NPLs in the banking sector in general, can be very costly. It cost South Korea some 15% of its GDP and 5–7% for the United States. For China, its total NPLs in the whole banking sector, including bad loans that had been transferred to the four AMCs plus a large amount of unidentified bad assets, could be close to 40% of its 2001 GDP, or some 3.8 trillion yuan. The cost of restructuring and reshaping China's banking system could therefore be an enormous burden on the government.[37]

---

[33] See P. Bottelier, "Implications of WTO Membership for China's State-Owned Banks and the Management of Public Finances: Issues and Strategies", *Journal of Contemporary China*, 11(32), 397–411, 2002.

[34] See T. Osborn, "Marketing China's Bad Loans", *Asian Wall Street Journal*, May 22, 2003.

[35] See Huang Jinlao, "Creating a Suitable Market Environment for Asset Management Companies", *Zhongguo Jinrong (China Finance)*, 1, 24, 2000.

[36] http://finance.sina.com.cn/g/g20030227/0838314988.shtml. Accessed on February 27, 2003.

[37] Ma and Fung estimated that the total NPLs of the big four state banks could have amounted to 3400 billion yuan at the end of 2001. See Guonan Ma and Ben S.C. Fung, "China's Asset Management Corporations", *BIS Working Paper No. 115*, Bank for International Settlements, 2002. Moreover, Huang pointed out that the existing NPLs are likely to rise, rather than fall, in the coming year before significant improvement in China's banking practice occurred. Due to the huge unrecognized bad assets, his estimate of NPL ratio was 35% in mid-2002. See Huang Yiping, "Is Meltdown of the Chinese Banks Inevitable?", *China Economic Review*, 13(4), 382–387, 2002.

Table 3.   Costs of restructuring financial sectors.

	Years	Fiscal Cost (% of GDP)	Peak in NPLs (%)
Argentina	1980–1982	13–55	9
Brazil	1994–1996	4–10	9
Columbia	1982–1987	5–6	25
Indonesia	1997–	45	64
Malaysia	1997–	12	24
Mexico	1994–1995	12–15	11
South Korea	1997–	15	19
United States	1984–1991	5–7	4

Source: See S. Green, "China: The Coming Market in Financial Services", *Sitrends.org*, May 2, 2002.

A Reform Problem, Not a Crisis

It is sufficiently clear that China's staggering NPLs with its state banks posed a serious threat to its banking system. Without resolving the NPL problem, China's banking sector would remain fragile and uncompetitive, and may eventually face a collapse. In any case, a large bad loan overhang impedes economic growth. With China then already in the WTO, there was also a rising concern that the high level of NPLs might bring about a collapse of confidence in domestic banks, thereby triggering a massive exodus of depositors to foreign banks.[38]

As pointed out earlier, because of China's peculiar institutional structure and its strong external economic balances, China was unlikely to repeat the Thailand-type or even the Japan-type of banking crisis. But at the same time, the Chinese government had to come to grips with the NPL problem by undertaking a thorough reform of both the banking sector and the SOEs. Specifically for banking reform, the needed measures include a massive recapitalization of the state banks and extensive liberalization of the financial sector.[39] In short, enormous reform efforts were required.

It is well known that China loathed to take up radical reform steps. It preferred a gradualist approach and counted heavily on its ability to

---

[38]"China's NPLs: Ticking Time Bomb", *Asia Times*, December 7, 2002.

[39]Jonathan Anderson, "How to Fix China's Banking System", *Asian Wall Street Journal*, March 28–30, 2003.

sustain high economic growth. A rapidly growing economy provided not only a favourable institutional environment for reform but also the needed resources to gradually digest the NPLs over time. There was no necessity for a direct bailout[40] and China was still able to muddle through.[41]

[40] S.M. Harner, "China's Banks Don't Need a Bailout", *Asian Wall Street Journal*, June 4, 2003.
[41] As Andy Rothman of the CLSA Emerging Market Brokerage put it, "I am not worried that the banking system is going to collapse over the next year. On the numbers you can mount a case for a doom-and-gloom scenario or the exact the opposite. In practice, they tend to muddle through." *Far Eastern Economic Review*, November 14, 2002, p. 34.

10

RAPIDLY CHANGING EXPORT STRUCTURE

Introduction

When Deng Xiaoping started to transform China's socialist economy in 1978, he introduced not just market reform but also the open-door policy at the same time. Ever since, "reform and the opening up" has become one single official expression, gaige kaifang (or "reform and opening-up"). In contrast to the reform experiences of the East European transitional economies like Poland and Hungary, China treated market reform and the open economy virtually as one integrated process, with the two interacting with each other — market reform will lead to a more open economy, which in turn will create demand or pressures for more reform.

Foreign trade in all centrally planned economies has been considered only a "marginal activity" under the autarkic principle, theoretically just a means to get rid of the surplus output from the central plan and to make up for domestic deficiencies. China under Mao Zedong had stretched such autarkic principle even further by emphasizing an all-round "self- reliance". Thus, China's total foreign trade in 1978 stood at only 9.7% of its GDP, or 4.6% for the export-GDP ratio.

In introducing market reform, Deng perceived the potentially important role of foreign trade in the marketization process because he was from the outset deeply influenced by successful development experiences of China's neighbouring economies like Japan and the four newly industrialized economies (NIEs) of South Korea, Taiwan, Hong Kong and Singapore. All these economies had experienced dynamic economic growth for a sustained period by pursuing the export-oriented development strategies. Deng wanted China's economy to follow suit by making it open and outward-looking.

Thus in 1979, shortly after introducing the reform plan, Deng immediately set out to establish four Special Economic Zones (Shenzhen, Zhuhai, Shantou and Xiamen) to facilitate foreign trade and foreign direct investment (FDI). China's foreign trade growth had since started to take off, with the trade-GDP ratio steadily rising to 31.8% in 1993 and peaking at 57.3% on the eve of the global financial crisis in 2008. During this period (1979–2008) trade had been growing at double-digit rate a year.

True to the export-oriented development model, exports had grown faster than imports, giving rise to chronic trade surplus for most of the years. Accordingly, export-GDP ratio rose from 4.6% in 1978 to 15.6% in 1993 and then peaked at 32% in 2008. Since then, the export-GDP ratio started to decline as China's export growth had slowed from double-digit to single-digit rates. Apart from the global economic slowdown, China's exports had started to lose comparative advantage due to rising costs and increasing wages along with the appreciation of the Renminbi.

For all these export-oriented East Asian economies, including China, exports have been an important engine of their economic growth during their periods of economic take-off. And their dynamic exports were mainly driven by labour-intensive manufactured products until the time when these exports started to lose their comparative advantage. For China with a huge population — what the Nobel economist Arthur Lewis called the existence of abundant but redundant rural labour, it had basically no choice except to follow the labour-intensive mode of industrialization.

This chapter highlights China's changing export structure in the first two decades of China's open-door policy, which was also the critical phase of China's export growth, driven predominantly by labour-intensive manufactured exports. Subsequently, such an export structure started to undergo rapid transformation. Zhu Rongji clearly had a hand first in promoting export growth through his reform of the exchange rate (1994) and the state-owned enterprises, and then in catalyzing the transformation of the export structure as he was preparing China for accession to the World Trade Organization (WTO).

Thus, China's exports over the first two decades of "reform and opening up" had grown at a hefty annual rate of 17%, from US$14 billion in 1979 to US$249 billion in 2000. Following such dynamic trade growth, China's export structure had also been radically transformed, with the share of manufactured products increased to 90% in 2000 from 47% in 1980.

In the early 1990s, light industrial manufactures like textiles, clothing and footwear (TCF) became the dominant export items, given China's comparative advantage in such labour-intensive goods. Even more dramatically, these traditional labour-intensive manufactures were rapidly replaced in the second half of the 1990s by non-traditional items like machinery and electronics whose share in total exports steadily increased from 30% in 1995 to 42% in 2000, while that of TCF declined from 29% in 1995 to 25% in 2000.

Of equal significance is the fact that high-tech items, which constituted 5% of total exports in 1996, rose to 15% in 2000. Along with China's industrial restructuring and upgrading, Chinese exports were no longer confined to low value-added or labour-intensive products and its export commodity structure had also become more diversified.

While maintaining its strong specialization in traditional industries like TCF, China has also succeeded in building up its comparative advantage for the more technology-intensive exports. China's ability to move up the technology ladder owed a great deal to a growing number of foreign-invested enterprises (FIEs) which were (and still are today) using China as an export base to manufacture those non-traditional manufactures at low cost.

Indeed, FIEs had played a crucial role in spearheading China's non-traditional exports as well as helping China capture an increasing share of the developed-country markets for such exports. China's share of the US electronics market, for instance, soared from a mere 2% in 1990 to 9.7% in 2000, comparable to that of the NIEs but higher than that of the ASEAN-4 (Indonesia, Malaysia, the Philippines and Thailand). China was then exerting a lot of competitive pressures on these ASEAN-4, which shared many similar export items as China's. Once China was in WTO, more FDI would flow into China to exploit its large domestic market and take advantage of the economies of scale effect. China would then pose even greater competitive challenges to Association of Southeast Asian Nations (ASEAN), which lacked such cost structures.

In short, China on the eve of joining the WTO was already a huge and diverse economy with a large pool of low-cost labour and an adequate pool of skilled labour capable of producing both low value-added as well as certain technological and capital-intensive goods for the world market.

By 2013, China had already been the world's largest exporting country. The share of TCF declined to just 15% of total exports while China had also *become the world's largest exporter of high-tech goods, surpassing the US, EU and Japan. At Zhu Rongji's time, in 1995, when the share of TCF products peaked at 28.6% of total exports, high-tech products accounted for only 6.8%. By 2010, China's high-tech exports totalled US$492 billion, accounting for 31.2% of its total manufacturing exports.*

China might well be the world's largest exporter of goods in total value terms. But it should be stressed that processing trade has made up about half of its exports, thereby implying that real domestic value-added to China is only half of the nominal amount of the export. This is all the more the case for China's high-tech exports. As China is a popular home to numerous regional and global production networks, an overwhelming share of China's high-tech exports are actually produced by foreign-invested firms in China, thereby yielding very low domestic value-added to China.

The much publicized made-in-China iPhone is the case in point. China's assembling an iPhone, which sold for US$179, created a total value-added of only US$6.5 to itself, mainly for the labour cost and not for technology. Nonetheless, the export of such a "made-in-China" iPhone carried a high nominal export price and hence grossly exaggerating China's high-tech exports in value terms.

It suffices to say that China's export structure continues to change and evolve along with China's economic growth and overall structural change. Xi Jinping is currently putting a strong emphasis on restructuring and rebalancing the Chinese economy with a view to render its future growth more domestic demand driven. At the same time, Xi has also stressed the importance of higher quality economic growth, with growth to be more driven by productivity increases and innovation.

The shape of the future is sufficiently clear. China's export growth is set to slow further while the overall export structure will also change. The commodity composition of China's future exports will be made up still less of the traditional labour-intensive products, while the share for high-tech products with higher domestic value-added will increase.

Dynamic Export Growth*

China, in the early 2000s, had emerged as a major trading economy in the world. Over the past two decades, China's exports had increased at a hefty

---

*The original version of this chapter was written jointly with Miss Sarah Chan.

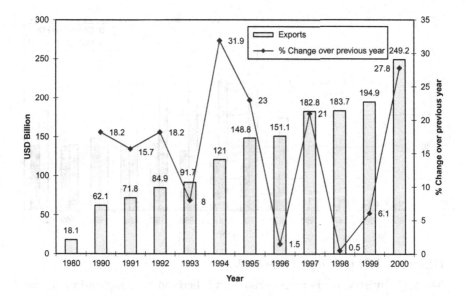

Figure 1.   Export trends in China, 1980–2000.

Sources: *China Customs Statistics Yearbook 1999*; and *China's Customs Statistics (Monthly Exports & Imports)*, December 2000.

annual rate of 17% from US$13.7 billion in 1979 to US$249.2 billion in 2000. In the 1997 Asian financial crisis, most Asian economies witnessed their export growth plunge to negative territory. China's export growth also became stagnant, growing at a mere 0.5% in 1998, compared to 21% in 1997. However, China's export growth was able to rebound quickly at 6% in 1999 and then shoot up to the startling double-digit rate of 28% in 2000 (Figure 1). China by then became the world's ninth largest exporting nation.

It is well known that China's dynamic export growth is an integral part of its equally dynamic economic growth. More specifically, China's rapid expansion of foreign trade, especially after the early 1990s, can be attributed to its large inflow of FDI. China then had become the most favoured destination of all developing countries for FDI. Even without WTO membership, China was attracting more FDI than the rest of Asia combined. From 1988 to 2000, actual or utilized FDI increased at an average rate of 23% per annum to reach a cumulative total of US$339 billion (Figure 2). FDI contributed most significantly to China's phenomenal

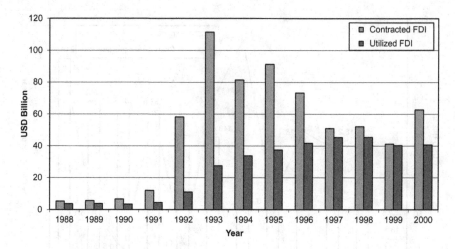

Figure 2.   FDI in China, 1988–2000.

Sources: Ministry of Foreign Trade and Economic Cooperation, *China Statistical Yearbook*, various issues.

export growth as FIEs[1] had grown to account for almost half of all exports from China. As shown in Figure 3, FIEs were responsible for 48% of China's total exports in 2000, up from 20% in 1992.

The rise of China's formidable export machine had already been widely noted and in fact felt in many industrial-country markets, especially the USA. What had come as quite a surprise to many was the significant shift that China's export structure had undergone at that time. The first phase of this shift was marked by the rise of manufactured products at the expense of primary commodities like food, minerals and agriculture.

In the second part of the 1990s, the composition of China's manufactured exports experienced another rapid but no less significant change, marked by the rise of non-traditional exports like machinery and electronics products and other "hi-tech" goods at the expense of traditional labour-intensive manufactures like TCF. Few economies had ever achieved such a remarkable export diversification in such a short span of time. China's then emerging export engine, based on the more capital- and

---

[1] FDI includes investment in the three types of FIEs, namely, fully foreign-owned enterprises, equity joint ventures and contractual joint ventures (cooperative enterprises).

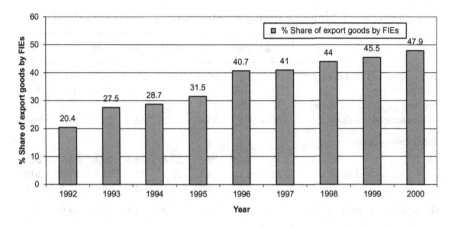

Figure 3.   FIE's contribution to China's exports, 1999–2002.

Sources: Percentage shares calculated from data in various issues of *China Statistical Yearbook*; and *China's Customs Statistics (Monthly Exports & Imports)*, December 20002.

technology-intensive activities, would have had profound implications for some ASEAN economies if it were to spearhead China's new round of export expansion after its accession to the WTO.

Rapid Change in Export Structure

Under central planning, foreign trade in Maoist China, as in other Soviet-typed economies, was largely a "residual item" with scant regard for the principle of comparative advantage. Foreign trade was used mainly as a means of acquiring scarce products and getting rid of surplus items. When China started its economic reform in 1979, foreign trade operated to maximize foreign exchange earnings to help economic reform and development. In 1980, China's export trade was dominated by primary commodities such as agricultural products and minerals, which accounted for slightly more than half of its total exports while a wide range of labour-intensive manufactured products made up the rest.

As China started to industrialize rapidly on account of its successful economic reform and open-door policy, its exports also began to mount. Along with the rapid expansion of exports had been the rapid change in the commodity composition of foreign trade. The share of Chinese

Table 1.   China's changing export structure from 1980–2000.

	1980	1990	1995	1996	1997	1998	1999	2000
Total exports (US$ billion)	18.1	62.1	148.8	151.1	182.8	183.7	194.9	249.2
% distribution	100	100	100	100	100	100	100	100
Primary products (% share)	53.4	25.6	14.4	14.5	13.1	11.2	10.2	10.2
Manufactured goods (%)	46.6	74.4	85.6	85.5	86.9	88.8	89.8	89.8
Traditional items								
(a) TCF:	22.9	24.9	28.6	27.8	28.3	26.6	25.7	24.9
(i) Textiles and apparel	21.9	22.3	24.1	23.1	23.6	22.0	21.2	20.9
(ii) Footwear	1.0	2.6	4.5	4.7	4.7	4.6	4.5	4.0
(b) Toys and sporting goods	—	—	3.6	4.0	4.1	4.2	4.0	3.7
Non-Traditional items								
(c) Machinery and electronics:	—	17.9	29.5	31.9	32.5	36.2	39.5	42.3[a]
(i) Light industrial & electrical machinery	—	7.8	7.7	8.0	7.9	8.2	9.0	n.a.
(ii) Mechanical appliances & transport equipment	—	4.0	10.7	11.7	12.0	13.3	14.0	n.a.
(iii) Electronics	—	6.1	11.1	12.2	12.6	14.7	16.5	22.1[b]
(d) Hi-tech items	—	—	6.8	5.08	5.3	11.0	13.0	15.0*

Note: (1) Blank spaces marked with "—" mean insignificant.
   (2) n.a. denotes not readily available.
   (3) [a] denotes December 2000 figure obtained from www.cei.gov.cn.
   (4) [b] denotes preliminary figure of electronics and information exports from www.mii.gov.cn.
   (5) *denotes figure extracted from www.china.com, "China's hi-tech exports up 50% in 2000".
   (6) Hi-tech products for export were mainly products in machinery, electronics, information, materials, biology and pharmaceutical industries.
   (7) For hi-tech products in 1998, data on total volume of exports and imports take into account adjustments of the different mix of hi-tech goods. Figure in 1998 may include a larger mix of items considered to be hi-tech and which have high technological content. Some of these items may be products manufactured in the machinery, electronic, materials, chemical or pharmaceutical industries.

Source: *China Foreign Economic Statistics, 1979–1991*; *Almanac of China's Foreign Economic Relations and Trade*, various issues; *China Statistical Yearbook 2000*; *China Customs Statistics Yearbook*, various issues; *China's Customs Statistics* (*Monthly Exports & Imports*), December 2000, *China's Latest Economic Statistics, December 2000*; China Chamber of Commerce for Import and Export of Machinery and Electronic Products, http://www.cccme.cn.net, (2000); China Council for the Promotion of International Trade, http://www.ccpit.org; *China Electronics Industry Yearbook*, various issues; *China Machinery Industry Yearbook*, various issues.

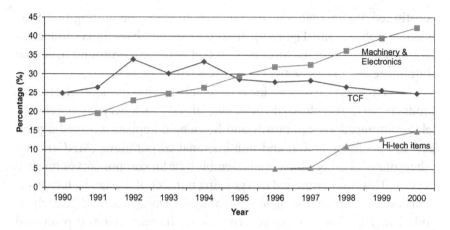

Figure 4. Trends of China's manufactured exports, 1990–2002.

Sources: Percentage shares calculated from data given in various issues of Almanac of *China's Foreign Economic Relations and Trade, China Customs Statistics Yearbook* and *China Machinery Industry Yearbook* (relevant years).

manufactured exports rose steadily from 47% of total exports in 1980 to 90% in 2000 (Table 1). In the process, light, labour-intensive industrial products such as TCF, toys, travel and sport goods, etc., became the dominant export items for which China undoubtedly enjoyed strong comparative advantage due to its abundant low-wage labour supply.

Along with its rapid industrial expansion, China was making efforts to restructure and upgrade its industrial sector, placing increasing emphasis on the development of the more capital- and technology-intensive new "pillar industries" — including IT, machinery, electronics and autos among others. Changes in the industrial structure eventually led to changes in the export composition, which had become increasingly evident in the second part of the 1990s. In 1995, as shown in Figure 4, exports of electronics and machinery products exceeded the TCF items for the first time.

In fact, non-traditional machinery and electronics goods had over the years grown to dominate China's export structure, rising from 32% in 1996 to 42% in 2000. They had gradually displaced the traditional TCF items whose share declined from 28% in 1996 to only 25% in 2000. Of equal significance is the fact that "hi-tech" items (mainly products in electronics, information, machinery, materials, biotech and pharmaceutical industries) constituted 5% in 1996 and rose to 15% in 2000, amounting to US$37 billion[2] (Table 1 and Figure 4). It suffices to say that China's industrial economy and its manufactured exports had achieved a profound structural shift by the end of the 1990s.

In retrospect, the rise in exports of machinery and electronics products such as industrial tools, specialized machinery, auto vehicles, telecommunications equipment and household appliances, owed a great deal to FIEs from Taiwan and multinational corporations (MNCs) from other countries using China as an assembly base for components or finished exports. This was manifested in a growing number of foreign hi-tech firms which started up in Guangdong (mainly in Dongguan and Shenzhen) and Shanghai. The Chinese government on its part had also promoted such hi-tech FDI (see Appendix for hi-tech FDI promotion measures.). Consequently, FIEs, apart from providing an impetus for China's own industrial reform and industrial upgrading, had also been a major driving force behind China's hi-tech exports.

While maintaining its strong specialization in traditional industries like TCF, China had succeeded in building up comparative advantage in the new and technologically more advanced activities such as telecommunications equipment (cellular phones), electrical apparatus or consumer electronics (TVs, radios, refrigerators, air conditioners, etc.) and industrial electronic components and products (such as computers and computer accessories including printers, disk drives, keyboards, switching systems, etc.). China was also making efforts to develop itself into a key manufacturing centre for semiconductor chips.[3]

Rapid growth of China's combined machinery and electronics exports can be seen in its increase in value from US$21 billion in 1995 to US$46 billion in 1999 (Table 2). The FIEs were largely responsible for the fast growth of these exports, with their share rising from 46% of the total in 1995 to 60% in 1999. For electronics exports, the role of FIEs was even

---

[2]"China's Hi-Tech Exports Up 50 Percent in 2000" (www.china.com).

[3]At that period, about 86% of China's semiconductors had to be imported from Taiwan, South Korea, USA and Japan. With the setting up of two large joint ventures in Shanghai — Shanghai Grace Semiconductor Manufacturing and Semiconductor Manufacturing International — China's chip production capacity were greatly boosted. "Taiwan holds upper hand in chips battle", *South China Morning Post* (April 2, 2001).

Table 2. Machinery and electronics exports by FIEs and domestic enterprises, 1995–1999 (value: US$ billion).

Value: US$ billion

	1995		1996		1997		1998		1999	
	Value	% of Total Exports	Value	% of Total Exports	Value	% of Total Exports	Value	% of Total Exports	Value	% of Total Exports
FIEs:										
• Wholly foreign-owned enterprises	8.3	20.1	12.2	25.4	16.7	28.1	20.7	31.0	25.5	33.0
• Joint ventures	9.2	20.0	11.9	24.7	14.7	24.7	16.6	24.9	17.9	23.2
• Cooperative enterprises	2.6	5.9	2.8	5.8	3.0	5.0	3.0	4.5	2.8	3.7
Total	**20.6**	**46**	**26.9**	**55.9**	**34.4**	**57.8**	**40.3**	**60.4**	**46.2**	**59.9**
Domestic Enterprises:										
• State-owned enterprises (SOEs)	22.5	51.3	20.3	42.1	23.7	40.0	24.9	37.5	28.1	36.5
• Collectively-run enterprises	0.7	1.7	1.0	2.0	1.2	2.1	1.5	2.2	2.1	2.7
• Individual holdings	0.003	0.007	0.003	0.005	0.006	0.01	0.03	0.05	0.2	0.2
Total	**23.2**	**53**	**21.3**	**44.1**	**24.9**	**42.1**	**26.4**	**39.8**	**30.4**	**39.4**

Note: Percentages may not be exact due to rounding errors.
Sources: China Machinery Industry Yearbook, various issues.

more important as their share increased from 53% in 1993 to 74% in 1999 (Table 3). In short, export-oriented FDI had been instrumental in beefing up China's export capacity in non-traditional and more capital-intensive items like electronics equipment and components.

Implications for ASEAN

In many ways, the pattern of China's export diversification, particularly with regard to the role played by FDI, is quite similar to what had taken place in the ASEAN economies. However, what made China different from ASEAN is the fact that China had by far a much larger pool of both skilled as well as non-skilled labour. Furthermore, China had a large domestic market for all sorts of products, high-tech or low-tech, to take advantage of the economies of scale effect. With lower costs generated as a result of high volume production, China was thus able to enjoy its natural cost advantage compared to ASEAN and other smaller developing countries.

As already broached earlier, the fundamental reason for the rapid growth of China's non-traditional and more capital-intensive exports was due to China's success in attracting FDI. Export-oriented FDI had been particularly important in helping China capture the markets of industrialized countries for such exports. Compared with ASEAN and the other developing regional economies, the growth of China's non-traditional exports was far more dynamic in terms of market expansion. This immediately brings to the fore the potential adverse impact on ASEAN of the future onslaught of China's non-traditional exports to the world market.

As illustrated in Figure 5, although the electrical and electronic exports of the ASEAN-4 and the NIEs combined were significantly higher than China's, China was rapidly taking on these Asian competitors, as evident in its increasing share of the US market for these products over the years. In 1990, for instance, China's share of the US electronics market was only around 2% but this share increased to 9.7% by 2000, comparable to 8.4% for Taiwan and 9.8% for South Korea, and higher than the ASEAN-4 countries — 9.2% for Malaysia, 1.02% for Indonesia, 3.0% for the Philippines and 4.5% for Thailand. China was set to overtake both the NIEs (which are relocating their production bases to China) and the ASEAN-4 whose export

Table 3.   Electronics exports by FIEs and domestic enterprises (value: US$ billion).

Value: US$ billion

	1993		1994		1995		1996		1997		1998		1999	
	Value	% of Total X	Value	% of Total X	Value	% of Total X	Value	% of Total X	Value	% of Total X	Value	% of Total X	Value	% of Total X
FIEs:														
— Foreign-owned enterprises	1.5	18.1	2.6	20.8	4.4	26.4	6.9	32.1	9.5	35.4	10.1	39.5	16.4	42.0
— Joint ventures	2.2	27.8	3.5	28.0	4.9	29.5	7.1	33.0	8.9	32.9	7.3	28.3	10.9	28.0
— Cooperative enterprises	0.6	7.5	1.0	8.4	1.3	7.6	1.4	6.5	1.4	5.3	1.2	4.8	1.4	3.6
Total:	4.3	53.4	7.1	57.2	10.6	63.5	15.4	71.6	19.8	73.6	18.6	72.6	28.7	73.6
Domestic enterprises:														
— SOEs	—		—		—		5.8	27	6.8	25.1	6.7	26.1	9.7	24.9
— Collectively-run enterprises	—		—		—		—		0.4	1.4	0.3	1.3	0.6	1.5
— Individual holdings	—		—		—		—		0.002	0.008	0.07	0.03	0.04	0.1
Total	—		5.3	42.6	5.9	35.5	—		7.2	26.5	7.1	27.4	10.3	26.5

Note: (1) Percentages may not be exact due to rounding errors.
(2) "% of total X" refers to % of total exports.
Sources: China Electronics Industry Yearbook, various issues.

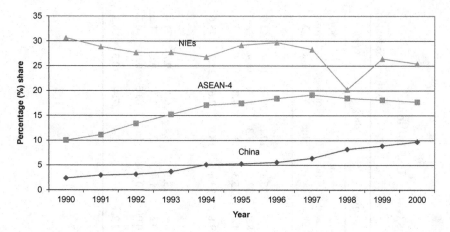

Figure 5.   East Asian electrical and electronic exports to US market, 1990–2000.

Sources: US Census Bureau, US Department of Commerce.

competitiveness fast eroded by China's growing strength in these non-traditional items.[4]

The WTO Effect

China's basic comparative advantage *vis-à-vis* other developing Asia-Pacific economies became even more pronounced after China's accession to WTO. For ASEAN, China's WTO membership was supposed to bring about both opportunities and challenges. In the longer run, ASEAN economies should benefit from increased access to China's markets. At that phase of development, however, China and ASEAN tended to be more competitive than complementary with each other, as far as manufactured exports and FDI were concerned.

Both China and ASEAN share a great deal of similarity in their export structures, for the traditional labour-intensive TCF items as well as non-traditional items like consumer electronics. Moreover, both are

---

[4]China's top electric appliance maker, Haier, for instance, had penetrated the US market to compete against entrenched foreign firms on the basis of price and quality. It had established a plant in the US to manufacture consumer electronics like refrigerators and air-conditioners. *Far East Economic Review*, March 29, 2001.

economically oriented towards the industrialized countries of the West and Japan. As shown in Table 4, in 1999, 57% of China's total exports and 57.5% of ASEAN-4's (average) were destined for the industrialized countries.[5] In other words, ASEAN would compete head on with China in the developed countries' markets in the export of both traditional and non-traditional manufactured goods.

For Japan and other smaller NIEs, rising costs and increasing wages had forced them to pass on their comparative advantage for labour-intensive products to their neighbouring economies with lower costs. But China is a rare continental-sized economy with such great diversity that it can contain the evolution of comparative advantage within its own borders. As it had already happened, the more developed coastal regions of China were transferring their losing comparative advantage in labour-intensive products in the coastal region to Central and Western China, which were then the focus of China's future development efforts. This means that China, for years, could continue to flood the world market with low-cost manufactured items even when many parts of China have achieved middle-income status.

As stressed earlier, the ASEAN-4 economies were already facing increasing competitive pressures from China in the export of non-traditional manufactured goods. Lest anyone should forget this, China actually started to industrialize in the 1950s — China's famous "Liberation" trucks were rolling out from the Changchun No. 1 Auto Plant back in July 1956[6] — well ahead of ASEAN and even the NIEs. Consequently, China's industrial base was by far larger and more established than that of any country in ASEAN. Most of China's electronics and hi-tech exports were spearheaded by FIEs. An increasing share would come from China's own domestic firms once they had completed their restructuring and upgrading after China's WTO entry.

---

[5] Accordingly, the level of Sino-ASEAN trade is also insignificant, particularly if Singapore (which is a member of ASEAN) is excluded from the group. China's exports to ASEAN-4 were only 3.2% of its total exports while China as a market for the ASEAN-4 was small too, ranging from 2.7% for Malaysia to just 1.6% for the Philippines. See John Wong, "Regional Implications of China's Reform and Development", paper presented at the International Conference on ASEAN, organized by Taiwan Comprehensive Research Institute, Taipei, November 16–20, 2000.

[6] The authors are grateful to Dr Lu Hanchao for this information.

Table 4. Intra-regional trade in East Asia, 1999.

	Total Exports (USD million)	To Industrialized Countries (%)				China %	NIEs %	ASEAN-4 %	East Asia %	East Asia less Japan %
		Total	USA	Japan	EU					
China	194,931	57	21.5	16.6	16	—	27.3	3.2	47.1	30.5
Japan	419,207	53.7	31.1	—	18.7	5.6	21.6	8.6	35.8	35.8
NIEs										
South Korea	143,647	50.5	20.6	11	15.8	9.5	14.1	7.7	42.3	31.3
Taiwan	121,590	n.a.	25.4	9.8	15.7	2.1	26.7	7.3	45.9	36.1
Hong Kong	173,793	49.4	23.9	5.4	16.9	33.4	6.4	3.2	48.4	43
Singapore	114,730	45.6	19.2	7.4	15.5	3.4	15.7	23.4*	49.9	42.5
ASEAN-4										
Indonesia	57,282	55.7	16.1	20	15.3	4.8	23.4	5.7	53.9	33.9
Malaysia	84,550	53	21.9	11.6	16	2.7	28.5	6.3	49.1	37.5
Philippines	35,474	63.6	29.6	13.1	19.3	1.6	23.8	6.9	45.4	32.3
Thailand	61,797	57.5	21.5	14.5	17.8	3.6	19	7.3	44.4	29.9

Notes: (1) East Asia region here comprises Japan, China, the four NIEs and ASEAN-4.
(2) *Figure for Indonesia is not available.
(3) n.a. denotes not available.

Sources: IMF, *Direction of Trade Statistics Yearbook 2000*; Statistics Department, Taiwan Ministry of Economic Affairs, http:/ / www. moea.gov.tw (2000).

In 1999, China produced 43 million colour TV sets, 13 million washing machines and 12 million refrigerators.[7] Chinese factories had obviously already acquired the right technology and the right cost structures (i.e., economies of scale) to produce these consumer durables efficiently and cheaply to out-compete others.[8] After China's accession to WTO, ASEAN would have an economically resurgent China to reckon with, one that would be dualistic in nature, capable of producing both low value-added as well as technology- and capital-intensive goods for the world market.

---

[7] *China Statistical Yearbook 2000.*

[8] For a more detailed discussion of China's industrial competitiveness after WTO, see Guy Liu Shaojia, "China's WTO Accession and the Impact on Its Large Manufacturing Enterprises", *East Asian Institute Contemporary China Series No. 30* (Singapore 2001).

APPENDIX

China Encourages New and High Technology Investment

The Ministry of Foreign Trade and Economic Cooperation (MOFTEC) and the Ministry of Science and Technology had drawn up policies to promote exports of new and high technology products. For instance, all high technology products would be included in the category of encouraged investment projects in order to attract foreign funds, while some new and high technology development zones were given the same treatment as export processing zones and will enjoy export tax rebates. The main policies were as follows:

(1) Selected new and high technology development zones will be permitted to experiment as closed export processing zones, paving the way for the establishment of high technology parks. In these zones, closed supervision will be implemented and international practices will be followed to facilitate the entry and exit of commodities, people and capital. Import and export of goods in the zones will be exempt from customs duty and value-added tax (VAT), and import and export of general commodities will be free from quantitative restrictions. Goods supplied to these zones from other areas of the mainland will be regarded as exports, and may enjoy export tax rebates. In addition, extensive information networks will be provided for enterprises to enhance their competitiveness in the international market.

---

(2) Efforts will be made to encourage the use of foreign investment and import of advanced technology. Multinational corporations will be attracted to set up research and development (R&D) centres. All high technology industries will be categorized as 'encouraged' projects and imports of hardware and software will enjoy tariff and VAT exemptions. At the same time, relevant policies will be improved to encourage Chinese high technology enterprises to expand into the international market. Support will be provided to these domestic enterprises in establishing R&D centres, under-taking joint-venture and cooperative production, strengthening international technological exchanges, and employing foreign high-technology personnel.

(3) Non-electromechanical hi-tech products will enjoy the preferential policies for electromechanical products. Thus, enterprises exporting non-electromechanical hi-tech products will also enjoy full tax rebates, low interest rate export credit and policy export credit insurance.

(4) A risk investment fund will be established, with funds raised from both China and abroad to be managed by domestic and foreign specialists. Also, mature hi-tech product export enterprises will be allowed to raise capital directly in the domestic and foreign markets, and preference will be given to such enterprises to list at home and overseas.

(5) A special information network will be built. Financial assistance will be given to small and medium hi-tech enterprises to participate in exhibitions, promote new products and open new markets.

(6) Qualified hi-tech enterprises will be allowed to handle the import and export of their own products.

11

GOING GLOBAL: RISING OVERSEAS DIRECT INVESTMENT

Introduction

Thanks to his successful management of market reform, Zhu Rongji had been able to build up a powerful export engine for China, as shown in the last chapter. Exports had since been growing at double-digit rates throughout his tenure in office (first as Vice Premier and then Premier), and with the single exception of 1993, China had consistently chalked up a sizeable trade surplus year after year — in fact, till this day (2015). This, along with steady capital inflow in the form of foreign direct investment (FDI) and China's persistently high levels of domestic savings, had transformed China from a capital-deficient economy in the early years of economic reform to a capital-surplus economy with a net resource outflow during Zhu's last few years as Premier.

In 2002, on the eve of his stepping down as Premier, Zhu had succeeded in strengthening China's both current and capital account positions, respectively, with a huge trade surplus of US$30 billion (4.8% of total trade) and a large inflow of US$53 billion in FDI. Such a robust external balance was further boosted by China's sizeable foreign exchange reserves of US$286 billion, which was then the second largest in Asia after Japan. Zhu's experience of the 1997 Asian financial crisis (which at one time threatened the Renminbi) must have also contributed to his determination to build up a strong external balance for China's economy. Thus, China was able to sustain a significant capital outflow for more overseas investment, officially called "overseas direct investment" or ODI.

China's ODI programme was actually an integral part of the national "Going out" (zuo chu qu) or "Go Global" business strategy. It has since come to light that Zhu was also behind this "Go Global" policy. After the initial success of reforming the country's state-owned enterprises (SOEs), he wanted to expose China's large SOEs to greater international competition by urging them to invest overseas and establish a foothold in the world market. Specifically, he selected many strategic SOEs that belonged to the central government (yangqi) as "national champions" to spearhead the Go Global drive. This business strategy was formally announced at the Fifteenth Party Congress in 1997.

In the meanwhile, Zhu was actively preparing China for the World Trade Organization (WTO) membership. He wanted China's SOEs to be better prepared for international competition arising from greater integration of China into the global economy. Thus, in 2000, he set out to fine-tune the "Go Global" strategy. In short, the government played an active role in the ODI programme from the very beginning.

This chapter discusses China's ODI at its nascent phase, up to 2002, with its annual ODI outflow averaging at only about US$2 billion. Though small, the ODI was globally well diversified without displaying any sectoral concentration. But generally, there was a concentration of Chinese ODI in Hong Kong for trade and services, in Australia and Canada for securing raw materials; and in USA for acquiring advanced technology.

A lot of China's ODI were initially intended to facilitate China's trade expansion. The "non-trading" activities then mostly took the form of joint ventures (JVs) due to their limited financial resources and lack of knowledge of local conditions. Typically, Chinese enterprises overseas at that time were also quite small with the size of investment averaging around US$1 million. With weak management structures and lacking innovation ability, many Chinese firms appeared quite unprepared to cope with the fiercely competitive business environment outside their country.

Not surprisingly, Chinese enterprises were yet to make a significant impact on global markets. Given the limited presence of Chinese firms in world markets, it would seem that none of them would ever even come remotely close to the Global 500 ranks.

Viewed from a different angle, although the majority of Chinese overseas enterprises were large SOEs, some private firms among them had started to nurture global ambitions and were making forays into the world market. In the future, some Chinese indigenous enterprises could emerge more competitive and stronger as a result of domestic restructuring. They could then play a more important part in Chinese ODI and achieve more success in the global marketplace.

Specifically for China's investment in the ASEAN region, it was at that time still modest in absolute terms but seemed to grow rapidly. With the ASEAN–China Free Trade Agreement in the pipeline, ASEAN countries would become an even more important and attractive investment destination for Chinese businesses as they grow more savvy and outward oriented.

In retrospect, ODI in 2002 might seem to be a new phenomenon, but it was actually a turning point for the long-term growth of China's ODI. WTO membership had not only sparked off China's double-digit rates of economic growth for the following decade and a half, but also much facilitated the capital movement in and out of China, i.e., more FDI inflow and more ODI outflow. In 2013, China's inward FDI totalled US$118 billion while its ODI hit the record high of US$108 billion, a 50-fold increase from the mere US$2 billion in 2002. In 2014, China became a net capital exporter as its ODI, at US$116 billion, outnumbering its FDI for the first time.

In 2013, China already became the world's third largest investor after Germany and the USA. With China already taking measures to liberalize capital controls and further internationalizing the Renminbi, China is poised to be the leading global capital exporter in the years to come. Neither Zhu Rongji nor anyone in 2002 would have anticipated that three of the top 10 in the Global 500 in 2014 were Chinese SOEs (Sinopec, CNPC and State Grid), which had already become large players in the global investment scene.

In the perspective of East Asian development, the development of China's ODI is quite close to the historical experiences of Japan, Korea, Taiwan and Singapore, which had all followed the export-led development strategies, first chalking up trade surplus consistently and then becoming significant capital exporters. Their foreign forays were initially for the acquisition of natural resources and primary commodities, including energy, as well as securing their export markets overseas.

Subsequently, with rising wages and increasing costs, these East Asian economies were fast losing their original comparative advantage for labour-intensive manufactured exports, and hence their overseas investment drive involved the shift of those manufacturing bases to other less developed economies. At the same time, as they were restructuring and upgrading their industrial structure for high value-added activities, they were also pushing their ODI into developed countries in search of advanced technology, usually through acquiring overseas companies. It suffices to say that all these sound much like a textbook theory of what motivates a domestic enterprise to go out and become a multinational, namely, as corporate strategy, for market seeking, for resource seeking, for technology seeking, and so on.

In general, China's ODI development did follow broadly similar paths of its East Asian neighbours, and was motivated by the same underlying factors. But there are also significant differences. To begin with, China's Go Global strategy is state led and state driven, spearheaded primarily by its large SOEs whereas the Japanese and Korean multinationals were basically private enterprises — though many Singapore multinationals are also government-linked companies. As such, China's overseas entities had often run into political opposition in certain countries for "security reasons".

China is also a much greater economic entity, as compared to its East Asian neighbours. China, having a vast hinterland, would not hastily push out its labour-intensive production bases overseas. Furthermore, China's resource acquisition is far more wide-ranging and on a much bigger scale, as China's appetite for natural resources overseas seems to be insatiable! This explains why China's resource-seeking ODI is all over in Africa and Latin America.

By early 2015, China became historically the world's largest recipient of FDI amounting to US$1.3 trillion, larger than the total amount of what the United States had accumulated. At the same time, China was poised to become the global powerhouse for capital supply and FDI. With its "twin surplus" (surplus in both capital and current accounts) continuing unabated and with its foreign exchange reserves swelling to US$4 trillion, China is awash with capital and foreign exchanges. China is set to send more ODI overseas, but has also become a kind of "lender of last resort", playing the role of the IMF by bailing out several countries from their financial crisis: providing credit and loans to Russia, Argentina and Venezuela.

At the 22nd APEC Summit in Beijing in November 2014, President Xi Jinping put up China's own kind of "Marshall Plan" by pledging US$40 billion to assist countries in his proposed Silk Road zone for infrastructure development under the "One Belt for One Road". Earlier on, Xi introduced his grand diplomacy of building an Overland Silk Road from China to Central Asia, and the Maritime Silk Road through the South China Sea to

the Indian Ocean. Economic diplomacy is clearly at the heart of the Silk Road
strategy. China was also instrumental in creating the new Asian Infrastructure
Investment Bank (AIIB). In future, a lot of China's ODI ventures will spearhead
China's new diplomatic drives.

More ODI Outflow After "Go Global" Strategy

While China's success in attracting FDI had frequently grabbed newspaper
headlines, the rise in China's outward ODI in the early 2000s had largely
gone unnoticed. This is perhaps because China's ODI, in absolute terms,
remained relatively small. But it would certainly have strong growth
potential, and its future impact on its neighbouring ASEAN economies
would be particularly significant.

China was fast emerging as the world's foremost manufacturing powerhouse and it was in 2002 the world's fifth largest trading
nation. As China's economy continued with its dynamic growth, it
interacted more with other economies commercially and financially.
China followed the footsteps of Japan, South Korea and Taiwan and
invested more in the ASEAN economies, initially for trading and
raw materials acquisition, and later diversifying to include manufacturing and processing. The ASEAN–China Free Trade Agreement
further facilitated China's economic integration with the ASEAN
region.

Apart from the need to reach out to the global economy through trade
and investment, the Chinese economy was financially robust enough to
export capital. Thanks to its persistent trade surpluses and huge influx
of FDI, China, through most of the 1990s, had achieved a very strong
external balance with rising foreign exchange reserves, as shown in Table 1.
In fact, due to the positive saving–investment and export–import gaps, the
Chinese economy had, for years, experienced a net resource outflow. In
other words, China had become a capital surplus economy, ready to export
more capital. Furthermore, the government had at that time urged large
domestic enterprises, especially the SOEs to "go out" (*zuo chu qu*) to the
world market under its "Go Global" strategy. In short, China's economy saw
more capital outflow for investment purposes.

Table 1.   China's resource balance.

	Gross Domestic Savings (% of GDP)	Gross Domestic Investment (% of GDP)	Saving-Investment Gap (% of GDP)	Merchandise Trade Balance (USD billion)	External Balance of Goods (% of GDP)	Foreign Exchange Reserves (USD billion)
Average (1971–1980)	32.5	34.2	−1.7	—	—	—
Average (1981–1990)	30.8	30.5	0.3	−3	—	5
1985	33.6	38.4	−4.8	−15	−4.4	3
1986	34.6	38.9	−4.3	−12	−3.1	2
1987	38.4	39.7	−1.3	−4	−0.5	3
1988	37.6	30.1	7.5	−8	−1.3	3
1989	37.7	36.8	0.9	−7	−1.3	6
1990	37.9	35.2	2.7	9	2.4	11
1991	38.1	35.4	2.7	8	2.2	22
1992	38.3	37.3	1.0	4	1.1	19
1993	41.9	41.5	0.4	−12	−1.8	21
1994	42.6	41.2	1.4	5	1.3	52
1995	41.1	40.8	0.3	17	2.6	74
1996	41.1	39.6	1.5	12	2.4	105
1997	41.5	38.2	3.3	40	5.1	140
1998	39.8	37.7	2.1	44	1.9	145
1999	39.4	37.4	2.0	29	3.6	155
2000	38.0	37.1	0.9	24	3.2	166
2001	38.6	38.6	0	23	2.9	212
2002	38.7	38.5	0.2	30	3.4	287

Sources: *Asian Development Outlook* (relevant issues); *China Statistical Abstract*, 2002; *Economist Intelligence Unit*.

Geographical Distribution

Chinese overseas investment can be divided into investments made by trading and non-trading enterprises. Non-trading activities refer to manufacturing (processing and assembling), resource development (such as mining and forestry) and contracting works such as turnkey engineering/construction. Trading activities are generally service-oriented activities (like financial intermediation, distribution, transport and communications) which are trade-supporting in nature.[1]

China's outbound investment in "non-trading" activities was spread across the globe, with a strong concentration in some countries — United States, Canada, Hong Kong/Macau. These few countries alone accounted for one-third of the total cumulative value of Chinese overseas investment (Table 2). A significant proportion of Chinese ODI had also been attracted by Australia, along with other countries like Russia, Peru and Mexico. In terms of projects, the biggest recipient of Chinese outbound investment was the United States. Up till 2001, the US had attracted 329 projects, representing 11% of the total number of projects committed by the Chinese. Hong Kong/Macau was also a major recipient of Chinese investment, with a total of 324 Chinese-invested entities by 2001. Russia ranked a close third, just a few projects less than that of Hong Kong/Macau.

In Southeast Asia, most of the countries hosted a relatively smaller share of Chinese investment compared to some other nations like Mexico and Russia. Among the ASEAN countries, Thailand had attracted the most number of Chinese projects and garnered the largest share of Chinese investment, accounting for 4.4% of the total cumulative value of China's outbound investment. It was followed by Cambodia with approximately 2.7% of total Chinese investment in non-trading activities, compared to the relatively more developed ASEAN countries of Singapore and Malaysia whose share in China's investment was merely 0.7%. The Philippines had the least share of Chinese investment, accounting for only a meagre 0.3% of Chinese investment.

A comparison of the levels of Chinese overseas investment at the end of 1991 and 2001 indicates that the proportion of Chinese investment was gradually becoming more widely distributed. Although North America (US and Canada) was still the biggest destination for Chinese overseas investment, the region's share had declined relative to other regions like Europe, Asia, Latin America, etc. Important new targets for Chinese overseas investment during that period included Sub-Saharan Africa, the former

---

[1] Friedwich Wu and Yee Hansia, "China's Rising Investment In Southeast Asia: How ASEAN and Singapore Can Benefit", MTI report (www.mti.gov.sg), 2002.

Table 2.   Geographical distribution of China's accumulated overseas investment in non-trading activities (breakdown by country), 1979–2001.

	Projects		Chinese Investment	
Country	Number	% Share	Cumulative Value (US$ million)	% Share
Developed Countries				
United States	329	10.6	559	12.6
Canada	95	3.1	392	8.8
European Union*	137	4.4	68	15.3
Hong Kong and Macau	324	10.5	534	12.0
ASEAN**	*537*		*586*	*13.2*
Thailand	154	5.0	194	4.4
Singapore	94	3.0	33	0.7
Malaysia	82	2.7	33	0.7
Indonesia	45	1.5	58	1.3
Philippines	33	1.1	15	0.3
Vietnam	41	1.3	56	1.3
Cambodia	54	1.7	120	2.7
Laos	11	0.4	30	0.7
Myanmar	23	0.7	47	1.1
East Asia				
Japan	95	3.1	19	0.4
Korea	26	0.8	15	0.3
Rest of Asia				
Australia	118	3.8	351	7.9
New Zealand	17	0.5	47	1.1
India	11	0.4	18	0.4
Others				
Russia	297	9.6	130	2.9
Peru	13	0.4	200	4.5
Mexico	36	1.2	143	3.2

Notes: (1) *denotes data for Greece and Ireland are not available.

    (2) **denotes data for Brunei are not available.

    (3) MOFTEC data reveal mainly 'non-trade' figures. It excludes or at least do not contain information on a number of capital movements (e.g., in financial services).

Source: *Yearbook of Foreign Economic Relations and Trade, 2002.*

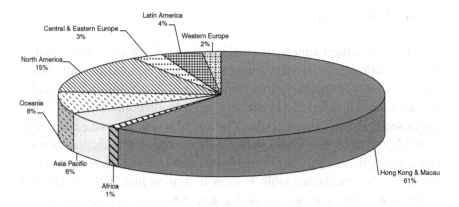

Figure 1. Geographical distribution of China's accumulated outward investment in trade-related activities, 1979–1994.

Note: Investment in trade services mainly comes from banks and other financial institutions. With the expansion of trade, credit business and remittance operations have increased.

Source: James Xiaoping Zhan, "Transnationalisation and Outward Investment: The Case of Chinese Firms", *Transnational Corporations*, 4(3), 67–100, 1995.

Soviet bloc (i.e., Commonwealth of Independent States) and the Middle East.

China's outward FDI in "trade" investments (a category for service activities) was also globally dispersed, although the pattern was different from that of China's outward FDI in non-trading activities. Up-to-date data are not readily available, but China's investments in trading activities were reported to be heavily concentrated in Hong Kong, and to a much lesser extent in Macau (Figure 1). Between 1979 and 1994, 61% of China's trade-related investment was located in Hong Kong and Macau as against the less than 9% of non-trade investment.[2] The relatively high proportion can be attributed to Hong Kong acting as a springboard for China's outward trade and investment, and serving as a channel for Chinese firms to raise capital.[3]

---

[2] Roger Strange, Jims Slater and Wang Limin (eds.), *Trade and Investment in China: The European Experience*, London, 1998.

[3] Hong Kong is the main conduit of foreign capital for China. It is also an entrepot trade and transshipment centre for China, providing vital transportation, storage, insurance, packaging and processing services."China 2020: Development Challenges in the New Century", *World Bank Report*, 1997.

Sectoral Distribution

Generally speaking, Chinese outward investment involves various business areas including trade, turnkey projects, resources exploration and extraction, processing, manufacturing, transport and communications, finance and insurance, medical and health services, consultation, hotels, etc.[4] Data on the sectoral distribution of China's outward investment were not readily available and as such, it would be beyond the scope of this chapter to make any meaningful analysis of the trends and patterns of Chinese ODI since 1980. The data available (Table 3) show that up to June 2001, investment in the trade-related or services sector accounted for over half of China's outward FDI.[5] In early 2000s, there were over 4400 Chinese foreign affiliates in this sector worldwide. The high percentage of China's capital outflows in the trade-related sector (57.2%) reflects that Chinese ODI was largely used to serve and promote the export of commodities.

As Table 3 indicates, up to the middle of 2001, the natural resources sector accounted for approximately 18% of China's outbound investment. Chinese foreign affiliates in this sector, primarily in minerals, forestry or ocean fisheries, were fewer in number compared to that established in the agricultural and manufacturing sectors but relatively larger in scale. Examples of ODI projects in this sector included a massive US$585 million acquisition of Indonesian oil and gas fields by China National Offshore Oil Corporation (CNOOC) in January 2001, as well as a US$394 million acquisition by Sinopec for a 75% stake in an oil field in North Africa.[6]

---

[4] Kevin G. Cai, "Outward Foreign Direct Investment: A Novel Dimension of China's Integration into the regional and global economy", *The China Quarterly*, 160 (December), 856–880, 1999.

[5] In trade-related activities like finance, Chinese banks were setting their eyes overseas, with notably the state-owned Bank of China (BOC) boasting operations in North America and Europe. BOC is also expanded into Jakarta as Indonesia's ethnic Chinese population, conservatively estimated at about seven million, makes the country a very attractive market for Chinese banks.

[6] Mainland companies were aggressively snapping up overseas assets. TCL, for instance, paid US$8 million for Germany's bankrupt Schneider Electronics in September 2002 to sell its wares under the brand name in order to break into the European market. Shanghai Baosteel paid US$30 million for a 46% stake in an Australian iron ore mining JV with Rio Tino PLC's Hamersley Iron unit, while PetroChina acquired Devon Energy's Indonesian oil and gas operations in 2002 for at least US$200 million. Shanghai Automotive was planning to

Table 3. Sectoral distribution of China's accumulated outward trade and non-trade flows, as of June 2001.

	Number of Enterprises	Contractual Value of Overseas Investment (USD million)
Trade/Services	4476	4450 (57.2)
Manufacturing (Processing & Assembling)	1580	1670 (21.5)
Resources Exploration	133	1430 (18.4)
Agriculture	142	150 (1.9)
Others	108	82 (1.1)
Total	6439	7782

Note: Figures in parentheses are percentage shares.
Source: Guo Ji Shang Bao, September 7, 2001.

It can also be inferred from Table 3 that till June 2001, the manufacturing sector accounted for approximately 22% of total contractual ODI. Chinese investment in this sector is usually characterized by relatively small-scale projects, labour-intensive production techniques and production of low value-added goods.[7] Manufactures such as textiles, bicycles, simple electrical appliances are industries where Chinese companies possessed a competitive edge, given that the Chinese economy was not ready to export technology-oriented capital.[8]

Investment Scale

Typically, the overseas investment projects that Chinese companies were involved in were comparatively small, except for a very few projects that were valued at over US$100 million. The scale of business operations tended

pay US$60 million for a 10% stake in GM's new Daewoo auto venture in South Korea. "A Global Shopping Spree for the Chinese", Business Week, November 18, 2002.

[7] Kevin G. Cai, "Outward Foreign Direct Investment: A Novel Dimension of China's Integration into the regional and global economy", The China Quarterly, 160 (December), 856–880, 1999.

[8] A few large conglomerates in technology-intensive industries such as aviation, astronautics and electronics had established foreign affiliates but such advanced technology-seeking projects were few in number. See Kevin G. Cai, The China Quarterly, 160 (December), 856–880, 1999.

to average around US$1 million, with the majority of companies having a scale of operations ranging between several hundred thousand and several million US dollars.

As seen from Table 4, among projects in non-trading activities, less than 40 involved an investment of over US$5 million by the Chinese partner. By the end of 2001, China had the most number of business projects in US, Hong Kong/Macau and Russia but these "non-trade" projects only had an average value of around US$1 million each. Among developed nations, the scale of Chinese investment in Canada was much larger than those in US and Hong Kong/Macau, with an average value of around US$4.1 million. This was followed by Australia and New Zealand where the average value per project were US$3 million and US$2.8 million, respectively. Investment projects in Australia, Canada and New Zealand were generally larger in scale since Chinese firms were mainly involved in natural resources development and backed financially by the Chinese government.

In developing countries such as Latin America or Africa, China committed the least number of projects in Benin, Zambia and Mexico compared to developed countries like Australia, the US or Hong Kong. However, the average investment value was relatively higher, ranging from around US$4 million to US$8 million per project. In Asia, particularly among the ASEAN countries, Laos and Myanmar hosted the least number of Chinese projects compared to the rest of their ASEAN neighbours. However, the average value of Chinese investment (around US$2 million) in Laos and Myanmar exceeded the average investment value of projects committed in the rest of the ASEAN member states, including Singapore (US$0.4 million), Thailand (US$1.3 million) and Malaysia (US$0.4 million).

Organizational Patterns

China's ODI mostly took the form of JVs or various cooperative projects with foreign partners. But almost all Chinese overseas ventures in banking and trade-supporting areas were wholly Chinese-owned.[9] In JVs, Chinese firms were generally inclined to hold a majority equity stake so as to control the operation of ventures. Apart from the host country's policy

---

[9]Kevin G. Cai, "Outward Foreign Direct Investment: A Novel Dimension of China's Integration into the Regional and Global Economy", *The China Quarterly*, 16 (December), 856–880, 1999.

Table 4. Average scale or size of overseas Chinese investment projects in non-trading activities, end-2001.*

Country	Number of Projects	Value of Investment (USD million)	Average Investment Value (USD million)
Peru#	11	19.6	15.4
Georgia	3	25.1	8.4
Zambia	17	134.1	7.9
Benin	4	16.7	4.2
Guinea Bissau	1	4.2	4.2
Canada	95	391.8	4.1
Mexico	36	142.9	4.0
Yemen	10	35.9	3.6
Cuba	4	14.0	3.5
DR Congo	7	24.2	3.5
Chile	6	20.87	3.5
Guyana	5	17.3	3.5
Honduras	5	16.2	3.2
Brazil	31	95.4	3.1
Zimbabwe	11	33.3	3.0
Qatar	4	12.1	3.0
Australia	118	351.1	3.0
New Zealand	17	46.9	2.8
Tanzania	14	39.5	2.8
Laos	11	30	2.7
Papua New Guinea	17	44.1	2.6
Mozambique	6	14.6	2.4
Cambodia	54	119.6	2.2
Myanmar	23	47.3	2.1
Egypt	17	30.6	1.8
Columbia	5	9.1	1.8
Romania	9	15.9	1.8
United States	329	559	1.7
Hong Kong and Macau	324	533.7	1.6
India	11	18.1	1.6
Bermuda	9	13.6	1.5
Vietnam	41	56.1	1.4
Thailand	154	193.8	1.3
Italy	10	12.6	1.3
South Africa	83	110.8	1.3
Jordan	9	9.7	1.1
Pakistan	18	19	1.1
Belarus	2	2.2	1.1

(Continued)

Table 4.   (*Continued*)

Country	Number of Projects	Value of Investment (USD million)	Average Investment Value (USD million)
Kyrgyzstan	22	22.1	1.0
Kenya	21	18.5	0.9
Nigeria	33	31.1	0.9
Mongolia	62	53.2	0.9
Switzerland	4	3	0.8
Mauritius	20	16.7	0.8
UK	16	10.5	0.7
Rwanda	4	2.9	0.7
France	16	10	0.6
Korea	26	15	0.6
Philippines	32	14.5	0.5
Singapore	94	33	0.4
Malaysia	82	32.5	0.4
Russia	297	129.7	0.4
Spain	13	4.2	0.3
Japan	95	18.5	0.2

Notes: (1) Average investment value = Value of investment/number of projects.

(2) *denotes countries are ranked according to the highest average investment value of projects committed by the Chinese.

(3) #The substantial investment in Peru is actually due to Shougang (Capital) Iron and Steel purchasing a Peruvian iron mining company in November 1992, the largest overseas investment project that the Chinese SOE had ever been involved.

Sources: Figures for average investment value calculated from data in *Almanac of China's Foreign Economic Relations and Trade*, 2002; Wu Hsiu-ling and Chen Chien-hsun, "An Assessment of Outward Foreign Direct Investment from China's Transitional Economy", *Europe-Asia Studies*, 53(8), December 1, 2001.

of prohibiting wholly foreign-owned enterprises, Chinese firms usually tended to engage in JVs with foreign counterparts due to limited financial resources, lack of knowledge of local conditions, minimizing various risks, or utilizing the wide distribution networks of local partners.[10]

The entry mode of Chinese ODI projects was largely decided by the financial resources, international experience and technological ability

---

[10] *Ibid.*

of specific Chinese firms.[11] Some SOEs with financial backing from the Chinese government preferred to invest overseas through mergers and acquisitions (M&A), for instance, in the resources extraction areas. Increasingly, there was M&A activity among the non-state-owned TNCs, particularly from the coastal Jiangsu and Zhejiang provinces that are historically the cradle of Chinese private businesses. Some of these dynamic private firms had merged with or acquired other foreign firms in order to obtain advanced technologies or promote the sale of the company's products on the world market. In some instances, M&A was also used as a channel to raise funds from the overseas market.[12] Generally, M&A by Chinese firms tended to occur in developed foreign countries where the system of laws and regulations was more developed.

An Overall Assessment

During those years, Chinese enterprises overseas were yet to make an impact in global markets with instantly recognizable brand names or distinctive logos around the world. Even home-grown established firms like Changhong, the world's second largest colour television manufacturer, was yet to gain worldwide prominence.[13] Chinese managers had focussed on building their businesses in the world's fastest growing consumer market before embarking on the expensive and risky venture of building a brand overseas.[14] Given the still limited presence of Chinese firms in world markets at that time, those hundreds of household names in China would

---

[11] *Ibid.*

[12] Instances of M&A by Chinese private firms have included the Wanxiang (Universal Joints) Group Company's acquisition of a listed American firm — the Universal Automotive Industries (UAI) Inc., and the merging of Jinyi Conglomerate (a Chinese company from Hangzhou specializing in food products) with a Singapore retailer — eWorld of Sports.

[13] It was reported that Changhong at that time beat electronics giants from Japan, South Korea and America to win a contract to supply Iraq with one million digital satellite colour TV receivers. The US$50 million contract enabled Changhong to become the first mainland enterprise to enter the post-war Iraqi market amid fierce competition from overseas rivals. "Changhong wins Iraq TV contract", *The Standard*, May 6, 2003.

[14] Legend Group, for instance, is the mainland's biggest PC maker but makes only 7% of its sales overseas. "Breaking into the Name Game", *Business Week*, March 31, 2003.

not come remotely close to the Global 500 ranks.[15] For some which made to the list, they were small players in terms of assets and revenues.[16] Admittedly, Chinese enterprises were still organizationally weaker and relatively smaller in scale compared to their international counterparts from developed countries like the US, Europe or Japan.

The stark fact remained that China, as a developing economy that had newly opened to market reform, had not been able to produce companies that could compete fiercely in the international market. Due to the legacy of the command economy, China's private, state-owned and collective firms had weak ownership structures that impeded growth and efficiency. Private firms were facing discrimination in securing bank loans and were unable to make large scale or long-term investments. Collective firms, which were owned by county- and village-level governments, were not flexible enough in responding to a rapidly changing market environment, while the SOEs faced the notorious problems of overstaffing, outdated management and mounting stockpiles of debt.[17] If Chinese companies at home were not well managed, their overseas branches or affiliates cannot be expected to be much better.

Another reason for the structural weakness of China's domestic firms was China's fragmented industrial structure, with too many industries and too many production lines for the same range of products. In China, M&A were often precluded by local protectionism, where provincial and municipal governments often defied economic rationality by treating local companies as their own and discouraging takeovers by outsiders.[18]

---

[15] Nearly half of Global 500 top companies were from US, Japan and Europe. China, despite being the world's sixth largest economy, had only 11 companies admitted to the prestigious group in 2001. All of them were SOEs: State Power (60th), China National Petroleum (81st), Sinopec (86th), China Telecom (214th), Industrial and Commercial BOC (243rd), BOC (277th), China Mobile (287th), Sinochem (311st), China Construction Bank (389th), COFCO (392th), Agricultural BOC (471st). *Fortune* magazine (www.fortune.com).

[16] The assets, profits, productivity and R&D spending of leading Chinese firms were a fraction that of the Global 500. Even the top Chinese industrial firm, with annual sales of US$6.1 billion, lagged behind the smallest of the Global 500, which had sales of US$8.9 billion. "Shoot the Moon", a *Business China* report from the *Economist Intelligence Unit (EIU)*, February 28, 2000.

[17] *Ibid.*

[18] *Ibid.*

Furthermore, most of the Chinese firms neither had the capability for innovations nor did they have the business acumen to survive in a highly competitive international environment.[19]

In short, Chinese companies remained woefully unprepared to deal with the competitive global business environment. When Chinese firms ventured abroad, they often had misconceptions about the host countries. Their business plans generally failed to address the business climate, marketing, operational efficiency and foreign regulations of the host countries.[20] They also frequently misgauged the additional costs, prospective competition and management complexities of the foreign marketplace.[21] It was further reported that Chinese companies tended to run the operations as if they were in China, and some would even engage friends or family members to advise them on how to run their businesses overseas.[22] Faced with such a myriad of problems, it is little wonder that most Chinese companies were yet to make a real impact in world markets.

Nonetheless, China's ODI had been impressive compared to many other developing nations. Within a span of just two decades, China's overseas investment had been globally dispersed with operations in more than 160 countries. With China's increasing integration into the world economy after the WTO, Chinese ODI would be expected to accelerate with more firms expanding rapidly abroad.[23] This was exactly what the government had in mind when it started to promote the "Go Global" policy.

---

[19]A MOFTEC survey indicated that in 2000, 55% of Chinese overseas enterprises (mostly in the manufacturing industry) were profitable, with some 28% breaking even and 17% operating at a loss. However, these figures are perhaps overly optimistic, given the doubtful accounting practices and often-inflated profit reporting system adopted by Chinese companies. Allan Zhang, "Going Abroad: China's Corporations Go Global", a report by PriceWaterhouseCoopers, September 2002.

[20]"Going Out: Other Side of Business Equation", *China Business Weekly*, April 22, 2003 (www.chinadaily.com.cn/bw).

[21]*Ibid.*

[22]*Ibid.*

[23]In 2000, China's government approved US$108 million in investments in ASEAN countries. In 2001, it approved US$188 million in new investment, a 74% jump. Actual Chinese investment should be significantly higher than the approved total, as Chinese companies are known to circumvent official foreign-currency controls by investing through offshore entities.

In particular, China was flexing its economic muscle in the ASEAN region; Chinese firms were reportedly grabbing local market shares aggressively for manufactured items like motorcycles and other consumer products. With the free trade agreement established between China and ASEAN around 2010, Southeast Asia became an even more important and attractive investment destination for Chinese businesses as they grow more savvy and outward oriented.

In those days, the majority of Chinese enterprises overseas were predominantly large SOEs. There were indications that some non-state-owned firms had started to nurture global ambitions and followed the SOEs in making forays into the world markets, although most of non-state firms were small and medium-sized companies.[24] In time to come, as Chinese indigenous non-state enterprises would emerge to be more competitive and stronger as a result of domestic restructuring, they could also separately spearhead Chinese ODI overseas and be successful in the global marketplace.

---

[24] According to UNCTAD in its World Investment Report 2002, non-state-owned firms had investments in over 40 countries, not only in Asia but also in other parts of the world. Among leading non-state-owned TNCs were the Huawei Technologies, the Wanxiang Group and Zheng Tai Group.

12

CHINA'S ECONOMY 2003: POISED FOR NEXT LAP OF HIGH GROWTH

Introduction

Zhu Rongji formally stepped down in March 2003. What was the state of the economy that he left behind? 2003 is a good vintage point for the Chinese economy to look back and look forth.

Zhu had already built up the growth momentum for the economy in the last few years of his office. The year 2002 ended with a hefty 9.1% growth, and the economy was heading for even stronger growth for 2003, which eventually chalked up a double-digit rate of 10.1% despite the outbreak of the Severe Acute Respiratory Syndrome (SARS). Zhu must have been very pleased with himself that he was handing over a sound economy — high growth with low inflation, to his successor Wen Jiabao.

In 1992, Zhu took over a much chaotic and overheating economy, sparked off by Deng Xiaoping's Nanxun. He had spent a lot of time and efforts including introducing many tough measures, to bring down overheating, as already discussed in early chapters. Then the Asian financial crisis struck in 1997. Though China was not directly hit by this regional crisis, its external and domestic environment for economic growth had sharply deteriorated, with the economy actually heading for a deflation in the post-crisis years. Thus, Zhu had to change gears in order to reverse the growth trends. And he had succeeded beyond his expectations.

When Zhu started as Vice Premier in 1992, China's per-capita GDP was 1,900 yuan. Zhu left office as Premier in 2003 with China's per-capita GDP rising more than five folds to 10,500 yuan. Annual economic growth for his period in office, 1991–2003, was 10.1%, a truly sterling growth performance in an overall sense.

Little did Zhu realize at that time that China's economy after his departure in 2003 was actually turbocharged to even high rates of growth! Growth since 2003 averaged at 12% a year along with reasonable price stability (i.e., no overheating) until China was struck by the global financial crisis in 2008. In all fairness, Zhu should share some of the credit for such spectacular growth performance after 2003.

With hindsight, it is sufficiently clear that Zhu's efforts in pushing vigorously for the reform of the state-owned enterprises (SOEs) and banking reform plus his measures to allow greater privatization had without doubt laid a strong precondition for the economy to achieve such high growth. By 2003, China's economy was extensively marketized. With few exceptions such as those in the strategic state sectors, market was a basic guide for resource allocation in most areas.

More significantly, the various measures introduced by Zhu to prepare for China's entry to the World trade Organization (WTO), including greater liberalization of the market and the further opening up of China to foreign trade and foreign investment, were conducive to growth. Officially, China became a member of WTO on December 11, 2001, but months before that many large foreign corporations had already come to China, vying to establish a good "beach-head" first. Thus, foreign direct investment (FDI) in 2002 increased to US$53 billion from $47 billion in 2001 and further to US$61 billion for 2004. Fixed investment went up to 4.6 trillion yuan in 2002 from 4.0 trillion yuan of 2001 and further up to 5.6 trillion yuan for 2004. Exports in 2002 went up to US$326 billion from US$266 of 2001, and further up to $438 billion for 2004.

In this way, China's economy in 2003 was all gearing up for the next phase of hyper growth at double-digit rates, based on rising domestic investment and increasing external demand (exports minus imports). In historical perspective, the year 2003 marks the critical point of China's economic take-off, for which Zhu had indeed created all the important preconditions.

After 2003, China's heavy industry from iron and steel and petrochemicals to automobile expanded rapidly. Infrastructure building from highways to ports and airports also sped up. In the meanwhile, a lot of other export-oriented manufacturing activities like consumer electronics and a wide variety of labour-intensive products had grown even more rapidly as China became a home for numerous regional and global production networks. All these activities were responsible for China's post-2003 dynamic growth.

Specifically for China's economic growth in 2003, which was initially estimated to be around 9%, but was subsequently revised up to 10.1%, the highest since 1995. Such impressive growth was mainly fuelled by a sharp rise in both domestic demand — particularly domestic investment (growing at 30% year-on-year) and external demand (with exports growing at a stunning 35%).

At that time, many foreign observers had come to realize that China's GDP accounts had significantly understated China's actual levels of economic activities. This was in sharp contrast to the frequent accusation by foreign commentators, a few years ago, against the same statistical system for having inflated China's economic growth numbers. In fact, China's National Statistical Bureau was then just taking measures to overhaul its reporting and computation systems in order to better capture the under-reported activities, particularly in the service sector. This explains the upward revision of China's growth series as well as its total and per-capita GDP.

The spillover effects of China's high economic growth were increasingly felt by its Asian neighbours. Apart from the surge in Chinese tourists, China imported a lot more from these economies than China's exports to them, thereby operating as Asia's second engine of economic growth after Japan.

Hectic economic growth had started creating new problems. Rapid industrial growth and rising affluence aggravated energy shortages, particularly the electricity supply in the urban areas. Rising car ownership (4.4 million units of new automobile in 2003) had also increased China's dependency on oil imports. China in 2003 was set to import more oil than Japan.

In 2003, dynamic export growth already created problems for China. Its chronic trade surplus brought about bilateral trade frictions with the USA, with the US government continuing to pressurize China to revalue its Renminbi. This issue, then and later, was quite clear. While the appreciation of the Renminbi would not help reduce the US trade imbalance with China, it could damage China's fragile financial sector while also hurting its export competitiveness.

Nonetheless, China policy makers soon began to realize the need for making the Renminbi exchange mechanism more flexible and liberalizing *some aspects of capital controls. In the longer run, China would still need to address the issue of the financial sector reform.*

With the memory of fighting the tough inflation in the mid-1990s still fresh in their minds, some officials got jittery over the hectic growth in 2003 and its potential for economic overheating in 2004. Money supply in 2003 shot up to 21% because of the influx of foreign capital. Nonetheless, inflation was still mild.

More obvious was the phenomenon of "sectoral overheating", with over-investment and over-production in some industries or sectors (e.g., automobile, steel, cement, refrigerators, etc.) existing side by side with under-investment and bottlenecks in others. This was actually more a problem of structural imbalance. Nonetheless, one of the government's major tasks in 2004 was to address such structural imbalance of the economy and to cool the overheated sectors.

Finally, China's spectacular economic growth in 2003 had not done enough to relieve the country's emerging socio-economic problems such as unemployment, income disparities and the plight of millions of peasants in the rural areas.

Looking back, many issues and problems from structural imbalance arising from over-production, over-investment and over-export to trade frictions and revaluation of the Renminbi, and the social aspects of growth had already surfaced in 2003 at the inception of China's new phase of hyper growth. Over a decade later, Xi Jinping is still coming to grips with those problems.

Hectic Growth is Back

China's economy in 2003 experienced highly impressive growth of 10.1%, despite some initial worries caused by the outbreak of the SARS. Actually, the preliminary official estimate in early December was only 8.5%, but the final figure came after adjustment.[1] In fact, key economic indicators like domestic investment, export growth and industrial production all served to show that the actual 2003 growth rate should at least be close to 10%.

---

[1]National Development and Reform Commissioner Ma Kai said on December 2, 2003 that China's economic growth for 2003 would be 8.5% (http://news.xinhuanet. com/fortune/2003-12/02/content_1208458.htm).

The spurt of high economic growth during that period together with rapid structural change in the economy had rendered China's traditional GDP accounting system seriously outdated, e.g., many new economic activities, particularly those pertaining to the contribution of the service sector were not adequately reflected in existing GDP growth accounts. China's National Bureau of Statistics was then overhauling its reporting and computation systems, not only to improve data quality but also to better capture the under-reported "underground economic activities". This had resulted in an upward revision of China's GDP growth series as well as its total and per-capita GDP.[2]

With 10% growth, China in 2003 was the best performing economy in the region, which had been slowly recovering from the global recession. China's growth performance was all the more creditable considering that the outbreak of SARS in the early summer had at one time threatened to derail China from its high-growth path, as indeed the second quarter growth plunged to 6.7% from the 9.9% in the first quarter. In the third quarter, growth quickly rebounded to 9.1% (Figure 1).

2003 was a kind of banner year for China with special significance: (1) It marked the 25th anniversary of China's economic reform, which was formally launched by Deng Xiaoping in December 1978 following the endorsement by the Third Plenum of the Party's 11th Central Committee. China's success in economic reform over the past two decades is well known, as evidenced by the average annual economic growth of over 9% since 1979. The achievement of 2003 was certainly considered by Beijing as yet another manifestation of this success. (2) 2003 was the first year of China's new leadership under Hu Jintao and Wen Jiabao. Their leadership was put to the test by the SARS outbreak shortly after they were at the helm. Economic success had greatly facilitated their power transition as well as bolstered their confidence in coming to grips with several rising challenges on both foreign and domestic fronts. (3) As shown in Figure 2, China's growth trends had been declining from 14.2% in 1992 to 7.1% in 1999, and the 2003 strong growth signalled a new sustainable growth trend of around 10% a year for the next few years.

---

[2] See "Statistics System Receive Overhaul", *China Daily*, December 14, 2003.

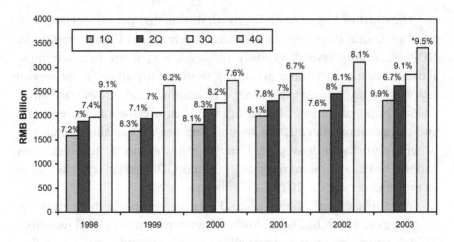

Figure 1.   China's quarterly growth rate, 1998–2003.*

Note: The level of quarter GDP is in current price and the quarter growth rate is calculated in constant price.

Sources: The People's Bank of China, *Quarterly Statistical Bulletin*, various issues; *China Monthly Economic Indicators* (October 2002 issue).

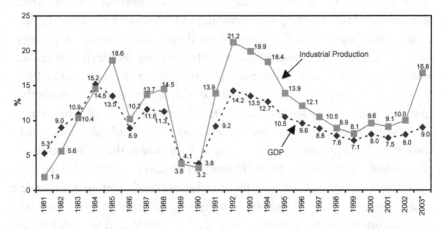

Figure 2.   Growth of GDP and industrial production, 1981–2003.

Note: GDP data in 2003 is estimated; industrial production data is from January to November.

Sources: *China Statistical Yearbook 2002*; *China Monthly Statistics*, October 2003; website of National Bureau of Statistics of China, December 2003 (http://www.stats.gov.cn).

Indeed, China achieved several new economic milestones in 2003. As a result of many years of surging exports and the continuing influx of FDI (FDI for 2003 about the same as for 2002, i.e., US$52.7 billion),[3] China had built up a very strong external economic balance, which was exerting pressures on the *Renminbi* to appreciate. As China's major trade partners like USA, Japan and EU had been calling on Beijing to revalue the *Renminbi*, this actually encouraged the further inflow of speculative foreign capital, which in turn led to a sharp rise in domestic money supply as well as the swelling of China's foreign exchange reserves to the record level of US$400 billion (the world's second largest) at the end of 2003.

On the domestic industrial front, China's automobile, steel, cement, building materials and a wide variety of electronics and electrical machinery industries turned out record levels of output in 2003. Some service activities were even brisker, particularly for housing transactions, car sales, and domestic and outbound tourism. Many of these key economic indicators pointed unmistakably to a buoyant or even overheated economy, leading some foreign observers to argue that China's existing GDP accounts had significantly understated China's actual levels of economic activities. This shift in perception represents a sharp contrast to the frequent foreign accusation against the same statistical system for having inflated China's economic growth numbers!

China's rising economic prosperity was already visible to visiting foreigners, and its spillovers were also increasingly felt by its Asia-Pacific neighbours. Apart from the surge in Chinese tourists to other Asian countries, China's imports from Japan, Korea, Taiwan, Singapore, Indonesia, Malaysia, the Philippines, Thailand, India and Australia had exceeded its exports to these economies, thereby incurring trade deficits with them, which were offset by China's trade surplus with USA and EU (Figure 3). Clearly, these Asia-Pacific economies were tapping China's vast domestic market and its growing demand for consumer goods, capital equipment and raw materials. In other words, China's economy was operating increasingly as Asia's second locomotive of economic growth after Japan.

---

[3] "Foreign Trade Volume to Hit US$840 billion", *China Daily*, December 29, 2003.

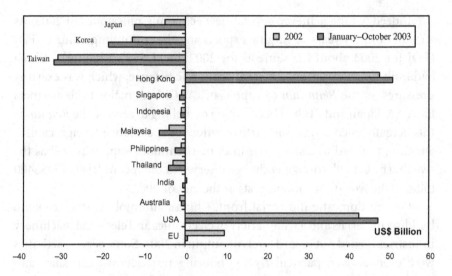

Figure 3.   China's trade balance with selected countries.

Sources: China Monthly Customs Statistics (December 2002), Ministry of Commerce website (mofcom.gov.in).

Besides creating a new source of growth for the region, China was also catalyzing the regional economic integration process in East Asia. In 2002, China took a bold initiative to conclude a Free Trade Agreement (FTA) with the ASEAN countries, thereby pressuring Japan and Korea to follow suit. In June 2003, China signed the Closer Economic Partnership Arrangement (CEPA) with Hong Kong and subsequently with Macau. CEPA was obviously aimed at the eventual integration of the Greater China economies after the inclusion of Taiwan in future. In October 2003, Wen Jiabao attended the ASEAN Summit in Bali and worked out arrangements with Japan and Korea to boost Northeast Asian tripartite cooperation.

All these foreign economic initiatives clearly serve as a powerful catalyst for the long-term economic integration of East Asia with potentially profound geo-economic implications. Without doubt, China's successful economic growth had given its new leadership the needed confidence and capacity to effectively conduct such kinds of economic diplomacy.

However, China's hectic economic growth in the second half of 2003 had also taken its toll in the form of potential economic overheating. The large influx of foreign capital stoked inflation by increasing money supply and hence too much liquidity. This in turn fuelled domestic investment and real estate speculation. At the same time, rising domestic demand and the export boom brought about a sharp rise in manufacturing activities, which aggravated power shortages. As if this is not enough, for the first time in many years, food prices[4] and energy prices rose in the urban areas. These were signs of economic overheating.

Worse still, economic overheating existed side by side with over-production of light industrial goods, growing structural unemployment in the urban areas and continuing stagnation in certain rural sectors. In short, China's economic boom was underpinned by a serious sectoral imbalance characterized by chronic deflation in some sectors and inflationary pressures in others.

The annual year-end national economic work conference called for "suitable structural adjustment" in order to sustain stable growth. Measures were proposed to rein in over-expansion of such industries as automobile, property, steel and refrigerators in order to head off a potential glut. This slowed down the overall growth momentum in the first half of 2004.

Strong Sources of Economic Growth

The Chinese economy, taking advantage of the positive WTO effects, experienced strong growth of 8% in 2002. High growth momentum spilled over to the first quarter of 2003, which chalked up a hefty 9.9% growth (Figure 1). At the beginning of 2003 when the global economy at large was still in the doldrums, China was conspicuously the bright spot. However, China's economy soon came down with only 6.7% growth in the second quarter due to the outbreak of SARS. SARS struck the Chinese economy much like a random "external shock". In retrospect, the overall adverse economic effects of SARS were surprisingly mild, even though the crisis had exposed the weaknesses in China's healthcare system. The epidemic was quite effectively contained once the central government took the matter seriously.

---

[4]China's grain output fell from the peak of 512 million tons in 1998 to 457 million tons in 2002. For the first time in six years, grain prices started to soar in autumn of 2003: wheat prices up by 32% in the northeast; corn prices up by 50% and so on. See Antoaneta Bezlova, "Grain Prices Hikes Ring Alarm Bells in China" (www.atimes.com).

More importantly, China as a large, diverse economy was inherently much more resilient against such a shock. SARS mainly took its toll on tourism, travel business and retail sectors in some urban centres, while agricultural and industrial production (which is the mainstay of the economy) suffered relatively little disruption. Hence, the Chinese economy could quickly shrug off the effects of SARS and started to bounce back in the third quarter with 9.1% growth, thereby resuming its high growth momentum for the rest of the year.

The pattern of economic growth in 2003 was pretty much similar to that of 2002 except that all the major sources of economic growth for 2003 were much stronger than those for 2002. For a huge economy like China, as can be expected, domestic demand (i.e., domestic consumption and domestic investment) regularly accounts for nearly 80% of its total demand, thereby constituting the dominant source of its economic growth. As shown in Figure 4, total household consumption for first 11 months of 2003 increased by 9%, compared to 5% in 2002, indicating that the economy as a whole had largely shaken off the deflation of the past few years.

The purchase of automobile by the growing urban middle class and of household appliances for their newly acquired homes had come to

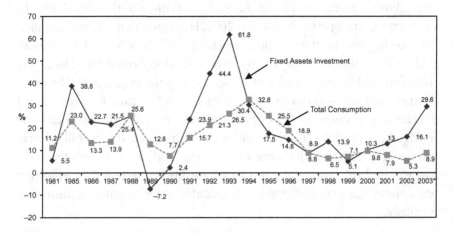

Figure 4.   Growth of fixed assets investment and total consumption, 1981–2003.*

Note: *2003 data is from January to November.

Sources: *China Statistics Yearbook 2002*; *China Monthly Statistics*, October 2003; website of National Bureau of Statistics of China, December 2003 (http://www.stats.gov.cn).

constitute a new source of domestic consumption. Furthermore, China's retail sector was beginning to feel the emergence of the more consumption-oriented post-reform generation, which was the product of China's one-child family policy. With steady rise in affluence, these new sources of spending would further change China's patterns of domestic consumption in the years to come.

For the growth of domestic demand in 2003, of far more importance had been the sharp rise in fixed assets investment in the first 11 months to 30%, compared to the 16% of 2002. Not since the early 1990s had China's fixed investment grown at such a high rate. Last time (from the early to mid-1990s), such high levels of domestic investment had given rise to double-digit rates of GDP growth and then high inflation, prompting the former Premier Zhu Rongji to introduce draconian macroeconomic control measures to cool down the economy. Accordingly, Chinese policy makers were getting a bit concerned that the economy might be overheating again. In any case, such a high rate of investment was not sustainable, and it could certainly lead to over-investment and over-production in such industries as automobile, steel and real estate.

The economic upsurge in 2003 was also fuelled by an explosive growth of external demand. As shown in Figure 5, China's exports in 2003 chalked up a stunning 35% year-on-year growth to reach a record level of US$430 billion — total trade for 2003 amounting to US$840 billion, with China becoming the world's fourth largest trading nation after USA, Japan and European Union (EU).[5] In 1994, when exports registered a 32% hike, this led to GDP growth of 12.7%. Thus, the sharp export expansion in 2003 had made a substantial contribution to the overall GDP growth in 2003.

As USA remained China's top export market (Figure 6), China's strong export growth inevitably further widened the US trade deficit with China, which amounted to over US$100 billion according to US figures, but much less from Chinese official source. This was mainly because the American computation of Chinese exports to USA included a large amount of Chinese re-exports via Hong Kong.[6] It may be noted that despite China's huge trade

---

[5]"Ministry of Commerce: China's Total Trade this Year Could Reach US$840 Billion" (http://news.xinhuanet.com/fortune/2003-12/29/content_1251469.htm).

[6]In 2002, US trade deficit with China amounted to US$103 billion according to official US computation, but only US$42 billion by the Chinese side. Basically, the US regarded

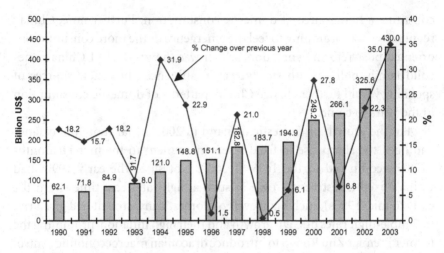

Figure 5.   China's exports, 1990–2003.

Sources: China Statistics Yearbook 2002; China Monthly Statistics, October 2000; website of National Bureau of Statistics of China, December 2003 (http://www.stats.gov.cn).

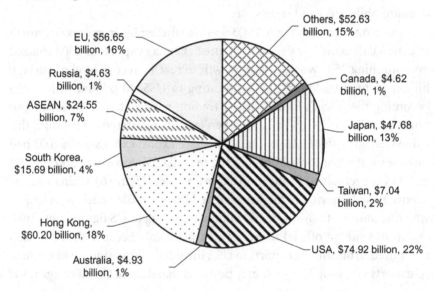

Figure 6.   Top 10 destinations for China's exports, January–October 2003 (US$ billion).

Source: Website of Ministry of Commerce of the P.R. China (http://www.mofcom.gov.cn).

surplus with USA, China's overall trade surplus for 2003 was expected to come down to around US$15 billion, as compared to US$30 billion for 2002. This was because China had incurred increasing trade deficits with its neighbouring economies, as shown in Figure 3.

One of the perplexing issues of the Chinese economy in 2003, as broached earlier, was whether or not existing official GDP figures had understated the actual levels of economic activities. Director of the National Statistical Bureau, Li Deshui, denied such deliberate government efforts to understate GDP growth.[7] Nonetheless, with explosive growth of both fixed assets investment (the highest since 1994) and exports (the highest since the open-door policy), it was hard to believe that the GDP accounts registered only 8.5% growth. Based on their historical time series, such unusual high levels of domestic investment and export growth should potentially give rise to a double-digit rate of GDP growth.

A closer look at the historical relationship between industrial pro-duction growth and GDP growth over the past two decades, as shown in Figure 2, also yields similar implications. From the past behaviour of these two time series, the growth of industrial production tends to be just a few percentage points above GDP growth, especially from the early 1990s onwards. Since "industry" then constituted 45% of China's total GDP, how would it be possible for China's overall GDP growth rate in 2003 to remain single digit while the industrial production had shot up to 17% (the highest since 1995) — unless one assumes zero or negative growth in the other sectors? Before China's National Statistical Bureau had rejigged its GDP accounts to reconcile these inconsistencies, China experts continued to be confounded by such downward bias in the official GDP growth figures at that time.

Chinese commodities shipped to America via Hong Kong (i.e., as HK's re-exports) or another third place as all imports from China. Yet, the US excluded American commodities transited to China via Hong Kong from its total exports to the mainland. This naturally overstated its trade deficit with China, see *Beijing Review*, November 27, 2003. It may further be added that most of Chinese exports to USA are manufactured products assembled in China, which contain many foreign-made parts and components, including those from Japan, Korea, Taiwan and USA. In other words, many "made-in-China" goods sold in the USA actually contain low Chinese domestic content, i.e., low value-added for China.

[7]"Director Li Deshui of the National Statistical Bureau: China Did Not Understate GDP Growth Rates" (http://news.xinhuanet.com./2003-11/20/content_1190001.htm).

With High Growth, Still More Worries

China's spectacular economic growth in 2003 did not spell unqualified blessings for the Chinese government. Specifically, high growth at that time had not done enough to relieve China's many short-term socio-economic woes. Since most of the growth activities were concentrated in the more developed areas along the coastal regions and selective pockets in the interior, this had not contributed much to narrowing China's regional development gaps or to reducing rural–urban income disparities. In particular, high economic growth had barely ameliorated the plight of many poor peasants in the rural areas.

More seriously, China's unemployment remained high, with the "registered unemployment rate" (which did not include the new *xiagang* or lay-offs from the SOEs) in urban areas then increasing to 4.7% from 4% in 2002.[8] Even prosperous Shanghai had started to face the unemployment problem.[9] This explains why the annual national economic conference in that year had singled out the important need to raise the incomes of the peasants and step up the re-employment of the laid-off workers.

While many old problems remained critical, hectic economic growth had created new ones such as energy shortages, particularly pertaining to power supply. Though China then globally ranked second to the US in installed electricity capacity (338 gigawatts in 2000), demand for electricity during those years had been increasing at double-digit rates (15% higher for 2003) due to rising urban affluence and rapid industrial expansion. Consequently, many regional grids including Shanghai and Guangzhou were under severe supply constraints.[10] The sharp rise in private car ownership in the past two years had also increased Chinese demand for imported oil, rising by 30% in 2003 to a record level of 82 million tons. China's oil imports in 2004 were then expected to exceed that of Japan to become the world's second largest oil importer after the USA.[11]

---

[8]"Concerns Spark 9 Million Jobs Scheme", *China Daily*, December 23, 2003.
[9]"Rise in Jobless Tops Shanghai Issues", *The Standard* (Hong Kong, December 5, 2003).
[10]"China in an Energy Quandary" (www.atimes.com); also (Mingpao.com/20031128/; www.chinanews.com.cn/n/2003-12-15/26/380967.html).
[11]www.chinanews.com.cn/n/2003-12-22/383745.html.

Likewise, China's dynamic export expansion had resulted in trade frictions with its largest export market, USA. Driven by electioneering politics, Washington had been pressurizing China to revalue the *Renminbi*. This issue was then already sufficiently clear. While any revaluation of the *Renminbi* would not much help reduce US trade imbalance with China, it could be highly damaging to China's still fragile financial sector burdened by a large amount of non-performing loans. Accordingly, China had at that time confirmed that it would continue with its present fixed exchange rate regime along with capital controls. At the same time, it had taken measures to make the *Renminbi* exchange-rate mechanism a little more flexible and to liberalize small-scale capital movements.[12] In the long run, China would still need to go for a flexible exchange rate in order to cope with the long-term appreciation trend of the *Renminbi*.

The burning economic issue for 2004 was, no doubt, how to avoid overheating. Chinese officials were still divided as to what "overheating" is exactly meant in the China context. It would certainly be unlike the kind of classical economic overheating it had experienced in the mid-1990s when inflation was rampant.

In 2003, as shown in Figure 7, the price increase was quite mild. However, money supply had shown a sharp rise to 21%, which was buoyed by the influx of capital and easy liquidity. In turn, easy credit had fuelled real estate speculation (Figure 8) and the over-expansion of certain "hot" industries like automobile, cement, steel and building materials. In this sense, China's economy was developing the phenomenon of "sectoral overheating".

In other words, the Chinese government in 2004 was facing the problem of serious structural imbalance as a result of the frenzied pace of economic growth in 2003. For certain industries, over-investment led to over-production, existing side by side with under-investment and bottlenecks in others. Former Premier Zhu Rongji used tough macroeconomic measures to bring down the overheated economy to soft landing. But it was not so easy for Premier Wen Jiabao to tackle the overheating issue at that time as the Chinese economy had become much more market driven.

---

[12]"Guidelines Set to Improve Yuan Exchange-Rate Mechanism", *China Daily*, December 4, 2003.

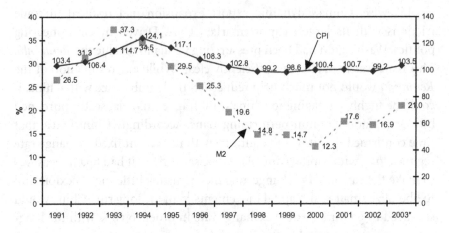

Figure 7.   Money supply and consumer price index, 1991–2003.*

Note: *2003 M2 data is from January to October; CPI data is of November.

Sources: China Statistics Yearbook 2002; *China Monthly Statistics*, October 2003; website of National Bureau of Statistics of China, December 2003 (http://www.stats.gov.cn).

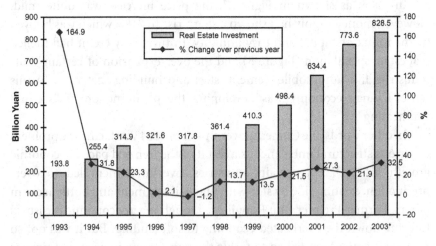

Figure 8.   Real estate investment, 1993–2003.*

Note: *2003 data is from January to November.

Sources: *China Statistics Yearbook 2002*; *China Monthly Statistics*, October 2003; website of National Bureau of Statistics of China, December 2003 (http://www.stats.gov.cn).

Still, measures were already undertaken to tighten credit and loans in order to cool down the overheated sectors.[13] But this also meant dampening economic growth. As for external demand, exports in 2004 were not expected to continue with such neck-breaking rate of 35% increases. On the other hand, the continuing recovery of the US economy ensured a strong demand for Chinese exports. On balance, there were still strong prospects for the Chinese economy to maintain strong growth in 2004.

---

[13]"Beijing Begins to Pay Heed to Sounds of Growth Strain", *Asian Wall Street Journal*, December 29, 2003.

13

POPULATION TRANSITION FROM RAPIDLY DECLINING FERTILITY RATES

Introduction

In 1999, China's population stood at 1.26 billion. Its natural growth rate fell to the low of 0.82%, down from 1.57% in 1992, as China implemented its family planning programme (Jihua shengyu zhengce) based on the "one-child policy" (OCP). This prompted Beijing to proudly declare that as a result of its successful family planning efforts, China had averted 330 million births, thereby saving the country a huge sum equivalent to its 1997 GDP.

By 2013, China's total population increased to 1.36 billion, or 7% more in 14 years. Its natural growth rate fell further to 0.49%, indicating that the OCP had been working well — in fact, too well! A lot of births must have also been prevented in this period. In this sense, China had successfully averted the potential "population time bomb".

The OCP had no doubt effectively brought down China's population growth for the period of 1979–1999. But it is difficult to say how much this policy had actually contributed to the still lower population growth for the next period of 1999–2013. This is because China's economy had achieved economic take-off during this period, and the resulting socio-economic forces would have inevitably slowed down population growth even without such stringent policy intervention.

Of greater importance are the broader socio-economic changes that are accompanying the population transition. Zhu Rongji had certainly welcomed the positive results of the OCP during 1979–1999 in terms of reducing the pressure of rapid population growth on his programmes of economic and social development. Because of the resulting smaller population, Zhu was able to channel a lot more of the scarce resources, instead of feeding the extra mouths, for useful economic development. Above all, lower population growth had made it much easier for him to tackle the thorny employment issue.

Indeed, Zhu as Premier had to give top priority to the country's unemployment problem. As China's economic development quickly picked up after Deng's Nanxun in 1991, a lot of surplus rural labour had been released from agricultural production and migrated to the urban areas as nongmin gong (or migrant workers) to seek modern sector employment. This, along with the annual new entrants to the labour force in the urban areas, had added mounting pressures to the government for employment creation.

Thus, as China's economic growth came down in the aftermath of the 1997 Asian financial crisis, Zhu had to struggle very hard to maintain economic growth at 8% (or his baoba), principally to protect employment. Subsequently, he had also to deal with 20 million or so laid-off workers (xiagang or "off post") from state-owned enterprises, as Zhu pushed this state sector to reform and restructure. In short, this sharp slowdown in population growth had been much a boon to Zhu's economic and social policies.

However, the situation in the second period had radically changed. China's population increased only 8% during 2003–2013, compared to 29% in the first period of 1979–1999. This means that the natural population decline due to the socio-economic factors (as a result of successful economic development) had reinforced the population controls policy to bring about a further drop in the natural growth rate — hence only 0.49% in 2013. When a population is experiencing a rapid slowdown in its natural growth, this will not only precipitate the rapid ageing of its population structure, but also bring about a serious repercussion in the labour market.

Technically speaking, the implementation of the OCP will inevitably bring about the rapid ageing of the population in the course of time. In fact, the ageing problem has started to surface in recent years, as evidenced by the rise of age-group of 65 from 6.9% in 1999 to 10.1% in 2014. As for the impact on the labour market, China's working age population, aged 15–59, started to decline for the first time in 2012. The decline has since continued, with the total labour force shrinking by 3.7 million in 2014.

Economist would argue that China's labour force has reached what may be called the typical Lewis' turning point, which implies that there is no more surplus labour in China, even though the situation does not translate into immediate labour shortages. But from the standpoint of economic development, China was running out of its "demographic dividend" that has fuelled the rapid growth of China's labour-intensive manufacturing industries. All these would surely have caused consternation to Zhu if he were still in charge. In other words, the OCP had obviously overshot its targets, turning a boon into a bane.

To better predict future population movements, demographers commonly use the more precise indicator of total fertility rate (TFR), which measures the average number of children that would be born alive to a woman during her entire reproductive years in accordance with the prevailing age-specific fertility rates. A TFR of 2.1 denotes the replacement-level fertility.

China's family planning officials preferred to use the term "natural population growth rate" instead of this more technical term, TFR. Hence, official figures for China's TFR were not available for all periods. This chapter discusses the overall implications of China's falling TFR around 2000.

Thus, China's TFR had steadily declined since 1979 as a result of its early adoption of family planning practices. The decline was later accelerated by the introduction of the draconian OCP, even though its effectiveness in the rural areas in the initial period had been highly debatable.

Overall, China has undergone two successful fertility transitions. The first took place in the 1970s, from high (pre-industrial) fertility to low fertility. The second occurred in the early 1980s under the impact of economic reform and rapid economic development, which brought fertility further down to below-replacement level. By the early 1990s, China's TFR was estimated to be around 1.8.

The most critical issue then was whether China had also undergone the <u>third</u> fertility transition from the late 1990s onwards, i.e., from below-replacement fertility to a substantially lower level. Chinese demographers at that time were not in total agreement amongst themselves. From the early 1990s onwards China ceased releasing its official TFR series. Perhaps even the Chinese government might be unsure of the actual TFR level.

Several official sample surveys in the 1990s show TFRs plunging to as low as 1.5. But the validity of these surveys had been disputed by Chinese demographers because of widespread under-reporting of births in the survey. Nonetheless, continuing rapid economic growth in the late 1990s, accompanied by strong anti-natal social changes (e.g., massive migration of rural youths to cities, sharp reduction in rural poverty, and elimination of illiteracy among the young and the middle-aged, particularly the women) must have caused fertility to dip further.

All things considered, we could reasonably assume that China's TFR in the late 1990s would be around 1.7, but moving towards 1.6. This means that China's total population could be easily capped at 1.4 billion in 2010, as officially targeted, and would eventually peak at 1.5–1.6 billion, possibly as early as 2030. This will then be the single most significant socio-economic achievement for China in the first quarter of this century.

With the fertility level apparently continuing to decline unabated, sooner or later the government would have to drop the unpopular OCP, which had outlived its usefulness amidst the thrust of radical economic and social transformation of China today. In any case, the OCP was originally meant to be a "policy only for one generation".

Then the study concludes ominously: in the experiences of other East Asian societies, when their fertility had declined to a very low level and built into the economic and social life of the people, even the subsequent adoption of pro-natal policy by their governments would be ineffective in reversing such declining trends. This may be a valuable lesson for Beijing.

Viewed from 2015, the above conclusion was actually very perceptive. After 1999, China's economy was steaming ahead with double-digit rates of economic growth along with fundamental social transformation, and this alone would have slowed down population growth. The OCP had merely further aggravated the decline. The average TFR level through the 2000s was around 1.6 and then fell further to 1.5 in recent years. Hence, China's total population in 2013 was 1.36 billion, and it was recently forecast that the population would peak in 2025 with a little over 1.4 billion, instead of 1.5–1.6 billion that was earlier projected when the OCP was initiated.

This follows that the OCP had long outlived itself, with socio-economic costs increasingly outweighing its initial benefits. The rapid deceleration of China's population growth in recent years had quickly turned into "bad demographics" with serious negative impact on China's future economic growth and social development. The fact that the OCP had continued for over three decades was partly because of bureaucratic inertia, as the National Population and Family Planning Commission had grown into a huge, self-interested organization until it was finally superseded by the National Health and Family Planning Commission in 2013.

In early 2014, the government finally put an end to the OCP in its original rigid form by relaxing the rules for having the second child. But it all seemed to have come too late, as there had been no popular response for the married couples to have an additional child, particularly in the urban areas. In Shanghai, 90% of its women of child-bearing age are qualified to have a second child; but only 5% had formally applied!

With continuing economic development and urbanization, the decision for a Chinese couple today to have children will increasingly depend on their total family incomes, wife's income, costs of bringing up children, opportunity costs in terms of leisure and the wife's career for having children, and so on. Such is the microeconomic theory of fertility behaviour associated with the Nobel laureate Chicago economist Gary Becker. In a sense, it is already too late for China's policy makers to realize that successful economic development is actually the most effective family planning policy.

Looking back, China's OCP has been dubbed the world's "greatest social experiment". It was largely a technocratic response to the highly complex issue of human fertility behaviour, which is shaped by all sorts of economic, social and cultural factors. It has since come to light that the OCP was originally put up by State Councillor Song Jian, a rocket scientist by profession, not by trained demographers. Song developed his "Theory of Population Control" based on simple extrapolation of China's population to reach 1.7 billion before 2000 and further to 2.7 billion in the following 50 years.

Such staggering numbers must have scared Deng Xiaoping and his economic planner Chen Yun to hastily accept the OCP. Both still had fresh memory of how Mao had struggled so hard (but failed) to feed China's teeming millions when China's population then was below 1 billion.

In the event, the OCP had turned out to be also the world's harshest population control programme. Those in charge of implementing this programme were largely bureaucrats and tough administrators. From the start, they introduced draconian measures to carry out this policy relentlessly, causing a lot of social sufferings and family pains along with a lot of negative social consequences like female infanticide and the resultant serious gender imbalance in the existing population. Whatever economic benefits that had yielded to the OCP must also be measured in the context of its high social costs.

Declining Fertility in the 1990s

China is the world's most populous nation. On November 12, 1999, when the world's total population reached six billion, China's own population (excluding Hong Kong, Macau and Taiwan) was officially put at 1.26 billion, accounting for 21% or one-fifth of the world's total. On November 1, 2000, China conducted its fifth national census, which was given the mammoth task of finding out more exact numbers relating to population size, its structure and its growth trends. Employing six million census workers, this census was the most comprehensive ever carried out in China. Because of its vast base, China's population, growing at whatever rate, would have had profound economic and social consequences for China and for the world.

In early 2000s, China's natural rates of population growth have been consistently on the decline. In 1999, the crude birth rate fell to 1.46%, down from 1.78% in 1979 when China started family planning. Since China's crude death rates for many years have been quite low (at around 0.6–0.7%) by international standards, its natural population growth rate (i.e., birth rate minus death rate, net of migration) in 1999 fell to an all-time low of 0.91%, from 1.44% in 1990 and 2.58% in 1970 (Table 1). In 1998, for the first time in China's modern history, its natural population growth rate was below the 1% benchmark.

In fact, China's official natural population growth rate in 1999 was comparable to that of Korea, Taiwan and Singapore, as can be seen from Table 2. Shanghai had actually experienced negative population growth for seven years in a row, with demographic trends similar to those in Japan and Western Europe. This prompted China's state population agency in 1999 to proudly declare its family programme a success. As a result, China averted 330 million births for the past 30 years, thereby saving the country a huge sum equivalent to its 1997 GDP.[1] Indeed, China won high praise from UN population experts for having achieved the "most successful family planning policy in the history of mankind in terms of quantity".[2] (Figure 1 shows China's demographic transition.)

---

[1] This is based on an estimated average cost of 40,000 yuan for raising a rural child for 16 years, and 110,000 yuan for an urban child. (*Mingpao* (Hong Kong, September 28, 1999).)

[2] "China Benefits Mankind", *China Daily*, October 13, 1999.

Table 1.   China's vital statistics, 1950–1999.

Year	Total Population (million)	Birth Rate (%)	Death Rate (%)	Natural Growth Rate (%)	Urban Population (%)
1950	552	3.70	1.80	1.90	11.18
1953*	588	3.70	1.40	2.30	13.31
1955	615	3.26	1.23	2.03	13.48
1960	662	2.09	2.54	−0.46	19.75
1964*	705	3.91	1.15	2.76	18.37
1965	725	3.79	0.95	2.84	17.98
1970	830	3.34	0.76	2.58	17.38
1975	924	2.30	0.73	1.57	17.34
1980	987	1.82	0.63	1.19	19.39
1982*	1017	2.23	0.66	1.57	21.13
1985	1059	2.10	0.68	1.43	23.71
1990*	1143	2.11	0.67	1.44	26.41
1991	1158	1.97	0.67	1.30	26.37
1992	1172	1.82	0.66	1.16	27.63
1993	1185	1.81	0.66	1.15	28.14
1994	1199	1.77	0.65	1.12	28.62
1995	1211	1.71	0.66	1.06	29.04
1996	1224	1.70	0.66	1.04	29.37
1997	1236	1.70	0.65	1.05	29.92
1998	1248	1.60	0.65	0.95	30.40
1999	1259	1.52	0.65	0.88	30.89

Note: * denotes a Census Year.
Sources: China Population Statistics Yearbook, 2000 and early years.

The "natural growth rate" is not an exact indicator of future demographic changes because it does not explain how the population growth comes about. Experts commonly use a more precise technical indicator such as the "total fertility rate" (TFR), which measures the average number of children that would be born alive to a woman during her entire reproductive period in accordance with prevailing age-specific fertility rates. The TFR, in providing a better picture of the fertility behaviour at the family level, can also predict future demographic movements more accurately for a particular period. Generally speaking, an average TFR of 2.1 (i.e., slightly more than two children per woman) denotes replacement-level fertility. During that period, however, Chinese family planning officials had avoided making public reference to TFR figures, probably because there was no clear

Table 2. Natural population growth rate in Asia.

| | Crude Birth and Death Rate & Natural Growth Rate (%) | | | | | | | | | | | | | | |
| | 1975 | | | 1980 | | | 1985 | | | 1990 | | | 1998 | | |
	B	D	N	B	D	N	B	D	N	B	D	N	B	D	N
China	2.30	0.73	1.57	1.82	0.63	1.19	2.10	0.68	1.42	2.10	0.63	1.47	1.60	0.65	0.95
Japan	1.71	0.63	1.08	1.36	0.62	0.74	1.19	0.63	0.56	0.99	0.67	0.32	0.96	0.75	0.21
NIEs															
Hong Kong	1.82	0.49	1.33	1.70	0.50	1.20	1.40	0.46	0.94	1.18	0.50	0.68	0.79	0.49	0.30
Korea	2.39	0.65	1.74	2.34	0.67	1.67	1.64	0.62	1.02	1.64	0.58	1.06	1.38	0.53	0.85
Singapore	1.77	0.51	1.26	1.71	0.52	1.19	1.66	0.52	1.14	1.84	0.48	1.36	1.32	0.46	0.86
Taiwan	2.30	0.47	1.83	2.34	0.48	1.86	1.80	0.48	1.32	1.66	0.52	1.14	1.24	0.56	0.68
ASEAN															
Cambodia	4.70	1.80	2.90	3.01	2.70	0.31	4.55	2.00	2.55	3.90	1.56	2.34	3.53#	1.17#	2.36#
Indonesia	4.00	1.70	2.30	3.45	1.30	2.15	3.05	1.12	1.93	2.76	0.90	1.86	2.25	0.75	1.50
Laos	4.20	2.20	2.00	4.50	2.10	2.40	4.20	1.90	2.30	4.47	1.60	2.87	4.13#	1.51#	2.62#
Malaysia	3.14	0.64	2.50	3.09	0.53	2.56	3.19	0.50	2.69	2.80	0.46	2.34	2.50	0.45	2.05
Myanmar	3.29	1.19	2.10	2.69	0.81	1.88	2.85	0.89	1.96	3.02	0.92	2.10	2.75	0.82	1.93
Philippines	2.91	0.64	2.27	3.37	0.87	2.50	3.22	0.79	2.43	3.18	0.74	2.44	2.84#	0.61#	2.23#
Thailand	2.71	0.56	2.15	2.29	0.53	1.76	1.88	0.44	1.44	2.23	0.70	1.53	1.73	0.65	1.08
Vietnam	4.10	1.60	2.50	3.94	1.23	2.71	3.40	0.80	2.60	3.11	0.89	2.22	2.56#	0.70#	1.86#

Notes: B = Crude birth rate; D = Crude death rate; N = Natural growth rate.
# denotes 1997 figure.
Sources: United Nations, *Statistics Yearbook for Asia and the Pacific 1999*; and *Statistical Yearbook of the Republic of China 2000*.

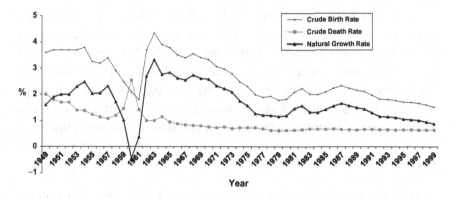

Figure 1. **Demographic transition in China, 1949–1999.**

official consensus on the accuracy of various TFR estimates that were then floating around.[3]

According to some foreign demographers, China's TFR has been steadily declining since the early 1970s due to the early adoption of the family planning policy.[4] The decline was later accelerated with the introduction of the radical OCP in 1980, even though its actual implementation in the rural areas had been mostly ineffective, especially in the early periods. By the end of the 1980s, China's TFR level was officially put at 2.2; but subsequent economic growth and concomitant social change since the early 1990s had brought it down to below replacement-level, with the TFR at around 1.8.

However, China in the late 1990s had witnessed the rise of even more powerful anti-natal forces (e.g., rising incomes, expanding education, rural industrialization, rapid urbanization, increasing rural–urban migration etc.) as a result of continuing dynamic economic and social change. Had China's TFR experienced a further decline to a substantially below replacement-level in the second part of the 1990s? A careful examination of various official sample surveys on TFR suggests that China's actual TFR by the late 1990s might have plunged to 1.7–1.6, slightly lower than that of South Korea and Taiwan.

---

[3]"Uncertainty the Only Sure Element in Population Statistics", *South China Morning Post*, July 4, 2000.

[4]Judith Banister, *China's Changing Population*, Stanford University Press, 1987.

With a TFR at 1.7 or 1.6 and slowly declining, China's total population could be easily capped at 1.4 billion in 2010, as officially targeted, and would eventually peak at 1.5–1.6 billion, possibly as early as 2030. This would then be the single most significant socio-economic achievement for China in the first quarter of this century. However, this positive demographic development will have to trade off against some long-term economic and social problems related to an ageing population and slower economic growth.

The Process of Fertility Transition

China's demographic transition in the second half of the 20th century from high birth and high death rates to low birth and low death rates had largely followed a predictable pattern, quite similar to that experienced in other East Asian economies. It suffices to say that China had a typical pre-industrial level of high fertility (TFR at 5.0 to 6.0) in the 1950s when social stability was restored after the civil war. This gave rise to China's first baby boom, which subsequently prompted Professor Ma Yinchu, a noted economist and President of Peking University, to espouse his "New Population Theory", calling for population control measures.

However, Chairman Mao, true to his Marxist ideology ("For every additional mouth, there will always be two additional hands"), came down very hard on Ma, and brought an abrupt end to the population debate. Not surprisingly, China's fertility throughout the 1960s remained high, except during the Great Leap Forward period of 1959–1962, when the population actually declined due to famine. By 1970, China's total population exceeded 800 million, exerting great pressures on the country's low-productivity collective farming. In response, the government introduced family planning programme, which caused the TFR to decline sharply from 5.8 in 1970 to a record low level of 2.7 in 1979, a remarkable reduction of more than 50% within one decade.[5]

Demographers have since recognized that China completed its first major fertility transition in the 1970s, from very high fertility to relatively low fertility.[6] From East Asian experiences, once the critical fertility

---

[5] The slogan of the time was: "*wan, xi, shao*" or "later marriage, wider spacing of children, and few children".

[6] See, e.g., P.M. Kulkarni and S. Rani, "Recent Fertility Declines in China and India: A Comparative View", *Asia-Pacific Population Journal*, 10(4), 1995. Also, J. Cleland and

transition begins, the momentum for its continuing decline would be sustained, thus inevitably bringing fertility down to replacement level. Why then did Beijing in January 1979 still introduce the controversial (or "notorious" in the eyes of many Western commentators) OCP? If completely successful, such a policy could technically bring China's TFR down to 1.0, which would be a highly "unnatural" level of fertility that could in theory de-populate China in the long run.

It seems clear that the Chinese leadership in 1978 were acutely aware of the serious potential demographic impact of the nation's large and youthful population. Because of high fertility in the preceding two decades and the existing large population base, China's total population, if left alone, would just continue to grow at least for one generation before stabilizing and decreasing, even if the TFR had already dropped to replacement level in 1978. Such is the familiar "hidden momentum of population growth", known to all demographers.

Whereas natural demographic changes are normally a long-term phenomenon, economic reform and development issues like employment creation call for immediate policy initiative. China's ageing leadership under Deng Xiaoping was simply too impatient to wait for the population decline to take its natural course, much less willing to see the fruits of economic reform "eaten up" by population expansion. Hence, their decision for a radical population control policy.

As expected, the OCP was initially strongly resisted by Chinese couples (particularly those living in rural areas), whose desire to have at least two children remained strong. The implementation of the OCP inevitably involved strong coercive measures, which easily gave rise to abuses and excesses at the local levels, such as forced abortion, infanticides, and a lop-sided sex ratio among the newly born. All these gave the OCP a bad image abroad. Nonetheless, the policy has remained in force to this day, even though it has been modified several times.[7] How then had the OCP fared over the past two decades?

C. Wilson, "Demand Theories of the Fertility Transition: An Iconoclastic View", *Population Studies*, 41(1), 1987.

[7] From the start, exceptions were made for minority ethnic groups, remarried couples without their own children and couples with retarded or handicapped children. In 1984, a major relaxation occurred in rural areas where couples with only one female child were allowed to have a second birth; and in mountainous and extremely poor areas, all couples

Many foreign commentators took the view that the OCP had failed, simply because there are limits to what any government can do to effectively force demographic changes. For China as a whole, the policy had clearly not been thoroughly implemented or its TFR then would have already plunged to an unnaturally low level of around 1. However, demographers had also conceded that the OCP had been successful in the urban areas.[8] In Chinese cities, the OCP had been widely accepted, partly because of rapidly growing anti-natal socio-economic changes (like better education for women) and partly because city governments had the required institutional resources to effectively enforce the policy.[9]

In the rural areas, the extended family has remained a vital institution for making decisions about production and consumption, and this naturally favours larger family size. Besides, most rural couples still have the deep-rooted desire for at least one male offspring to carry on with their family farm business as well as their family lineage. Therefore, the implementation of the OCP in the rural areas had been tardy and its results, spotty. However, what critics of the policy had apparently failed to realize is the fact that the OCP, like many other reform policies of the Deng era, embodied elements of Deng's pragmatism and flexibility as manifested in the motto: "Two steps ahead, if in trouble take one step back". The government knew only too well that enforcing such a severe policy would have required far more forceful measures than it was willing to use. After all, the OCP is an extreme policy, inherently unachievable even in the very long run.

This explains why the State Family Planning Commission, initially given the authority to maintain surveillance and monitoring of births, soon lost its power and prestige to become merely a weak, decentralized

---

were allowed to have a second birth. Nevertheless, the policy remained fully implemented in urban areas, except for couples who are themselves single children or who are remarried.
[8]According to a study, as early as in 1986, only 20% of urban women with one child had borne a second one compared to rural areas where the percentage was as high as 94%. See Feeney Griffith, Feng Wang, Mingkun Zhou and Baoyu Xiao, "Recent Fertility Dynamics in China: Results from the 1987 One Percent Population Survey", *Population and Development Review*, 15(2), 1989.
[9]Among the reasons, urban residents enjoy the institutional support of the state such as guaranteed full employment, free housing and medical care, and trusted the state to look after them in their old age, thus removing one of the traditional reasons for having more children to take care of them in old age.

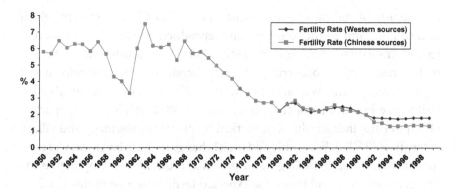

Figure 2.   China's TFR, 1950–1999.

Source: Columns 1 and 2, Table 3.

regulatory body, which often turned a blind eye to violations provided they were not too blatant and too excessive. The government was apparently prepared to allow the OCP in the rural areas to work its way through slowly, letting the underlying socio-economic forces finish the job.

Viewed from such a broad perspective, China's OCP had actually worked. It was instrumental in bringing about China's second fertility transition from low fertility to below-replacement fertility, a highly creditable achievement given China's present stage of economic development. According to the US Census Bureau, China's TFR since 1992 has consistently hovered around 1.8, a level comparable to that in Taiwan or South Korea, which are economically more developed than China (Figure 2).

Had TFR Fallen Far Below Replacement Level?

What was China's likely TFR level around 2000? Had it fallen further below the 1.8 "benchmark" level? To put it differently: Had China also undergone a third fertility transition in the late 1990s, from below-replacement fertility to a substantially lower level of fertility? Chinese demographers did not seem to be in total agreement amongst them. In the absence of officially confirmed figures, the answer remains a matter of guesswork, which nevertheless deserves our careful examination.

To begin with, China's first fertility transition in the 1970s from high fertility to low fertility did not come as a surprise to experts because of the two-decade of radical socialist transformation in Chinese society, which in turn undermined the "century-long reproductive norms".[10] The second fertility transition (starting in the early 1980s) from low fertility to below-replacement fertility, occurring under the impact of economic reform and rapid development, was also predictable. The reform brought about a visible rise in rural prosperity in the early 1980s, which in turn sparked off rapid rural industrialization marked by the rise of township and village enterprises (TVEs). Economic and social change in the urban areas was even more far-reaching. In demographic parlance, economic development is the best contraceptive; and hence the expected fertility decline in this phase.

In the 1990s, China experienced even higher levels of economic and social development, and from a larger base. The economy in the 1990s grew at an annual rate of 10.1%, compared to 9.3% in the 1980s. Industrialization had also spread from the original large urban clusters and special economic zones in the coastal region to the small and medium cities in many parts of China. In 1978, 68% of the labour force were engaged in farming; but the proportion decreased to only 47% in 1999.[11] The 1990s also witnessed massive migration of rural youths (the "floating population") into cities and towns to seek non-farm employment. Social progress in this period was no less impressive. The total number of people living under the poverty line decreased from 250 million at the beginning of economic reform in 1978 to 34 million in 1999; and illiteracy among the young and the middle-aged had been virtually eliminated by 1999.[12]

In fact, by 2000 China was a different society altogether, compared to 20 years ago. The total number of fixed-line telephone subscribers in 2000 reached 144 million, in addition to 85 million mobile phones in use, compared to only 1.2 million phone sets in 1978 and 5.4 million in 1990.[13] Such rapid socio-economic development must have triggered another spurt of fertility decline, causing the TFR to dip further.

---

[10]Peng Xizhe, "Current Fertility and Future Prospects in China" (Draft), Institute of Population Research, Fudan University, Shanghai, China.

[11] *China Statistical Yearbook 2000.*

[12]The White Paper, "China's Population and Development in the 21st Century", The Information Office of the State Council, December 2000.

[13]"Mobile Subscriptions Double", *South China Morning Post,* February 12, 2001. Also, *Mingpao,* February 10, 2001.

How much has the TFR actually declined? As can be seen from Table 3, there were no consistent official TFR series after 1992. All that was available to the public were some sample surveys conducted by the National Bureau of Statistics (NBS), which are technically competent but widely deemed to be unreliable due to serious undercounting caused by large numbers of unregistered households and unrecorded births forming the so-called "black population".[14]

From Table 3, both the 1992 and the 1997 sample surveys show an abrupt drop in fertility during 1991–1992 to well below-replacement levels (1.5–1.6), and even dropping further to 1.35 in 1996. This had since stirred up heated controversies among China's demographers.[15] Even the State Family Planning Commission openly questioned the validity of the TFR figures derived from the NBS' sample surveys.[16]

Since the mid-1990s, the NBS had conducted an annual sample survey (sampling ratio at 0.98%) of the "average number of live births per woman of child-bearing age", which had similarly plummeted from 1.99 in 1995 to 1.33 in 1999 (Table 3, Column 6). To be sure, the ratio of "live births per woman" is not exactly the same as the TFR (which is usually compiled on a cohort basis), and the former should theoretically be slightly lower than the latter, as many women in the sample have not lived through their entire child-bearing years and completed their fertility. Still, the ratio unmistakably points to sharply declining fertility trends in the late 1990s.

Since it is technically difficult to fault the NBS's sample surveys, the only rational explanation lies in the under-reporting of births during the survey. Treated as a random element, under-reporting can indeed occur in any population survey and even in the general population census. To explain such a large discrepancy, however, one needs to assume that the

---

[14] See, e.g., "Uncertainty the Only Sure Element in Population Statistics", *South China Morning Post*, July 4, 2000; and "China Losing 'War' on Births", *The Washington Post*, May 4, 2000.

[15] The NBS at one time had estimated China's TFR for 1983, 1984 and 1985, respectively at 1.96, 1.96 and 1.94, (implying that China's fertility had already reached below-replacement level in the early 1980s), which was subsequently proved to be wrong. The more accurate TFR numbers should be 2.42, 2.35 and 2.17, respectively. See Feng Litian, "China's Population Policy: Past, Present and Future", *Renkou Yanjiu* (*Population Research*), 24(4), 25, 2000.

[16] Peng Xizhe, *op cit.*, for more detailed arguments, see also, Zheng Yi, "Has China's Fertility in 1991–1992 Been Far Below the Replacement Level?", *Renkou Yanjiu*, 19(3), 1995.

Table 3.   Various estimates of China's TFR.

			TFR		
	Western Estimates		Chinese Official Estimates		
	1	2	3	4	5	6
Year	Banister and Feeney *et al.*	US Census Bureau	CPIRC	1997 Sample Survey	1992 Sample Survey	Average No. of Live Births Per Woman
1950	5.81	—	5.81	—	—	—
1953	6.05	—	6.05	—	—	—
1958	5.68	—	5.68	—	—	—
1959	4.31	—	4.30	—	—	—
1960	4.00	—	4.02	—	—	—
1961	3.29	—	3.29	—	—	—
1962	6.03	—	6.02	—	—	—
1965	6.07	—	6.08	—	—	—
1970	5.82	—	5.81	—	—	—
1971	5.44	—	5.44	—	—	—
1972	4.98	—	4.98	—	—	—
1973	4.54	—	4.54	—	—	—
1974	4.17	—	4.17	—	—	—
1975	3.58	—	3.57	—	—	—
1976	3.23	—	3.24	—	—	—
1977	2.85	—	2.84	—	—	—
1978	2.72	—	2.72	—	—	—
1979	2.75	—	2.75	—	—	—
1980	2.24	—	2.24	—	—	—
1981	2.69	—	2.63	—	—	—
1982	2.71	—	2.87	—	—	—
1983	2.35	—	2.42	—	—	—
1984	2.16	—	2.35	—	—	—
1985	2.27	—	2.20	—	—	—
1986	2.33	—	2.42	2.59	2.46	—
1987	2.45	—	2.59	2.66	2.57	—
1988	2.50	—	2.31	2.41	2.28	—
1989	2.40	—	2.25	2.40	2.24	—
1990	—	2.20	2.17	2.29	2.04	—
1991	—	2.00	2.01	1.75	1.66	—
1992	—	1.82	—	1.57	1.47	—
1993	—	1.81	—	1.51	—	—
1994	—	1.79	—	1.32	—	1.49
1995	—	1.76	—	1.33	—	1.99

(*Continued*)

Table 3. (*Continued*)

				TFR		
	Western Estimates		Chinese Official Estimates			
	1	2	3	4	5	6
	Banister and	US Census	CPIRC	1997	1992	Average
	Feeney	Bureau		Sample	Sample	No. of Live
Year	*et al.*			Survey	Survey	Births Per Woman
1996	—	1.78	—	1.35	—	1.42
1997	—	1.82	—	—	—	1.37
1998	—	1.82	—	—	—	1.38
1999	—	1.82	—	—	—	1.33

Sources: For Column 1, Judith Banister, *China's Changing Population*, Stanford University Press, 1987 and Feeney, G. and others, "Recent Fertility Dynamics in China: Results from the 1987 One Percent Population Survey", *Population and Development Review*, 15(2), 1989; Column 2, US Bureau of the Census; Column 3, China Population Information Research Centre (CPIRC); Columns 4 and 5, Guo Zhigang, "Lifetime Fertility of Chinese Women: A Look at the Recent Period Fertility Behaviour", *Rankou Yanjiu*, 1, 2000; and Column 6, *China Statistics Yearbook 1995*, and subsequent years.

under-reporting of the real number of births was practised systematically on a very large scale, virtually by most families and in most villages.[17] Such blatant under-reporting, occurring year after year, is hard to believe. This also implies that the riddle of China's exact TFR may never be resolved, not even by the 2000 Census, which was subject, in theory, to the same set of technical and social constraints that were responsible for the under-reporting in the past sample surveys.[18]

---

[17] An enterprise can easily under-report profits, which are mere numbers in the book. But a village official cannot hide the unregistered above-quota births (the so-called "black children") year after year. Furthermore, if a village official has allowed one family to have two or more children illegally, its neighbours in the same village will soon follow suit. And so will others in the neighbouring villages.

[18] For problems faced by the 2000 Census, see "China's Floating Population a Headache for Census", *Straits Times* (Singapore, September 22, 2000); "Census Extended Amid Fear and Confusion", *South China Morning Post*, November 11, 2000; and an article in Chinese on the 2000 population census, *Yazhou Zhoukan* (*Asian Week*, February 5, 2001).

If the NBS's sample survey results are not completely invalid, the question nonetheless remains: How is it possible for China's TFR to plunge to such a low threshold of 1.5–1.4 in such a short span of time? According to the World Bank, the average TFR for high-income economies in 1998 was 1.7, with a few developed countries such as Japan, Germany and Austria having a TFR of 1.4.[19] Russia and many East European countries were then plagued by even lower fertility levels because of rampant abortions and their many abnormal socio-economic problems.[20] For China, all things considered, one may, therefore, reasonably assume that its TFR would then stand at 1.7, but moving towards 1.6.[21]

Has OCP Outlived Its Usefulness?

In terms of pressure on the environment, food supply systems, and social and education services, the Chinese government should find its declining fertility a much welcome relief.[22] At the same time, a sharply declining fertility would also hasten the early arrival of an "ageing society", with a smaller proportion of productive population to support an expanding ageing cohort. For a married couple today who are themselves from one-child families and who also want to stop at one, their child in future will have to take care of six dependants, i.e., two parents and four grandparents.

---

[19] *World Development Report 2000/2001.*

[20] See "Abortion Still Rampant in the Former East Bloc", *International Herald Tribune*, February 16, 2001.

[21] In China's urban areas then, the one-child family was become the norm. In larger cities like Shanghai, Beijing and Guangzhou, the TFR was below 1 because of the postponement of marriage and rising education of women. In the more developed rural areas of the coastal region (which were also heavily populated), increasingly, young peasants were postponing their marriage in order to pursue non-farm occupations and accepting smaller family size, particularly when their first born happens to be a boy. Thus, with the urban population (30% of total population) having a TFR of 1.0 and the rural population (70% of total) having a below-replacement TFR, this yielded an overall TFR of 1.6–1.7 for China as a whole.

[22] At that time, Jiang Zemin, in a high-level seminar organized by the Central Committee of the Party, said, "Population control, resources and environmental protection will be the three crucial issues in China's march toward becoming a great power in the new century". He also stressed "the next few years will be a crucial time during which China must stabilize its birth rate at the current low level and improve population quality". *China Daily*, March 13, 2001.

In early 2000, those over 65 already constituted 10% of China's total population, and the proportion will reach 25% within three decades.

The labour force would eventually shrink. In fact, as a result of the steady fertility decline in the past three decades, the growth of China's labour force had already slowed down substantially, from 2.2% in the 1980s to 1.3% in the 1990s.[23] In the short term, however, China would continue to be burdened with the pressing task of creating jobs for the new entrants to the labour force. In other words, continuing fertility decline actually made no difference to the country's then unemployment problem. This suggests that the government should have started re-assessing the costs and benefits of its OCP, which in any case was supposed to be a "policy only for one generation".

Officially, the government had repeatedly stated that the OCP will stay.[24] At the same time, it had also manifestly eased the strict implementation of this policy.[25] In the urban areas, couples from one-child families can now have a second child while many rural families whose first child is a girl can have a second child. In many parts of rural China, especially in Guangdong and Fujian, some couples can even have more than three children after they have paid a specific sum of "fine" to the local government.[26] In the past, such flexibility was applied only to the ethnic minorities. As Zhang Weiqing, Minister of the State Family Planning Commission, plainly put it, "the family planning policy in China is not 'one-child policy' as many people especially Westerners think".[27]

Why does the government not just abolish this immensely unpopular policy, whose implementation has been politically and socially costly and its effectiveness highly debatable? The government appears to be unsure

---

[23] *World Development Report 2000/2001.*

[24] "Family Planning Policy to Continue", *China Daily*, October 12, 1999; and "One-Child Policy 'Must Stay'", *South China Morning Post*, March 13, 2000.

[25] "China Tries Easing One-Child Policy", *Asian Wall Street Journal*, February 5, 2001. Also, "Abuses Under One-Child Policy Lead to Rethink", *South China Morning Post*, December 20, 2000.

[26] "Guangdong Villages Accept Two Babies 'No Longer a Right'", *South China Morning Post*, January 14, 2000.

[27] "Nation Sticks to Family Planning for Long Term", *China Daily*, December 20, 2000. See also, "Two-Child Families Possible for Many", *China Daily*, February 1, 2000; and "Babies Break all the Rules in Remote Areas", *South China Morning Post*, August 13, 1999.

about just how far below the replacement level China's TFR has actually fallen: 1.7, 1.6 or even 1.5? It is even more uncertain if the fertility decline can be sustained. There is an underlying fear that the untimely scrapping of this policy could spark off an extensive resurgence of second births.

It may, however, be argued that since the OCP has been largely an urban phenomenon, its termination is not likely to produce a big baby boom in the urban areas, in view of the rapid socio-economic transformation of China's cities today. In any case, additional births in the urban areas could actually result in more "quality children", as it is generally believed that the more affluent and better-educated urban parents are better able to bring up children than their rural counterparts.

With fertility trends continuing to decline, sooner or later the government would have to drop the OCP altogether, which had outlived its usefulness amidst the thrust of radical economic and social transformation of China today. In the experiences of other East Asian societies, when their fertility had fallen to a very low level and built into the economic and social life of the people, even the subsequent adoption of pro-natal policies by their governments would be ineffective in reversing such declining trends. The Chinese leadership might well take heed of this lesson.

14

INCORPORATING CAPITALISM AND EMBRACING THE CAPITALISTS

Introduction

Capitalism has obviously played a central role in Zhu Rongji's entire economic reform process. Economic reform everywhere means allowing the market to play a more decisive role in resource allocation. China's "reform and opening up" policy that was introduced by Deng Xiaoping in 1979, marks a system shift from central planning or a state-dominated economy to one that is mainly market driven. In fact, the process of "marketization" itself is capitalism in action.

But there are also a lot of semantic complications. The pragmatic Deng had once forcefully argued that the market is not a monopoly of a capitalist system. Central planning does not equal socialism, because planning also exists in capitalism; neither does market economy equal capitalism, because the market can also exist in socialism.

What then is capitalism all about? The pure form of capitalism refers to an economic and social system in which all means of production are privately-owned and the "surplus value" is appropriated by the bourgeoisie through the market. In the real world, however, there is no such pure form of capitalist system, even in the United States, in which all means of production are supposed to be basically privately-owned and distribution is mostly done by the market.

Specifically for Deng and subsequently also for Zhu Rongji, the purpose of economic reform or bringing in the market mechanism was not intended to introduce capitalism per se to China, but merely as a means to employ certain capitalist economic instruments or policies so as to increase the efficiency in production and distribution. All along, particularly at the initial phases of economic reform, Deng made it a point to stress the state-domination in all key areas of industrial production and the prevalence of public ownership in the economy were the prerequisite for introducing market reform. When individual ownership or getihu was first publicly allowed, it was ideologically justified that China's socialism was then still at its primary stage so that it could allow the existence of some form of private ownership.

After the Tiananmen event, Deng had come to recognize the problems of China having such "limited version" of capitalism as manifested in its much troubled "half-reformed economy". Thus, he undertook the Nanxun (tour of South China) in early 1992 to boldly propagate his ideas of having a thorough-going market reform so as to introduce a "stronger" version of capitalism to China, which he eventually redefined as a "socialist market economy". In other words, as long as public ownership remained predominant (i.e., China being "Socialist"), all manners of capitalist practices were possible. Such was Deng's pragmatic way of treating capitalism. Subsequently most of China's high officials or technocrats, including Zhu Rongji, who were running economic reform, had taken to such a pragmatic approach.

Specifically for Zhu, his whole career in economic reform was basically a process of managing marketization by combining the tools of both free markets and state control. In implementation, he often mixed these tools in a highly flexible manner. In December 1990, shortly after the Tiananmen event as the top leadership was still divided over the direction of economic reform, Zhu launched the Shanghai Stock Exchange. This had naturally caused great consternation in the conservative wing of the Party in Beijing, as the existence of a stock market carries the very spirit of capitalism. But Zhu had apparently convinced Deng Xiaoping first, who had later openly endorsed this move in his Nanxun speech, to the effect that "if capitalist countries all have a stock market, why can't socialist China also have one. Just try it out first".

Soon afterwards, Zhu was transferred to Beijing and promoted to Vice Premier in charge of economic affairs especially economic reform. At the beginning, Zhu had to be ideologically very correct by emphasizing that his market reform measures were all undertaken under prevailing public ownership, and they were not meant to stoke the fire of capitalism in China, but merely to increase the efficiency of the economy. When he later came to tackle the reform of taxation reform and foreign exchange, he pushed ahead vigorously as purely an economic exercise.

However, as Zhu came to deal with economic overheating in the mid-1990s, the "macroeconomic control tools" that he had used, were made up more by administrative means than market tools. This is because China at that time had not yet developed effective macroeconomic fine-tuning techniques to be supported by market-based monetary and fiscal policies, as already explained in early chapters. Similarly for his grain acquisition policies, Zhu had all along relied more on administrative directives than economic levers such as market incentives. Hence, his farm policies had mixed results.

When Zhu came to tackle the state-owned enterprise (SOE) reform and the reform of the banking sector in the later part of the 1990s, he had changed tack. By this time, China's economic reform had been successful and the economy had already become extensively marketized. Private ownership had already been extended widely under the impact of market reform.

It may be argued that the growth of the private sector was mainly due to the removal of its institutional obstacles and ideological barriers rather than being the result of the government's active promotion. But with this, Zhu did not need to pay any more ideological lip-service to "public ownership" when he came to reforming the state sector. After all, the very idea of SOE reform was basically an encroachment or even a direct attack on the ideological sanctity of state ownership. Any serious attempt for any SOE reform would inevitably involve significant privatization in a real sense.

At the same time, Zhu, much like Deng before, had from the start embodied a deeply ambivalent attitude towards privatization. On the one hand, Zhu had clearly recognized capitalism as the most dynamic form of organizing production, not just because it can make the best use of technological progress to improve productivity, but also employ the best management practice as well as duly taking into account of individual incentives. On the other hand, he had to toe the Party's ideological line against openly advocating privatization, at least in terms of privatizing all the SOEs, as happened in the former Soviet Union. He had also realized the political need for the state to retain control of many large and strategic state enterprises.

In the event, Zhu managed to get out of the dilemma through some brilliant tactical manoeuvre, as discussed in an early chapter on SOE reform. First, he pushed for the corporatization of some large SOEs by converting them into "share-holding companies", and he rationalized this move as not being a form of "privatization". Later, as he closed down or hived off some small SOEs while retaining larger ones for restructuring (Zhuada Fangxiao), he would also not refer to this as a process of privatization. He could, in fact, argue that that many non-socialist countries still keep their state companies.

For any enterprise, what is most crucial to its performance lies in its conduct and behaviour, whether or not it is professionally managed and able to compete in an open market and operate with a hard budget constraint. This has little to do with whether the enterprise is state-owned, privately-owned or joint venture, so long as the management is properly separated from ownership. Viewed from a different angle, it is also true that a SOE is more likely to have political intervention in its market operation. In fact, many SOEs tend to follow a softer option by making profits through some form of monopoly created through their close links to the government.

Looking back, Zhu had scored significant breakthroughs in the initial round of SOE reform. But because of his gingerly approach to privatization (either due to the ideological constraint or his personal ambivalent attitude) his SOE reform had remained an "unfinished business", with some fundamental problems still lingering on to these days.

By 2013, the total number of SOEs fell further to 6,830 with a total employment of 64 million while private enterprises increased to 194,950 units, employing 82 million workers. Private enterprises generated a total sale of 330 trillion yuan, compared to 212 trillion yuan from SOEs. The former made more profits than the latter, and also delivered more taxes to the state. In a sense, China's economy is now clearly dominated by the non-state sector.

However, Xi Jinping was not satisfied with the overall performance of SOEs, particularly those big conglomerates directly controlled by the central government, the yangqi. A lot of their profits were derived from their monopoly position and privileged access to low-cost credit and so on. Xi wanted to deepen the SOE reform, pushing them to embrace the market further ("putting the market at the centre of their activities") and hence further privatization. He had already used his anti-corruption campaign to break up the oil giants (Petro China and CNOOC) and restructure several others. If Zhu Rongji were still in charge of the economy, he would certainly go along with Xi in all these.

Under Xi, economic reform is for further marketization, pure and simple. It is also a clear move towards capitalism, as the original ideological constraint *on the economy has already lifted. Capitalism is now openly incorporated as the best practice that will lead to greater economic efficiency and deliver higher economic growth.*

When Deng Xiaoping first propounded his concept of "a socialist market economy with Chinese characteristics", many of his followers at that time, including Zhu Rongji, had difficulty in visualizing this concept in the future. Is it going to develop into some form of "capitalism with Chinese characteristics" or just "socialism with Chinese characteristics", in a kind of "half-full" and "half-empty" conundrum? Now after two decades, the Chinese system is more like "capitalism with Chinese characteristics", as many China scholars have argued.

China has now openly embraced capitalism. In the process, the government or the Chinese Communist Party (CCP) has also embraced the capitalists. Was Zhu Rongji a "capitalist" at heart? At one time, particularly in the mid-1990s, some had argued that Zhu was primarily a "central planner" at heart, never an ardent believer in a truly free market. But this point of argument had become immaterial once the Party, originally formed for workers and peasants, officially started to admit capitalists into its ranks. This chapter is primarily about this and its broader implications.

Thus, at the 80th anniversary celebration of the CCP on July 1, 2001, Jiang Zemin as its Secretary-General of the Party called for the admission into the Party "outstanding elements" of society such as private entrepreneurs, professionals, technical and managerial personnel from non-state firms and multinational corporations (MNCs). Jiang's supporters hailed the initiative as a breakthrough that would allow the Party to discard its old dogmas, particularly the shackles of class.

However, some party ideologues had raised a great hue and cry. The strength of their opposition seemed to have taken Jiang by surprise. Some feared that such developments had tarnished Jiang's personal prestige. The backlash against Jiang's bold initiative, as reported overseas, might well have been exaggerated. What Jiang was doing is merely endorsing what had already been happening to the Party for years.

Private entrepreneurs had already gained much prominence since Deng Xiaoping's Nanxun in 2002. Their emergence had undermined the Party's orthodox ideology, which often had to take a backseat when the Party was dealing with the private sector. So, as business interests advanced, the Party would retreat. At the local level, many private entrepreneurs had already directly or indirectly participated in local politics to influence policy. Many had joined the Party. At the national level, however, political participation by private entrepreneurs at that time was small in number and remained low-keyed.

Reform and development had bourgeoisified and benefited many Party members and cadres. Jiang's public support of the capitalists was thus not going against the tide but merely a recognition of reality. In fact, the Party, to continue to grow and expand, must embrace the better educated and the most enterprising in society.

Admitting private entrepreneurs could also enable the Party to expand its social base and to revitalize itself. Mao could depend on class struggle and mass movements to govern China. With the Party's original power base fast being eroded amid rapid economic development and social change, Jiang did not have Mao's options. But the Party would have to incur some long-term costs. As some had feared, more bourgeoisies could spell more corruption within the Party, facilitating the rise of the "money for power" or the phenomenon of "money politics". Worse, the capitalists could one day even take over the Party's leadership.

This was actually already happening in many Party branches in the rural areas. Businessmen had reportedly used their financial power to manipulate local elections or simply took over local Party leadership.

Indeed, the capitalists in its ranks would certainly catalyze the transformation of the Party. In admitting capitalists, had the CCP unknowingly let in the Trojan horse? Jiang Zemin's original aim might just be to strengthen the Party-state by broadening its social base. And as the Party was to metamorphose, perhaps into a kind of social democratic party in future, Jiang would be given the credit for having paved the way for such a far-reaching change.

In this way, Jiang had left a legacy in both strengthening the Party and facilitating its transformation — a win–win situation for him. The loser, however, could then be the original CCP.

Indeed, the Chinese leadership today may be officially Communist and continue to label the Chinese system as socialist; but the society at large and the common people have long embraced capitalism. According to the latest Pew global survey (October 2014), 76% of the Chinese people had expressed strong support to free market, a proportion slightly higher than in the United States!

China is in fact widely regarded as a state capitalism. Its state sector may appear strong — as most of the large corporations in China today are SOEs; but this alone does not make China socialist, particularly since the growth of the economy as a whole is mainly private-sector driven. Furthermore, China's social structure from its weak social welfare system to its high income inequality (Gini coefficient at around 0.48) is more blatantly capitalist than socialist in nature.

According to the Hurun, a Shanghai-based organization that is regularly tracking the super-rich people in China, China has 1,271 billionaires in 2015. And 203 of them are members of China's Parliament, either in the China's National People's Congress or the Chinese People's Political Consultative Congress. Most of these super-rich are probably also members of the CCP. Jiang and Zhu have certainly achieved their original objectives way beyond expectations.

Opening Pandora's Box*

In his controversial speech celebrating the 80th anniversary of the CCP on July 1, 2001, Jiang Zemin made a speech calling on the Party to admit those "outstanding elements" of society such as private entrepreneurs, professionals, technical and managerial personnel from various non-state sectors, including those employed by MNCs.[1] According to Jiang, these were people who could also make a positive contribution to the rebuilding of China's socialism, and should therefore not be excluded from the Party. Whether they are politically progressive (*xianjin*) or backward (*luohou*) should not be judged purely on whether they are property-owning classes.

"Private entrepreneurs" — actually an official euphemism for "capitalists" or "private businessmen" — were hitherto publicly barred from the Party. The proposed membership relaxation had accordingly generated much enthusiasm from many private businessmen wanting to join the Party. Immediately after Jiang's speech, more than "100,000 private

---

*The original version of this chapter was jointly written with Professor Zheng Yongnian.

[1]Jiang Zemin, "Jiang Zemin Zai Qingzhu Zhongguo Gongchandang Chengli Bashi Zhounian Dahui Shang De Jianghau" (Jiang Zemin's Speech at the Conference Celebrating the Eightieth Anniversary of the CCP, July 1, 2001), *Renmin Ribao* (*People's Daily*, Beijing, July 2, 2001). Also, "Entrepreneurs from Non-Public Sector Hail Jiang's Speech", *Beijing Review*, August 9, 2001.

entrepreneurs" were reported to have submitted their applications to join the Party. The Party's organization department (headed by Zeng Qinghong) was planning to recruit 200,000 private entrepreneurs before the sixteenth Congress in September 2002.[2]

Traditionally, the CCP was supposed to represent the interests of only five major groups, i.e., workers, peasants, intellectuals, members of the People's Liberation Army (PLA), and government officials and cadres. Majority of the original rank and file of the Party was basically drawn from the "proletariat" background. In championing the causes of capitalists, Jiang's initiative was hailed by supporters as a theoretical breakthrough, throwing off the Party's old dogmas, particularly the shackle of class.

At the same time, for Jiang as General Secretary to openly embrace capitalists — the anti-thesis of the proletariat class — amounts to dropping an ideological bombshell on the conservative wing of the Party. Naturally, the Party's ideologues had raised a great hue and cry. The strength of the opposition from these Party diehards seemed to have taken Jiang by surprise.

The opposition came into the open with the publication on the Chinese Internet of a widely-circulated *Wanyan-shu* or "a petition of ten-thousand words", attributed to a group of conservative Party veterans led by long-time leftist critic Deng Liqun (aged 86, and no relation to Deng Xiaoping). Prior to Jiang's "July 1" speech, several provincial Party leaders, such as Deputy Party Secretary of Jilin Province Lin Yanzhi, had already spoken out against Jiang's scheme.

In brief, apart from being accused of breaching the Party's cardinal principle by courting members of the exploitative class, Jiang was blamed for his failure to address the burning issues of growing unemployment and widening income disparities, and his failure to hold formal consultations within the Party before making the announcement. Jiang was also criticized for promoting a personality cult for himself. This suggests that Jiang might not have had strong Party consensus on the issue, and that the resistance he had encountered was not just ideological but also political in nature.

In response, Jiang quickly ordered the closure of the two "theoretical" (i.e., ideological) magazines, *Zhenli De Zhuiqiu* (Seeking Truth) and

---

[2] *Ming Pao*, July 23, 2001.

Zhongliu (The Central-Pillar), which were the well-known mouthpieces of the leftists.[3] Subsequently, some leftist websites were also shut down.[4] Since then Party cadres throughout China, including officers of the PLA, had been instructed to hold study sessions of Jiang's "July 1 Speech".[5] How much had Jiang's personal prestige been tarnished by this move?

Jiang, as the head of the ruling group, certainly had no shortages of opponents: Falun Gong followers, losers from the economic reform such as *xiagang* (laid-off) workers of state enterprises, displaced rural migrants, disenchanted intellectuals and so on. But this motley group of opponents was unlikely to form a coalition with the Party's ideological diehards against Jiang. Nonetheless, it was clear that the issue might well complicate or even weaken Jiang's role in the ongoing arrangements for the coming leadership transition.

A big unknown to the outside is whether any factions at the Party's top leadership (e.g., Li Peng's) might have exploited the issue to jockey their own proteges against Jiang's own in the leadership line-up at the next Party Congress. The question would boil down to this: Did Jiang really have sufficient political clout to openly restructure the Party's ideological orthodoxy and remain unscathed?

A careful examination of all the relevant background would suggest that the backlash against Jiang's bold initiative, as reported overseas, might well have been overstated. In real terms, what Jiang was doing is merely an open endorsement of what had already been happening to the Party for years. China had been manifestly following capitalism after Deng Xiaoping officially sanctioned the "socialist market economy" concept in 1992. Following China's success in economic development and the rise in per-capita income, the Party (also the government) was getting more "middle-class" in character. For the Party to renew itself and to stay relevant, it certainly needed to recruit more younger and better-educated members, regardless of their class origins.

---

[3]"Showdown of Ideologies", *South China Morning Post*, August 15, 2001; and "Party Closes Leftist Journal that Opposed Jiang", *op cit.*, August 14, 2001.

[4]"Dissenting Leftist Websites Taken off (from) Internet", *South China Morning Post*, September 3, 2001.

[5]Jiang urged the armed forces to thoroughly understand the "July 1 Speech", *Ming Pao*, September 3, 2001.

The Party's organization department had revealed that almost half of its existing total membership was below 45 years old. More significantly, one in four of China's postgraduate students were already Party members and about one-third of China's university undergraduates had applied to join the Party.[6] Incidentally, most university students in China came from urban middle class background.

The CCP had also been transformed in a "technocratic" way. During Mao Zedong's time, the CCP was genuinely a revolutionary party with its members overwhelmingly from workers and peasants, who constituted 83% of the total membership in 1956 (this figure dropped to 52% in 1994). Furthermore, after his return to power, Deng started what may be called a "technocratic movement", replacing revolutionary cadres in Party leadership positions with technocrats.[7]

This was crystal clear at the pinnacle of the Party's power structure. All the seven Standing Committee members of the current Political Bureau and 18 of the 24 Political Bureau members may be classified as "technocrats". In short, the CCP had already ceased to be an ideologically oriented party led by revolutionaries; it had become one with a "full-fledged technocratic leadership."[8]

Strangely, neither the proponents nor the opponents had bothered to define what was precisely meant by an "entrepreneur", who, in the Schumpeterian sense is, a great innovator or risk-taking capitalist. In any society, there are precious few successful entrepreneurs. If an "entrepreneur" is defined broadly to mean just an ordinary capitalist or businessman, then one can find in China many "new capitalists" who have been created by the economic reform.

A broader definition of "new capitalists" would include, apart from conventional private businessmen, hundreds of thousands of Party cadres

---

[6]"Party More Attractive to Chinese Youth", *China Daily*, June 6, 2001.

[7]Hong Yong Lee, *From Revolutionary Cadres to Party Technocrats in Socialist China*; and Cheng Li, and David Bachman, "Localism, Elitism, and Immobilism: Elite Formation and Social Change in Post-Mao China", *World Politics*, 42(1), 64–94, 1989.

[8]Li Cheng and Lynn White, "The Fifteenth Central Committee of the Chinese Communist Party: Full-fledged Technocratic Leadership with Partial Control by Jiang Zemin", *Asian Survey*, xxxviii(3), 231–264, 1998; David Shambaugh, "The CCP's Fifteenth Congress: Technocrats in Command", *Issues and Studies*, 34(1), 1–37, 1998.

who started the profit-maximizing township and village enterprises (TVEs) as well as those who were assigned by the Party to run the privatized SOEs, both in China and overseas. These cadres were practically "capitalists" or more correctly, "bureaucratic capitalists" — often dubbed "Red Capitalists" overseas. Many of them were children of high-ranking officials, now called *Guan-er-dai*.

In short, reform and development had bourgeoisified numerous existing Party members and cadres. With rising affluence, there were fewer and fewer real "have-nots" among the Party's rank and file. Viewed in this context, Jiang was actually not swimming against the tide when he came out to support capitalists publicly. He could see clearly that for the Party to continue to grow and expand, it must embrace the better educated and the most enterprising in society, who, incidentally, would include many children of the ruling elite. Many of the Party ideologues opposing Jiang were themselves already marginalized. It seemed clear that Jiang's scheme would eventually prevail, unless the opposition was backed by a powerful group at the top with ulterior motives.

It may be argued that from the start Jiang had conceived the scheme of admitting capitalists and professionals to the Party as a very shrewd win–win move. Provided that he could ride out the initial resistance, Jiang would be seen as doing what was necessary to arrest the decay of the Party and he would eventually be credited for having revitalized the Party. Nevertheless, in the longer run, the presence of many capitalists and professionals in a primarily socialistic party would inevitably sharpen its internal contradictions and hasten its structural and ideological metamorphosis.

Ultimately, the main body of the Party might evolve into a kind of social democratic party, and for that Jiang would also be credited for opening the door to such a transformation. Mao was given full credit for creating a New China while Deng for starting economic reform. Jiang left as his legacy the successful transformation of the Party, one way or the other.

The Rise of the Capitalist Class

In the wake of the 1989 Tiananmen event, China's top leadership was engaged in a hot debate as to which direction China's economic reform and development should take — more socialistic or less socialistic (i.e., more capitalistic)? Alarmed by the sudden collapse of the Soviet Union as a result of its dismal failure in economic reform, Deng Xiaoping was determined to lead China boldly to a faster reform route via capitalistic means.

Deng espoused the idea during his famous *Nanxun* or tour of South China in early 1992. He urged Party leaders to liberate their thoughts and open up themselves so as to learn how China could best make use of the dynamic capitalist system to promote its economic growth. Deng's *Nanxun* put a quick end to the futile debate of "Mr. Socialism vs. Mr. Capitalism" among the Party's ideologues.[9] In effect, this also paved the way for the Party to accept a capitalist mode of economic development as its new orthodoxy, which in turn sparked off a decade of spectacular economic growth for China.[10]

In the pre-reform era, China under Mao Zedong was an ideologically organized society. As the noted China scholar Franz Schurmann correctly pointed out in the early 1960s, "Communist China is like a vast building made of different kinds of brick and stone. However it was put together, it stands. What holds it together is ideology and organization."[11] Armed with his own brand of ideology, Mao could therefore use the Party to mobilize peasants and workers for various political experiments, from the Great Leap Forward (1978) to the Cultural Revolution (1966–1976), in order to reshape China according to his own utopian ideals. In effect, Mao used totalitarian state power to destroy all possible private space and politicized Chinese society with scant regard for China's economic conditions.[12]

---

[9] It is worth noting that there had been heated debates in the intellectual circles about socialism and capitalism. For a collection of the articles appearing in the debates, see Zhang Wenmin *et al.* (eds.), *Zhongguo jingji da lunzhan* (Debating about China's Economy), 3 volumes, Beijing: Jingji guanli chubanshe, 1996, 1997 and 1998. What is important is that Deng's *Nanxun* speeches legitimated capitalistic development.

[10] For a more detailed discussion of the causes and effects of Deng's *Nanxun*, see John Wong and Zheng Yongnian (eds.), *The Nanxun Legacy and China's Development in the Post-Deng Era*, Singapore University Press and World Scientific, 2001.

[11] Franz Schurmann, *Ideology and Organization in Communist China*, University of California Press, 1968, p. 1.

[12] For example, Tang Tsou, *The Cultural Revolution and Post-Mao Reforms: A Historical Perspective*, The University of Chicago Press, 1986.

After Mao, Deng Xiaoping had to pick up the pieces by reviving the economy and rebuilding the Party. Deng followed a radically different path to organize society and manage the economy. He realized that too much ideological and political contention as manifested in Mao's numerous movements and campaigns would simply not be conducive to economic growth, which would require a certain pragmatism so as to exploit all sources of comparative advantage and productivity gains, regardless of their ideological origins.

Deng also realized that successful economic growth, in delivering more goods and material benefits to the people, would ultimately increase the Party's legitimacy. Consequently, Deng took a radical turn in 1992 by launching the concept of the "socialist market economy", which provided a fertile ground for society's most productive elements, the "private entrepreneurs", to emerge. Thus, the private sector had expanded rapidly along with the relative decline of the state sector. Private enterprises employing more than eight workers increased from 90,000 units in 1989 to 150,000 in 1999. In terms of output, the non-state sector had also grown rapidly along with the corresponding decline of the state sector, which in 1999 accounted for only 26% of total industrial output, down from 76% in 1980 (Table 1).

As can be expected, the rise of the entrepreneur class had brought about concomitant political and social changes, some of which carried negative consequences for China in the transitional stage. First, as people soon came to see that private businesses were highly profitable and the quickest way to increase their income and wealth, many government officials and Party cadres joined the private sector in a phenomenon known as *xiahai* (literally, "plunging into the sea").[13]

Second, many Party cadres and government officials who had chosen to stay on in the public sector soon learned how to market their official positions and *guanxi* (connection) for their own personal gain. This had led to a rapid growth of rent-seeking activities and open corruption, which had since developed into a serious endemic problem in China today.

---

[13] For a description, see John Wong, "The *Xia Hai* Phenomenon in China", *Ritsumeikan Journal of International Relations and Area Studies*, 6, 1–10, 1994.

Table 1.   Gross industrial output in China by different sectors, 1980–1999.

Year	Total (%)	SOEs (%)	Collective-owned Enterprises (%)	Individually-owned Enterprises (%)	Other Types of Enterprises (%)
1980	100	76.0	23.5	0	0.5
1985	100	64.9	32.1	1.9	1.2
1990	100	54.6	35.6	5.4	4.4
1991	100	56.2	33.0	4.8	6.0
1992	100	51.5	35.1	5.8	7.6
1993	100	47.0	34.0	8.0	11.1
1994	100	37.3	37.7	10.1	14.8
1995	100	34.0	36.6	12.9	16.6
1996	100	33.7	36.5	14.4	15.4
1997	100	29.8	35.9	16.9	17.4
1998	100	26.5	36.0	16.0	21.5
1999	100	26.1	32.8	16.9	24.2

Source: Calculated from *Zhongguo tongji nianjian 2000* (*China Statistical Yearbook 2000*), Zhongguo tongji chubanshe, 2000, p. 409.

When political power is freely traded for economic benefits, corruption becomes inevitable. Widespread corruption not only produces deleterious social (i.e., reducing equity) and economic (i.e., misallocating resources) effects, but also saps the Party apparatus at all levels. Previously, political loyalty was the main criterion for assessing Party cadres and government officials; money or pecuniary benefits have now come to be used as an important yardstick. Accordingly, the effective functioning of the Party as well as its image and legitimacy would have suffered. The end result had been the social decline of the Party.

In the meanwhile, the entrepreneur class had been rising high, socially and politically. Not surprisingly, the rise of this class has undermined the Party's ideological orthodoxy, making it difficult for the Party to employ its official ideology to regulate the daily life of Party cadres and government officials. In fact, when the Party came to deal with the private sector, especially in regard to certain business decisions involving maximization of profits, efficiency, or growth, the Party's official ideology often had to take a backseat. As the Party retreats, business interests advance.

At the local level, many private entrepreneurs had already directly or indirectly participated in local politics in order to influence policy. Many had joined the Party.[14] At the national level, however, political participation by private entrepreneurs remained small. For instance, only 46 out of more than 2,000 representatives of the Ninth Chinese People's Political Consultative Conference in 1998 were classified as "private entrepreneurs".[15] It follows that Jiang's "July 1" speech was largely aimed at the political participation of private entrepreneurs at the national level.

The Capitalists in Jiang's New Political Order

The Fifteenth Party Congress in 1997 had already legitimated the private sector, and a constitutional amendment in the following year further provided constitutional protection for private ownership. In February 2000, Jiang instructed Party members to study his new theory based on the concept of *San-ge dai-biao* (literally, the "Three Representatives"). According to this theory, the Party represents the "most advanced mode of productive force, the most advanced culture, and the interests of the majority of the population".[16]

The Three-Representative theory is undoubtedly the Party's strongest affirmation yet of the importance of the non-state sector in the economy. It also implies that the Party is flexible enough to accommodate the interests of the newly rising economic and social groups. Many had argued that Jiang's "Three-Representative" theory, put forth when he was about to pass on the Party leadership baton to the fourth-generation leaders under Hu Jintao, was originally meant to be his own ideological legacy after his departure.

---

[14] According to a survey, 13% of private businessmen joined the CCP in 1993. The proportion increased to 17% in 1997 and 20% in 2000. According to the same survey, by 2000, there were more businessmen in the Party than workers and peasants. See Li Qiang, Guanyu Siying Jingji (About the Private Economy), 2001.

[15] Jiang Nanyang, "Lun siying qiyezhu de zhengzhi cenyu" ("Political Participation by the Owners of Private Businesses"), in Zhang Houyi and Ming Zhili (eds.), *Zhongguo siying qiye fazhan baogao 1978–1998* (A Report of the Development of Private Enterprises in China, 1978–1998), Shehui kexue wenxuan chubanshe, 1999, pp. 103–117.

[16] The Xinhua News Agency, "Jiang Zemin tongzhi zai quanguo dangxiao gongzuo huiyi shang de jianghua", June 9, 2000 ("Comrade Jiang Zemin's Talk in National Party Schools Working Conference"), *People's Daily*, July 17, 2000.

Whatever his original intention, Jiang's theory had gone down quite well with the public. It provided clear indications that the Party was finally giving up its past ideological rigidity by its willingness to embrace rising economic and social elites. In short, the Party was seen to be getting politically and socially pluralistic. With such good public reaction, it seemed only logical for Jiang to make use of the occasion of the 80th Party anniversary to formally open the door to private capitalists and professionals.

Jiang's initiative was apparently motivated by other pragmatic political considerations as well. First, admitting private entrepreneurs was real proof that the Party had been adapting itself to China's changing political and social reality. As mentioned earlier, many private entrepreneurs were already Party members under a different disguise. What the Party leadership proposed to do today was to formally endorse their Party membership while allowing others to join as new members.

Second, by so doing, the leadership wanted to expand the Party's social base in order to revitalize itself. Over the years, the capitalist mode of economic development had radically changed China's class structure. With the decline of the political and ideological importance of workers and peasants, the Party had to embrace the rising new elites, from industrialists and international businessmen to property magnates and "dotcom" venture capitalists, in order to stay socially relevant. China then had 60 million registered stock and share buyers, roughly equal to the total Party membership!

Politically, the Party's initiative to embrace these new social elites or new economic interest groups was clearly calculated to bolster its one-party domination. Mao could depend on class struggle and mass movements to govern China, and he could count on the support of millions of poor peasants and workers. China was then a backward agricultural economy, with peasants accounting for 80% of the total labour force. Today, China is a growing industrial economy, with peasants constituting less than 50% of the labour force and many of them not even full-time farmers.

Specifically, Jiang (and much less the younger leaders in future) simply could no longer rule China by mass political mobilization as Mao once did, since the Party's original power base had been fast eroded. China was rapidly developing into a modern society, with 130 million hand-phones and close to 30 million Internet users. The economy was increasingly integrated into international capitalism on account of China's growing foreign trade, foreign investment and foreign tourism. The populace was also getting increasingly literate, especially in urban areas.

On the other hand, state governance in China was not yet highly institutionalized, and the rule of law not firmly rooted. For the Party to effectively rule such a vast and diverse country without sound democratic foundations, it was all the more crucial for the Party leadership to build up a broad social consensus with a coalition of various interests. Clearly, the Party just could no longer exclude the "outstanding elements" of society from the private sector. For China's emerging political order to remain viable, the Party had to be socially more broad-based.

Towards a Social Democratic Party?

However, the Party had to bear some long-term costs for admitting capitalists and professionals. Leftist critics had warned that the recruitment of the bourgeoisie into the Party would invite more corruption to the Party, leading to the potential rise of the "money for power" phenomenon. Some critics had even suggested that capitalists might one day even take over the Party's leadership.[17]

This was actually happening in some Party branches in the rural areas where businessmen were reported to use their financial power to manipulate local elections or simply took over local Party branches.[18] It suffices to say that with capitalists inside the Party, they would certainly act as potential catalysts to quicken the transformation of the Party. Judging by

---

[17] Lin Yanzhi, Deputy Secretary of Jilin province stated: "The key to controlling the socialist market economy is to control the bourgeoisie and its capitalistic component; the key to control the bourgeoisie is ensure that they are not in the Party, and the Party has to see clearly their true colour", "The CCP Must Lead and Control the New Bourgeoisie", *Zhengli de zhuiqiu* (Seeking Truth), No. 5, 2001, p. 7.

[18] Zhang Dejiang, Party Secretary of Zhejiang Provincial Committee of the CCP, also strongly opposed private entrepreneurs from joining the Party. Zhejiang was among the few provinces where the private sector had gained rapid development and had played an increasingly important role in the local economy and even politics. See, Zhang Dejiang, "Yao mingque siying qiyezhu buneng rudang" ("To Make Clear that Private Entrepreneurs Cannot Join the Party"), *Zhengli de zhuiqiu*, No. 5, 2001, p. 28. Zhang's original paper was published in *Dang de jianshe* (Party Construction), No. 4, 2000.

the way Chinese society was evolving, there was a real possibility that the Party, in admitting capitalists, had also let in the Trojan horse.

Jiang Zemin might have genuinely believed that he was doing what it took to strengthen the Party-state by broadening its social base. In the distant future, as the Party was stepping up its process of metamorphosis and evolving possibly into a kind of social democratic party, Jiang would still be favourably judged by history for leading the way for such a transformation. In short, he would have left a legacy in both strengthening the Party and facilitating its transformation — a win–win situation for him. The loser, however, was clearly the original CCP itself.

INDEX

Printed in the United States
by Baker & Taylor Publisher

Printed in the United States
By Bookmasters